Spring 5.0 Microservices

Second Edition

Build scalable microservices with Reactive Streams, Spring
Boot, Docker, and Mesos

This book is based on Spring Version 5.0 RC1

Rajesh R V

BIRMINGHAM - MUMBAI

Spring 5.0 Microservices

Second Edition

First published: June 2016

Second edition: July 2017

Production reference: 1120717

Published by Packt Publishing Ltd.
Livery Place
35 Livery Street
Birmingham
B3 2PB, UK.

ISBN 978-1-78712-768-5

www.packtpub.com

Credits

Author
Rajesh R V

Reviewer
Aditya Abhay Halabe

Commissioning Editor
Aaron Lazar

Acquisition Editor
Chaitanya Nair

Content Development Editor
Siddhi Chavan

Technical Editor
Abhishek Sharma

Copy Editor
Zainab Bootwala

Project Coordinator
Prajakta Naik

Proofreader
Safis Editing

Indexer
Aishwarya Gangawane

Graphics
Abhinash Sahu

Production Coordinator
Shraddha Falebhai

About the Author

Rajesh R V is a seasoned IT architect with extensive experience in diversified technologies and more than 18 years of airline IT experience.

He received a degree in computer engineering from the University of Cochin, India, and he joined the JEE community during the early days of EJB. During his course as an architect, he worked on many large-scale, mission-critical projects, including the new generation Passenger Reservation System (iFly Res) and next generation Cargo Reservation System (Skychain, CROAMIS) in the Airline domain.

At present, as a chief architect at Emirates, Rajesh handles the solution architecture portfolio spread across various capabilities, such as JEE, SOA, NoSQL, IoT, cognitive computing, mobile, UI, and integration. At Emirates, the Open Travel Platform (OTP) architected by him earned the group the prestigious 2011 Red Hat Innovation Award in the Carved Out Costs category. In 2011, he introduced the innovative concept of the Honeycomb architecture based on the hexagonal architecture pattern for transforming the legacy mainframe system.

Rajesh has a deep passion for technology and architecture. He also holds several certifications, such as BEA Certified Weblogic Administrator, Sun Certified Java Enterprise Architect, Open Group Certified TOGAF practitioner, Licensed ZapThink Architect in SOA, and IASA global CITA-A Certified Architecture Specialist.

He has written *Spring Microservices* and reviewed *Service-Oriented Java Business Integration* by Packt Publishing.

Acknowledgments

I would like to thank everyone at Packt who I've worked closely with to make my dream come true. Thanks to the reviewers; their in-depth reviews helped improve the quality of this book.

This book would have never been possible without the encouragement from my excellent colleagues at Emirates with whom I worked with and learned from. A very special thanks goes to Neetan Chopra, Senior Vice President, and Thomas Benjamin, CTO, GE Aviation, for their constant support and help. Special thanks to Daniel Oor and Tomcy John for their help.

A heartfelt thanks goes to my wife, Saritha, for her tireless and unconditional support that helped me focus on this book. Thanks to my kids, Nikhil and Aditya. I have taken away a lot of the time that I'd spend playing with them to write this book. A huge thanks goes to my father, Ramachandran Nair, and my mother, Vasanthakumari, for their selfless support that helped me reach where I am today.

About the Reviewer

Aditya Abhay Halabe is a full-stack web application developer at Springer Nature's technology division. His primary technology stack includes Scala, Java, micro-web services, NOSQL databases, and multiple frameworks such as Spring, Play, and Angular. He has a very good understanding of Agile development, with continuous integration, which includes knowledge of DevOps, Docker, and automated deployment pipelines.

He is passionate about his work and likes to take on new challenges and responsibilities. Previously, Aditya has worked as a consultant with Oracle, and as a software developer with John Deere.

www.PacktPub.com

For support files and downloads related to your book, please visit www.PacktPub.com.

Did you know that Packt offers eBook versions of every book published, with PDF and ePub files available? You can upgrade to the eBook version at www.PacktPub.com and as a print book customer, you are entitled to a discount on the eBook copy. Get in touch with us at service@packtpub.com for more details.

At www.PacktPub.com, you can also read a collection of free technical articles, sign up for a range of free newsletters and receive exclusive discounts and offers on Packt books and eBooks.

https://www.packtpub.com/mapt

Get the most in-demand software skills with Mapt. Mapt gives you full access to all Packt books and video courses, as well as industry-leading tools to help you plan your personal development and advance your career.

Why subscribe?

- Fully searchable across every book published by Packt
- Copy and paste, print, and bookmark content
- On demand and accessible via a web browser

Customer Feedback

Thanks for purchasing this Packt book. At Packt, quality is at the heart of our editorial process. To help us improve, please leave us an honest review on this book's Amazon page at https://www.amazon.com/dp/1787127680.

If you'd like to join our team of regular reviewers, you can e-mail us at customerreviews@packtpub.com. We award our regular reviewers with free eBooks and videos in exchange for their valuable feedback. Help us be relentless in improving our products!

Table of Contents

Preface

Microservices is an architecture style and a pattern in which complex systems are decomposed into smaller services that work together to form larger business services. Microservices are services that are autonomous, self-contained, and independently deployable. In today's world, many enterprises use microservices as the default standard to build large service-oriented enterprise applications.

Spring Framework has been a popular programming framework for the developer community for many years. Spring Boot removed the need to have a heavyweight application container, and provides a means to deploy lightweight, serverless applications. Spring Cloud combines many Netflix OSS components and provides an ecosystem to run and manage large-scale microservices. It provides capabilities such as load balancing, service registry, monitoring, Service Gateway, and so on.

However, microservices comes with its own challenges, such as monitoring, managing, distributing, scaling, discovering, and more, especially when deploying at scale. Adopting microservices without addressing common microservices challenges will lead to catastrophic results. The most important part of this book is a technology-agnostic microservices capability model that helps address all common microservice challenges.

The goal of this book is to enlighten readers with a pragmatic approach and provide guidelines to implement responsive microservices at scale. This book will give a holistic view of capabilities that are required to build microservices with examples. This book takes a deep dive into Spring Boot, Spring Cloud, Docker, Mesos, and Marathon. Upon completion of this book, you will understand how Spring Boot will be used to deploy autonomous services by removing the need to have a heavyweight application server. You will also learn different Spring Cloud capabilities, as well as realize the use of Docker for containerization, Mesos, and Marathon for compute resource abstraction and cluster-wide control.

I am sure you will enjoy each and every section of this book. Also, I honestly believe that this book adds tremendous value in successfully conceiving microservices into your business. Throughout this book, I have used practical aspects of microservices implementation by providing a number of examples, including a case study from the travel domain. At the end of this book, you will have learned how to implement microservice architectures using Spring Framework, Spring Boot, and Spring Cloud. These are battle-tested, robust tools for developing and deploying scalable microservices. Written to the latest specifications of Spring, with the help of this book, you'll be able to build modern, internet-scale Java applications in no time.

What this book covers

Chapter 1, *Demystifying Microservices*, gives you an introduction to microservices. This chapter covers the background, evaluation, and fundamental concepts of microservices.

Chapter 2, *Related Architecture Styles and Use Cases*, covers the relationship with Service-Oriented Architecture, the concepts of cloud native and Twelve Factor applications, and explains some of the common use cases.

Chapter 3, *Building Microservices with Spring Boot*, introduces building REST and message-based microservices using the Spring Framework and how to wrap them with Spring Boot. In addition, we will also explore some core capabilities of Spring Boot.

Chapter 4, *Applying Microservices Concepts*, explains the practical aspects of microservices implementation by detailing the challenges that developers face with enterprise-grade microservices.

Chapter 5, *Microservices Capability Model*, introduces a capability model required to successfully manage a microservices ecosystem. This chapter also describes a maturity assessment model, which will be useful when adopting microservices at enterprise level.

Chapter 6, *Microservices Evolution – A Case Study*, takes you to a real-world case study of microservices evolution by introducing BrownField Airline. Using the case study, explains how to apply microservices concepts learned in the previous chapter.

Chapter 7, *Scale Microservices with Spring Cloud Components*, shows you how to scale previous examples using Spring Cloud stack capabilities. It details the architecture and different components of Spring Cloud and how they integrate together.

Chapter 8, *Logging and Monitoring Microservices*, covers the importance of logging and monitoring aspects when developing microservices. Here, we look at the details of some of the best practices when using microservices, such as centralized logging and monitoring capabilities using open source tools and how to integrate them with Spring projects.

Chapter 9, *Containerizing Microservices with Docker*, explains containerization concepts in the context of microservices. Using Mesos and Marathon, it demonstrates next-level implementation to replace the custom life cycle manager for large deployments.

Chapter 10, *Scaling Dockerized Microservices with Mesos and Marathon*, explains auto-provisioning and deployment of microservices. Here, we will also learn how to use Docker containers in the preceding example for large-scale deployments.

Chapter 11, *Microservices Development Life Cycle*, covers the process and practices of microservices development. The importance of DevOps and continuous delivery pipelines are also explained in this chapter.

What you need for this book

Chapter 3, *Building Microservices with Spring Boot*, introduces Spring Boot, which requires the following software components to test the code:

- JDK 1.8
- Spring Tool Suite 3.8.2 (STS)
- Maven 3.3.1
- Spring Framework 5.0.0.RC1
- Spring Boot 2.0.0. SNAPSHOT
- spring-boot-cli-2.0.0.SNAPSHOT-bin.zip
- Rabbit MQ 3.5.6
- FakeSMTP 2.0

In Chapter 7, *Scale Microservices with Spring Cloud Components*, you will learn about the Spring Cloud project. This requires the following software component, in addition to those previously mentioned:

- Spring Cloud Dalston RELEASE

In Chapter 8, *Logging and Monitoring Microservices*, we will see how centralized logging can be implemented for microservices. This requires the following software stack:

- elasticsearch-1.5.2
- kibana-4.0.2-darwin-x64
- logstash-2.1.2

Chapter 9, *Containerizing Microservices with Docker*, demonstrates how we can use Docker for microservices deployments. This requires the following software components:

- Docker version (17.03.1-ce)
- Docker Hub

Chapter 10, *Scaling Dockerized Microservices with Mesos and Marathon,* uses Mesos and Marathon to deploy Dockerized microservices into an autoscalable cloud. The following software components are required for this purpose:

- Mesos version 1.2.0
- Docker version 17.03.1-ce
- Marathon version 3.4.9

Who this book is for

This book will be interesting for architects who want to know how to design robust internet-scale microservices in Spring Framework, Spring Boot, and Spring Cloud, and manage them using Docker, Mesos, and Marathon. The capability model will help architects device solutions even beyond the tools and technologies discussed in this book.

This book is primarily for Spring developers who are looking to build cloud-ready, internet-scale applications to meet modern business demands. The book will help developers understand what exactly microservices are, and why they are important in today's world, by examining a number of real-world use cases and hand-on code samples. Developers will understand how to build simple Restful services and organically grow them to truly enterprise-grade microservices ecosystems.

Conventions

In this book, you will find a number of text styles that distinguish between different kinds of information. Here are some examples of these styles and an explanation of their meaning.

Code words in text, database table names, folder names, filenames, file extensions, pathnames, dummy URLs, user input, and Twitter handles are shown as follows: "RestTemplate is a utility class that abstracts the lower-level details of the HTTP client."

A block of code is set as follows:

```
@SpringBootApplication
public class Application {
  public static void main(String[] args) {
    SpringApplication.run(Application.class, args);
  }
}
```

When we wish to draw your attention to a particular part of a code block, the relevant lines or items are set in bold:

```
@Component
class Receiver {
  @RabbitListener(queues = "TestQ")
  public void processMessage(String content) {
    System.out.println(content);
  }
}
```

Any command-line input or output is written as follows:

```
$java -jar target/bootrest-0.0.1-SNAPSHOT.jar
```

New terms and **important words** are shown in bold. Words that you see on the screen, for example, in menus or dialog boxes, appear in the text like this: "If the services are being build up fresh using the Spring Starter project, then select **Config Client**, **Actuator**, **Web** as well as **Eureka Discovery** client."

Warnings or important notes appear like this.

Tips and tricks appear like this.

Reader feedback

Feedback from our readers is always welcome. Let us know what you think about this book-what you liked or disliked. Reader feedback is important for us as it helps us develop titles that you will really get the most out of.
To send us general feedback, simply e-mail feedback@packtpub.com, and mention the book's title in the subject of your message.
If there is a topic that you have expertise in and you are interested in either writing or contributing to a book, see our author guide at www.packtpub.com/authors.

Customer support

Now that you are the proud owner of a Packt book, we have a number of things to help you to get the most from your purchase.

Downloading the example code

You can download the example code files for this book from your account at http://www.packtpub.com. If you purchased this book elsewhere, you can visit http://www.packtpub.com/support and register to have the files e-mailed directly to you.

You can download the code files by following these steps:

1. Log in or register to our website using your e-mail address and password.
2. Hover the mouse pointer on the **SUPPORT** tab at the top.
3. Click on **Code Downloads & Errata**.
4. Enter the name of the book in the **Search** box.
5. Select the book for which you're looking to download the code files.
6. Choose from the drop-down menu where you purchased this book from.
7. Click on **Code Download**.

Once the file is downloaded, please make sure that you unzip or extract the folder using the latest version of:

- WinRAR / 7-Zip for Windows
- Zipeg / iZip / UnRarX for Mac
- 7-Zip / PeaZip for Linux

The code bundle for the book is also hosted on GitHub at https://github.com/PacktPublishing/Spring-5.0-Microservices-Second-Edition. We also have other code bundles from our rich catalog of books and videos available at https://github.com/PacktPublishing/. Check them out!

Downloading the color images of this book

We also provide you with a PDF file that has color images of the screenshots/diagrams used in this book. The color images will help you better understand the changes in the output. You can download this file from https://www.packtpub.com/sites/default/files/downloads/Spring5.0MicroservicesSecondEdition_ColorImages.

Errata

Although we have taken every care to ensure the accuracy of our content, mistakes do happen. If you find a mistake in one of our books-maybe a mistake in the text or the code-we would be grateful if you could report this to us. By doing so, you can save other readers from frustration and help us improve subsequent versions of this book. If you find any errata, please report them by visiting http://www.packtpub.com/submit-errata, selecting your book, clicking on the **Errata Submission Form** link, and entering the details of your errata. Once your errata are verified, your submission will be accepted and the errata will be uploaded to our website or added to any list of existing errata under the Errata section of that title.

To view the previously submitted errata, go to https://www.packtpub.com/books/content/support and enter the name of the book in the search field. The required information will appear under the **Errata** section.

Piracy

Piracy of copyrighted material on the Internet is an ongoing problem across all media. At Packt, we take the protection of our copyright and licenses very seriously. If you come across any illegal copies of our works in any form on the Internet, please provide us with the location address or website name immediately so that we can pursue a remedy.

Please contact us at copyright@packtpub.com with a link to the suspected pirated material.

We appreciate your help in protecting our authors and our ability to bring you valuable content.

Questions

If you have a problem with any aspect of this book, you can contact us at questions@packtpub.com, and we will do our best to address the problem.

Demystifying Microservices

1

Microservices is an architecture style and an approach for software development to satisfy modern business demands. Microservices are not invented, it is more of an evolution from the previous architecture styles.

We will start the chapter by taking a closer look at the evolution of microservices architecture from the traditional monolithic architectures. We will also examine the definition, concepts, and characteristics of microservices.

By the end of this chapter, you will have learned about the following:

- Evolution of microservices
- Definition of microservices architecture with examples
- Concepts and characteristics of microservices architecture

Evolution of microservices

Microservices is one of the increasingly popular architecture patterns next to **Service Oriented Architecture** (**SOA**), complemented by DevOps and Cloud. Its evolution has been greatly influenced by the disruptive digital innovation trends in modern business and the evolution of technology in the last few years. We will examine these two catalysts--business demands and technology--in this section.

Business demand as a catalyst for microservices evolution

In this era of digital transformation, enterprises are increasingly adopting technologies as one of the key enablers for radically increasing their revenue and customer base. Enterprises are primarily using social media, mobile, cloud, big data, and **Internet of Things (IoT)** as vehicles for achieving the disruptive innovations. Using these technologies, enterprises are finding new ways to quickly penetrate the market, which severely pose challenges to the traditional IT delivery mechanisms.

The following graph shows the state of traditional development and microservices against the new enterprise challenges, such as agility, speed of delivery, and scale:

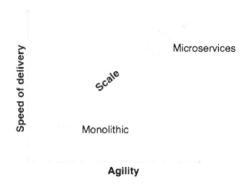

 Microservices promises more agility, speed of delivery, and scale compared to traditional monolithic applications.

Gone are the days where businesses invested in large application developments with turnaround times of a few years. Enterprises are no longer interested in developing consolidated applications for managing their end-to-end business functions as they did a few years ago.

The following graph shows the state of traditional monolithic application and microservices in comparison with the turnaround time and cost:

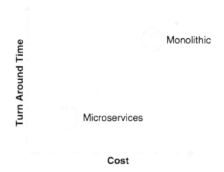

 Microservices provides an approach for developing quick and agile applications, resulting in a lesser overall cost.

Today, for instance, airlines are not investing in rebuilding their core mainframe reservation systems as another monolithic monster. Financial institutions are not rebuilding their core banking systems. Retailers and other industries are not rebuilding heavyweight supply chain management applications, such as their traditional ERP's. Focus has been shifted from building large applications to building quick win, point solutions that cater to the specific needs of the business in the most agile way possible.

Let's take an example of an online retailer running with a legacy monolithic application. If the retailer wants to innovate their sales by offering their products personalized to a customer based on the customer's past shopping preferences and much more, or they want to enlighten customers by offering products to customer based on propensity to buy a product.

In such cases, enterprises want to quickly develop a personalization engine or an offer engine based on their immediate needs, and plug them into their legacy application, as shown here:

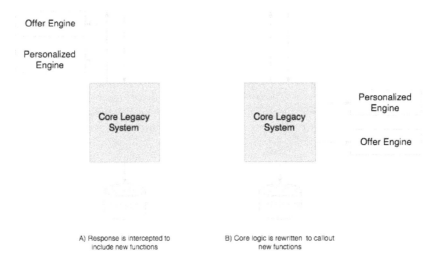

As shown in the preceding diagram, rather than investing on rebuilding the **Core Legacy System**, this will either be done by passing the responses through the new functions, as shown in the diagram marked **A**, or modifying the **Core Legacy System** to call out these functions as part of the processing, as shown in the diagram marked **B**. These functions are typically written as microservices.

This approach gives organizations a plethora of opportunities to quickly try out new functions with lesser cost in an experimental mode. Business can later validate key performance indicators change or replace these implementations if required.

 Modern architectures are expected to maximize the ability to replace its parts and minimize the cost of replacing them. Microservices' approach is a means to achieve this.

Technology as a catalyst for microservices evolution

Emerging technologies have made us rethink the way we build software systems. For example, a few decades ago, we couldn't even imagine a distributed application without a two-phase commit. Later, **NoSQL** databases made us think differently.

Similarly, these kinds of paradigm shifts in technology have reshaped all layers of software architecture.

The emergence of HTML 5, CSS3, and the advancement of mobile applications repositioned user interfaces. Client-side JavaScript frameworks, such as Angular, Ember, React, Backbone, and more, are immensely popular due to their capabilities around responsive and adaptive designs.

With cloud adoptions steamed into the mainstream, **Platform as a Services** (**PaaS**) providers, such as Pivotal CF, AWS, Sales Force, IBM Bluemix, Redhat OpenShift, and more, made us rethink the way we build middleware components. The container revolution created by **Docker** radically influenced the infrastructure space. Container orchestration tools, such as **Mesosphere DCOS**, made infrastructure management much easier. Serverless added further easiness in application managements.

Integration landscape has also changed with the emerging **Integration Platform as a Services** (**iPaaS**), such as Dell Boomi, Informatica, MuleSoft, and more. These tools helped organizations stretch integration boundaries beyond the traditional enterprise.

NoSQL and **NewSQL** have revolutionized the space of the database. A few years ago, we had only a few popular databases, all based on relational data modeling principles. Today, we have a long list of databases: **Hadoop**, **Cassandra**, **CouchDB**, **Neo 4j**, and **NuoDB**, to name a few. Each of these databases addresses certain specific architectural problems.

Imperative architecture evolution

Application architecture has always been evolving alongside with demanding business requirements and evolution of technologies.

Different architecture approaches and styles, such as mainframes, client server, *n*-tier, and service oriented were popular at different times. Irrespective of the choice of architecture styles, we always used to build one or the other forms of monolithic architectures. Microservices architecture evolved as a result of modern business demands, such as agility, speed of delivery, emerging technologies, and learning from previous generations of architectures:

**Monolithic
Architecture**　　　　　　　**Microservices
Architecture**

Microservices help us break the boundaries of the monolithic application and build a logically independent smaller system of systems, as shown in the preceding diagram.

 If we consider the monolithic application as a set of logical subsystems encompassed with a physical boundary, microservices are a set of independent subsystems with no enclosing physical boundary.

What are Microservices?

Microservices are an architectural style used by many organizations today as a game changer to achieve high degrees of agility, speed of delivery, and scale. Microservices gives us a way to develop physically separated modular applications.

Microservices are not invented. Many organizations, such as Netflix, Amazon, and eBay had successfully used the divide and conquer technique for functionally partitioning their monolithic applications into smaller atomic units, each performing a single function. These organizations solved a number of prevailing issues they were experiencing with their monolithic application. Following the success of these organizations, many other organizations started adopting this as a common pattern for refactoring their monolithic applications. Later, evangelists termed this pattern microservices architecture.

Microservices originated from the idea of **Hexagonal Architecture**, which was coined by Alister Cockburn back in 2005. Hexagonal Architecture, or Hexagonal pattern, is also known as the **Ports and Adapters** pattern.

 Read more about Hexagonal Architecture here:
`http://alistair.cockburn.us/Hexagonal+architecture`

In simple terms, Hexagonal architecture advocates to encapsulate business functions from the rest of the world. These encapsulated business functions are unaware of their surroundings. For example, these business functions are not even aware of input devices or channels and message formats used by those devices. Ports and adapters at the edge of these business functions convert messages coming from different input devices and channels to a format that is known to the business function. When new devices are introduced, developers can keep adding more and more ports and adapters to support those channels without touching business functions. One may have as many ports and adapters to support their needs. Similarly, external entities are not aware of business functions behind these ports and adapters. They will always interface with these ports and adapters. By doing so, developers enjoy the flexibility to change channels and business functions without worrying too much about future proofing interface designs.

The following diagram shows the conceptual view of Hexagonal Architecture:

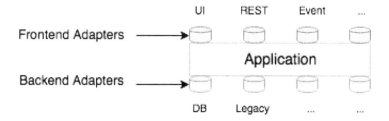

In the preceding diagram, the application is completely isolated and exposed through a set of frontend adapters, as well as a set of backend adapters. Frontend adaptors are generally used for integrating UI and other APIs, whereas backend adapters are used for connecting to various data sources. Ports and adapters on both sides are responsible for converting messages coming in and going out to appropriate formats expected by external entities. Hexagonal architecture was the inspiration for microservices.

When we look for a definition for microservices, there is no single standard way of describing them. Martin Fowler defines microservices as follows:

> *"The microservice architectural style is an approach to developing a single application as a suite of small services, each running in its own process and communicating with lightweight mechanisms, often an HTTP resource API. These services are built around business capabilities and independently deployable by fully automated deployment machinery. There is a bare minimum of centralized management of these services, which may be written in different programming languages and use different data storage technologies."* --(http://www.martinfowler.com/articles/microservices.html)

The definition used in this book is as follows:

 Microservices is an architectural style or an approach for building IT systems as a set of business capabilities that are autonomous, self contained, and loosely coupled.

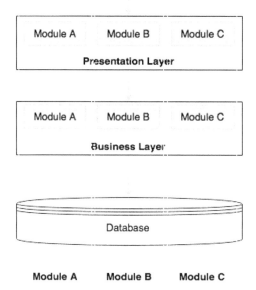

The preceding diagram depicts a traditional *n*-tier application architecture, having a **Presentation Layer**, **Business Layer**, and **Database Layer**. Modules **A**, **B**, and **C** represent three different business capabilities. The layers in the diagram represent separation of architecture concerns. Each layer holds all three business capabilities pertaining to that layer. The presentation layer has web components of all three modules, the business layer has business components of all three modules, and the database host tables of all three modules. In most cases, layers are physically spreadable, whereas modules within a layer are hardwired.

Let's now examine a microservices-based architecture:

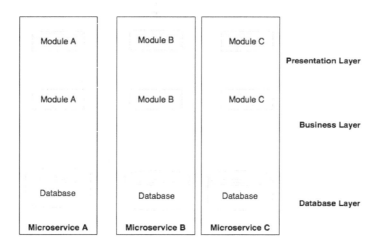

As we can see in the preceding diagram, the boundaries are inversed in the microservices architecture. Each vertical slice represents a microservice. Each microservice will have its own presentation layer, business layer, and database layer. Microservices are aligned towards business capabilities. By doing so, changes to one microservice does not impact others.

There is no standard for communication or transport mechanisms for microservices. In general, microservices communicate with each other using widely adopted lightweight protocols, such as HTTP and REST, or messaging protocols, such as **JMS** or **AMQP**. In specific cases, one might choose more optimized communication protocols, such as **Thrift**, **ZeroMQ**, **Protocol Buffers**, or **Avro**.

Since microservices are more aligned to business capabilities and have independently manageable life cycles, they are the ideal choice for enterprises embarking on DevOps and cloud. DevOps and cloud are two facets of microservices.

DevOps is an IT realignment to narrow the gap between traditional IT development and operations for better efficiency.

Read more about DevOps at `http://dev2ops.org/2010/02/what-is-dev ops/`.

Microservices - The honeycomb analogy

A honeycomb is an ideal analogy for representing the evolutionary microservices architecture:

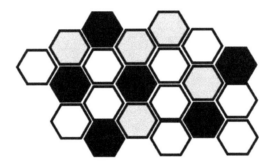

In the real world, bees build a honeycomb by aligning hexagonal wax cells. They start small, using different materials to build the cells. Construction is based on what is available at the time of building. Repetitive cells form a pattern, and result in a strong fabric structure. Each cell in the honeycomb is independent, but also integrated with other cells. By adding new cells, the honeycomb grows organically to a big, solid structure. The content inside the cell is abstracted and is not visible outside. Damage to one cell does not damage other cells, and bees can reconstruct those cells without impacting the overall honeycomb.

Principles of microservices

In this section, we will examine some of the principles of the microservices architecture. These principles are a must have when designing and developing microservices. The two key principles are single responsibility and autonomous.

Single responsibility per service

The single responsibility principle is one of the principles defined as part of the **SOLID** design pattern. It states that a unit should only have one responsibility.

 Read more about the SOLID design pattern at `http://c2.com/cgi/wiki ?PrinciplesOfObjectOrientedDesign`.

It implies that a unit, either a class, a function, or a service, should have only one responsibility. At no point do two units share one responsibility, or one unit perform more than one responsibility. A unit with more than one responsibility indicates tight coupling:

As shown in the preceding diagram, **Customer**, **Product**, and **Order** are different functions of an e-commerce application. Rather than building all of them into one application, it is better to have three different services, each responsible for exactly one business function, so that changes to one responsibility will not impair the others. In the preceding scenario, **Customer**, **Product**, and **Order** were treated as three independent microservices.

Microservices are autonomous

Microservices are self-contained, independently deployable, and autonomous services that take full responsibility of a business capability and its execution. They bundle all dependencies including the library dependencies; execution environments, such as web servers and containers; or virtual machines that abstract the physical resources.

One of the major differences between microservices and SOA is in its level of autonomy. While most of the SOA implementations provide the service-level abstraction, microservices go further and abstract the realization and the execution environment.

In traditional application developments, we build a war or a ear, then deploy it into a JEE application server, such as **JBoss**, **Weblogic**, **WebSphere**, and more. We may deploy multiple applications into the same JEE container. In the microservices approach, each microservice will be built as a fat jar embedding all dependencies and run as a standalone Java process:

	Microservice A	Microservice B
	Service Implementation	Service Implementation
Application A (ear/war)		
	Dependent Libraries	Dependent Libraries
Application B (ear/war)		
	Service Listener (HTTP)	Service Listener (HTTP)
JEE Application Server		
	JRE	JRE
Container / Virtual Machine	**Container**	**Container**
Physical Machine	Physical Machine	

Microservices may also get their own containers for execution, as shown in the preceding diagram. Containers are portable, independently manageable, and lightweight runtime environments. **Container** technologies, such as Docker, are an ideal choice for microservices deployments.

Characteristics of microservices

The microservices definition discussed earlier in this chapter is arbitrary. Evangelists and practitioners have strong, but sometimes, different opinions on microservices. There is no single, concrete, and universally accepted definition for microservices. However, all successful microservices implementations exhibit a number of common characteristics. Therefore, it is important to understand these characteristics rather than sticking to theoretical definitions. Some of the common characteristics are detailed in this section.

Services are first class citizens

In the microservices world, services are first class citizens. Microservices expose service endpoints as APIs and abstract all their realization details. The internal implementation logic, architecture, and technologies, including programming language, database, quality of services mechanisms, and more, are completely hidden behind the service API.

Moreover, in the microservices architecture, there is no more application development, instead organizations will focus on service development. In most enterprises, this requires a major cultural shift in the way applications are built.

In a customer profile microservice, the internals, such as data structure, technologies, business logic, and so on, will be hidden. It wont be exposed or visible to any external entities. Access will be restricted through the service endpoints or APIs. For instance, customer profile microservices may expose register customer and get customers as two APIs for others to interact.

Characteristics of service in a microservice

Since microservices are more or less like a flavor of SOA, many of the service characteristics defined in the SOA are applicable to microservices as well.

The following are some of the characteristics of services that are applicable to microservices as well:

- **Service contract**: Similar to SOA, microservices are described through well-defined service contracts. In the microservices world, JSON and REST are universally accepted for service communication. In case of JSON/REST, there are many techniques used to define service contracts. JSON Schema, WADL, Swagger, and RAML are a few examples.
- **Loose coupling**: Microservices are independent and loosely coupled. In most cases, microservices accept an event as input and respond with another event. Messaging, HTTP, and REST are commonly used for interaction between microservices. Message-based endpoints provide higher levels of decoupling.
- **Service abstraction**: In microservices, service abstraction is not just abstraction of service realization, but also provides complete abstraction of all libraries and environment details, as discussed earlier.
- **Service reuse**: Microservices are course grained reusable business services. These are accessed by mobile devices and desktop channels, other microservices, or even other systems.

- **Statelessness**: Well-designed microservices are a stateless, shared nothing with no shared state, or conversational state maintained by the services. In case there is a requirement to maintain state, they will be maintained in a database, perhaps in-memory.

- **Services are discoverable**: Microservices are discoverable. In a typical microservices environment, microservices self-advertise their existence and make themselves available for discovery. When services die, they automatically take themselves out from the microservices ecosystem.

- **Service interoperability**: Services are interoperable as they use standard protocols and message exchange standards. Messaging, HTTP, and more are used as the transport mechanism. REST/JSON is the most popular method to develop interoperable services in the microservices world. In cases where further optimization is required on communications, then other protocols such as Protocol Buffers, Thrift, Avro, or Zero MQ could be used. However, use of these protocols may limit the overall interoperability of the services.

- **Service Composeability**: Microservices are composeable. Service composeability is achieved either through service orchestration or service choreography.

 More details on SOA principles can be found at `http://serviceorientat ion.com/serviceorientation/index`.

Microservices are lightweight

Well-designed microservices are aligned to a single business capability; therefore, they perform only one function. As a result, one of the common characteristics we see in most of the implementations are microservices with smaller footprints.

When selecting supporting technologies, such as web containers, we will have to ensure that they are also lightweight so that the overall footprint remains manageable. For example, Jetty or Tomcat are better choices as application containers for microservices as compared to more complex traditional application servers, such as Weblogic or WebSphere.

Container technologies such as Docker also helps us keep the infrastructure footprint as minimal as possible compared to hypervisors such as VMware or **Hyper-V**.

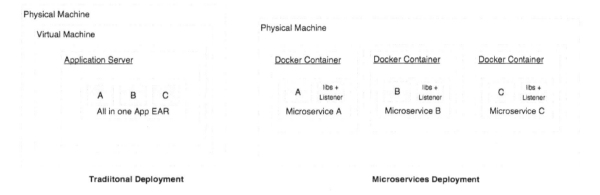

As shown in the preceding diagram, microservices are typically deployed in Docker containers, which encapsulate the business logic and needed libraries. This helps us quickly replicate the entire setup on a new machine, a completely different hosting environment, or even move across different cloud providers. Since there is no physical infrastructure dependency, containerized microservices are easily portable.

Microservices with polyglot architecture

Since microservices are autonomous and abstract everything behind the service APIs, it is possible to have different architectures for different microservices. A few common characteristics that we see in microservices implementations are as follows:

- Different services use different versions of the same technologies. One microservice may be written on Java 1.7 and another one could be on Java 1.8.
- Different languages for developing different microservices, such as one microservice in Java and another one in **Scala**.
- Different architectures such as one microservice using **Redis** cache to serve data while another microservice could use MySQL as a persistent data store.

A polyglot language scenario is depicted in the following diagram:

REST/JSON	REST/JSON
Erlang	Java
Elastic Search	My SQL
Hotel Search	**Hotel Booking**

In the preceding example, since **Hotel Search** is expected to have high transaction volumes with stringent performance requirements, it is implemented using **Erlang**. In order to support predictive search, **Elastic Search** is used as the data store. At the same time, Hotel Booking needs more **ACID** transactional characteristics. Therefore, it is implemented using MySQL and Java. The internal implementations are hidden behind service endpoints defined as REST/JSON over HTTP.

Automation in microservices environment

Most of the microservices implementations are automated to a maximum, ranging from development to production.

Since microservices break monolithic applications into a number of smaller services, large enterprises may see a proliferation of microservices. Large numbers of microservices are hard to manage until and unless automation is in place. The smaller footprint of microservices also helps us automate the microservices development to deployment life cycle. In general, microservices are automated end to end, for example, automated builds, automated testing, automated deployment, and elastic scaling:

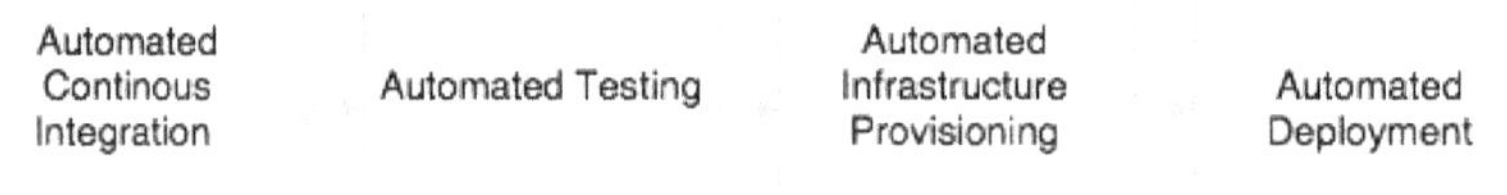

Automated Continous Integration	Automated Testing	Automated Infrastructure Provisioning	Automated Deployment

As indicated in the diagram, automations are typically applied during the development, test, release, and deployment phases.

Different blocks in the preceding diagram are explained as follows:

- The development phase will be automated using version control tools, such as Git, together with **continuous integration** (**CI**) tools, such as Jenkins, Travis CI, and more. This may also include code quality checks and automation of unit testing. Automation of a full build on every code check-in is also achievable with microservices.
- The testing phase will be automated using testing tools such as **Selenium**, **Cucumber**, and other **AB testing strategies**. Since microservices are aligned to business capabilities, the number of test cases to automate will be fewer compared to the monolithic applications; hence, regression testing on every build also becomes possible.
- Infrastructure provisioning will be done through container technologies, such as Docker, together with release management tools, such as Chef or Puppet, and configuration management tools, such as Ansible. Automated deployments are handled using tools such as Spring Cloud, **Kubernetes**, **Mesos**, and Marathon.

Microservices with a supporting ecosystem

Most of the large scale microservices implementations have a supporting ecosystem in place. The ecosystem capabilities include DevOps processes, centralized log management, service registry, API gateways, extensive monitoring, service routing, and flow control mechanisms:

Microservices work well when supporting capabilities are in place, as represented in the preceding diagram.

Microservices are distributed and dynamic

Successful microservices implementations encapsulate logic and data within the service. This results in two unconventional situations:

- Distributed data and logic
- Decentralized governance

Compared to traditional applications, which consolidate all logic and data into one application boundary, microservices decentralize data and logic. Each service, aligned to a specific business capability, owns its own data and logic:

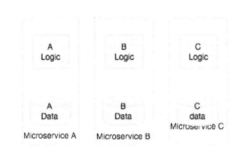

Logical System Boundary (as in monolithic)

The dotted line in the preceding diagram implies the logical monolithic application boundary. When we migrate this to microservices, each microservice, **A**, **B**, and **C**, creates its own physical boundaries.

Microservices don't typically use centralized governance mechanisms the way they are used in SOA. One of the common characteristics of microservices implementations are that they are not relaying on heavyweight enterprise-level products, such as an **Enterprise Service Bus** (**ESB**). Instead, the business logic and intelligence are embedded as a part of the services themselves.

A retail example with ESB is shown as follows:

A typical SOA implementation is shown in the preceding diagram. **Shopping Logic** is fully implemented in the ESB by orchestrating different services exposed by **Customer**, **Order**, and **Product**. In the microservices approach, on the other hand, shopping itself will run as a separate microservice, which interacts with **Customer**, **Product**, and **Order** in a fairly decoupled way.

SOA implementations are heavily relaying on static registry and repository configurations to manage services and other artifacts. Microservices bring a more dynamic nature into this. Hence, a static governance approach is seen as an overhead in maintaining up-to-date information. This is why most of the microservices implementations use automated mechanisms to build registry information dynamically from the runtime topologies.

Antifragility, fail fast, and self healing

Antifragility is a technique successfully experimented with at Netflix. It is one of the most powerful approaches to build fail-safe systems in modern software development.

 The antifragility concept is introduced by Nassim Nicholas Taleb in his book, *Antifragile: Things That Gain from Disorder*.

In the antifragility practice, software systems are consistently challenged. Software systems evolve through these challenges, and, over a period of time, get better and better to withstand these challenges. Amazon's Game Day exercise and Netflix's **Simian Army** are good examples of such antifragility experiments.

Fail Fast is another concept used to build fault-tolerant, resilient systems. This philosophy advocates systems that expect failures versus building systems that never fail. Importance has to be given to how quickly the system can fail, and, if it fails, how quickly it can recover from that failure. With this approach, the focus is shifted from **Mean Time Between Failures** (**MTBF**) to **Mean Time To Recover** (**MTTR**). A key advantage of this approach is that if something goes wrong, it kills itself, and the downstream functions won't be stressed.

Self-Healing is commonly used in microservices deployments, where the system automatically learns from failures and adjusts itself. These systems also prevent future failures.

Microservices examples

There is no *one size fits all* approach when implementing microservices. In this section, different examples are analyzed to crystalize the microservices concept.

An example of a holiday portal

In the first example, we will review a holiday portal--**Fly By Points**. **Fly By Points** collects points that are accumulated when a customer books a hotel, flight, or car through their online website. When a customer logs in to the **Fly By Points** website, they will be able to see the points accumulated, personalized offers that can be availed by redeeming the points, and upcoming trips, if any:

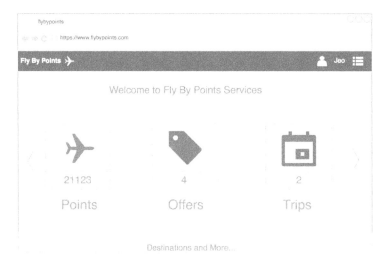

Let's assume that the preceding page is the home page after login. There are **2** upcoming trips for **Jeo**, **4** personalized offers, and **21123** points. When the user clicks on each of the boxes, details will be queried and displayed.

Holiday portal has a Java, Spring-based traditional monolithic application architecture, as follows:

As shown in the preceding diagram, Holiday portal's architecture is web-based and modular with clear separation between layers. Following the usual practice, Holiday portal is also deployed as a single war file deployed on a web server such as **Tomcat**. Data is stored in an all encompassing backing relational database. This is a good fit for the purposes of architecture when the complexities are less. As the business grows, the user base expands and the complexity also increases.

This results in a proportional increase in the transaction volumes. At this point, enterprises should look for rearchitecting the monolithic application to microservices for better speed of delivery, agility, and manageability:

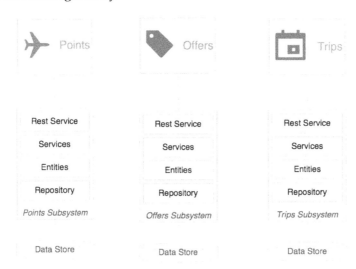

Upon examining the simple microservices version of this application, we will immediately see a few things in this architecture:

- Each subsystem has now become an independent system by itself--a microservice. There are three microservices representing three business functions--**Trips**, **Offers**, and **Points**. Each one has its internal data store and middle layer. The internal structure of each service remains the same.
- Each service encapsulates its own database as well as its own HTTP listener. As opposed to the previous model, there is no web server and there is no war. Instead, each service has its own embedded HTTP listener, such as Jetty, Tomcat, and more.
- Each microservice exposes a rest service to manipulate the resources/entities that belong to that service.

It is assumed that the presentation layer is developed using a client-side JavaScript MVC framework, such as Angular JS. These client-side frameworks are capable of invoking REST calls directly.

When the web page is loaded, all three boxes, **Trips**, **Offers**, and **Points**, will be displayed with details such as points, number of offers, and number of trips. This will be done by each box independently making asynchronous calls to the respective backend microservices using REST. There is no dependency between the services at the service layer. When the user clicks on any of the boxes, the screen will be transitioned and will load the details of the clicked item. This will be done by making another call to the respective microservice.

An example of a travel agent portal

This third example is a simple travel agent portal application. In this example, we will see both synchronous REST calls as well as asynchronous events.

In this case, portal is just a container application with multiple menu items or links in the portal. When specific pages are requested, for example, when the menu is clicked or a link is clicked, they will be loaded from the specific microservices:

The architecture of the **Travel Agent Portal** backed with multiple microservices is shown as follows:

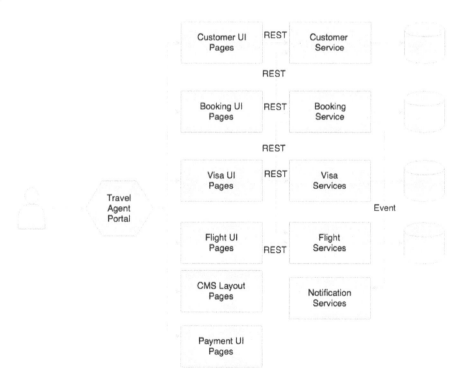

When a customer requests a booking, the following events will take place internally:

- The travel agent opens the flight UI, searches for a flight, and identifies the right flight for the customer. Behind the scenes, the flight UI will be loaded from the Flight microservice. The flight UI only interacts with its own backend APIs within the Flight microservice. In this case, it makes a REST call to the Flight microservice to load the flights to be displayed.

- The travel agent then queries the customer details by accessing the customer UI. Similar to the flight UI, the customer UI will be loaded from the Customer microservices. Actions in the customer UI will invoke REST calls on the Customer microservice. In this case, the customer details will be loaded by invoking appropriate APIs on the Customer microservice.

- Then the travel agent checks the visa details to see the eligibility to travel to the selected country. This will also follow the same pattern as mentioned in the previous two points.

- Then the travel agent makes a booking using the booking UI from the Booking microservices, which again follows the same pattern.

- The payment pages will be loaded from the Payment microservice. In general, the payment service will have additional constraints, including the **Payment Card Industry Data Security Standard** (**PCIDSS**) compliance, such as protecting and encrypting data in motion and data at rest. The advantage of the microservices approach is that none of the other microservices need to be considered under the purview of PCIDSS as opposed to the monolithic application, where the complete application comes under the governing rules of PCIDSS. Payment also follows the same pattern described earlier.

- Once the booking is submitted, the **Booking Service** calls the flight service to validate and update the flight booking. This orchestration is defined as a part of the Booking microservices. Intelligence to make a booking is also held within the Booking microservices. As a part of the booking process, it also validates, retrieves, and updates the Customer microservice.

- Finally, the Booking microservice sends a booking event, which the **Notification Services** picks up, and sends a notification to the customer.

The interesting factor here is that we can change the user interface, logic, and data of a microservice without impacting any other microservices.

This is a clean and neat approach. A number of portal applications could be built by composing different screens from different microservices, especially for different user communities. The over all behavior and navigation will be controlled by the portal application.

The approach has a number of challenges unless the pages are designed with this approach in mind. Note that the site layouts and static contents will be loaded from the **Content Management System** (**CMS**) as layout templates. Alternately, this could be stored in a web server. The site layout may have fragments of User Interfaces, which will be loaded from the microservices at runtime.

Microservices benefits

Microservice offers a number of benefits over the traditional multi-tier monolithic architectures. This section explains some of the key benefits of the microservices architecture approach.

Supports polyglot architecture

With microservices, architects and developers get flexibility in choosing the most suitable technology and architecture for a given scenario. This gives the flexibility to design better fit solutions in a more cost-effective way.

Since microservices are autonomous and independent, each service can run with its own architecture or technology, or different versions of technologies.

The following image shows a simple, practical example of polyglot architecture with microservices:

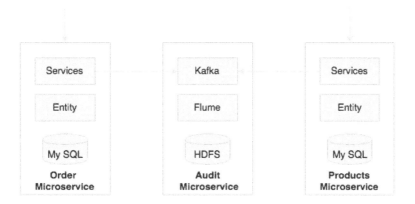

There is a requirement to audit all system transactions and record transaction details such as request and response data, users who initiated the transaction, the service invoked, and so on.

As shown in the preceding diagram, while core services like Order microservice and Product microservice use a relational data store, the Audit microservice persists data in a **Hadoop File System** (**HDFS**). A relational data store is neither ideal nor cost effective to store large data volumes, like in the case of audit data. In the monolithic approach, the application generally uses a shared, single database that stores the **Order**, **Product**, and **Audit** data.

In this example, audit service is a technical microservice using a different architecture. Similarly, different functional services could also use different architectures.

In another example, there could be a Reservation microservice running on Java 7, while a Search microservice could be running on Java 8. Similarly, an Order microservice could be written on Erlang, whereas a Delivery microservice could be on the Go language. None of these are possible with a monolithic architecture.

Enables experimentation and innovation

Modern enterprises are thriving toward quick wins. Microservices is one of the key enablers for enterprises to do disruptive innovation by offering the ability to experiment and Fail Fast.

Since services are fairly simple and smaller in size, enterprises can afford to experiment with new processes, algorithms, business logic, and more. With large monolithic applications, experimentation was not easy, straightforward, or cost effective. Businesses had to spend a large sum of money to build or change an application to try out something new. With microservices, it is possible to write a small microservice to achieve the targeted functionality, and plug it into the system in a reactive style. One can then experiment with the new function for a few months. Moreover, if the new microservice is not working as expected, change or replace it with another one. The cost of change will be considerably less compared to the monolithic approach:

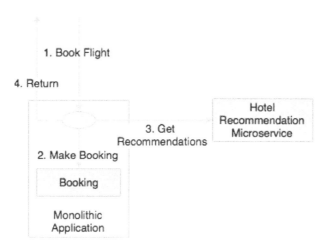

In another example of an airline booking website, the airline wants to show personalized hotel recommendations in their booking page. The recommendations have to be displayed on the booking confirmation page.

As shown in the preceding diagram, it is convenient to write a microservice that can be plugged into the monolithic applications booking flow rather than incorporating this requirement in the monolithic application itself. The airline may choose to start with a simple recommendation service, and keep replacing it with newer versions until it meets the required accuracy.

Elastically and selectively scalable

Since microservices are smaller units of work, it enables us to implement selective scalability and other **Quality of Services (QoS)**.

Scalability requirements may be different for different functions in an application. Monolithic applications are generally packaged as a single war or an ear. As a result, applications can only be scaled as a whole. There is no option to scale a module or a subsystem level. An I/O intensive function, when streamed with high velocity data, could easily bring down the service levels of the entire application.

In the case of microservices, each service could be independently scaled up or down. Since scalability can be selectively applied for each service, the cost of scaling is comparatively less with the microservices approach.

In practice, there are many different ways available to scale an application, and this is largely constraint to the architecture and behavior of the application. The **Scale Cube** defines primarily three approaches to scale an application:

- X-axis scaling, by horizontally cloning the application
- Y-axis scaling, by splitting different functionality
- Z-axis scaling, by partitioning or sharding the data.

 Read more about Scale Cube at `http://theartofscalability.com/`.

When Y-axis scaling is applied to monolithic applications, it breaks the monolithic into smaller units aligned with business functions. Many organizations successfully applied this technique to move away from monolithic application. In principle, the resulting units of functions are inline with the microservices characteristics.

For instance, on a typical airline website, statistics indicates that the ratio of flight search versus flight booking could be as high as 500:1. This means one booking transaction for every 500 search transactions. In this scenario, search needs 500 times more scalability than the booking function. This is an ideal use case for selective scaling:

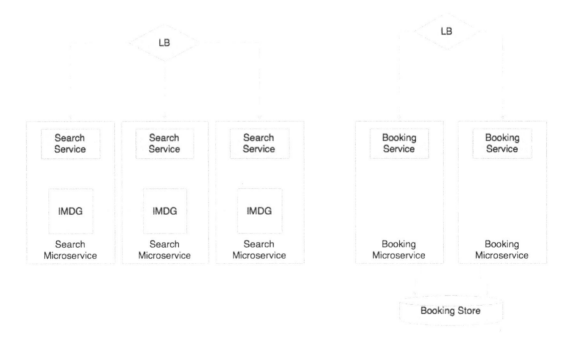

The solution is to treat search requests and booking requests differently. With a monolithic architecture, this is only possible with Z scaling in the scale cube. However, this approach is expensive, as, in Z scale, the entire codebase will be replicated.

In the preceding diagram, Search and **b** are designed as different microservices so that Search can be scaled differently from Booking. In the diagram, Search has three instances and Booking has two instances. Selective scalability is not limited to the number of instances, as shown in the preceding diagram, but also in the way in which the microservices are architected. In the case of Search, an **In-Memory Data Grid** (**IMDG**) such as Hazelcast can be used as the data store. This will further increase the performance and scalability of Search. When a new Search microservice instance is instantiated, an additional IMDG node will be added to the IMDG cluster. Booking does not require the same level of scalability. In the case of Booking, both instances of the Booking microservices are connected to the same instance of the database.

Allows substitution

Microservices are self-contained independent deployment modules, enabling us to substitute one microservice with another similar microservice.

Many large enterprises follow buy-versus-build policies for implementing software systems. A common scenario is to build most of the functions in-house and buy certain niche capabilities from specialists outside. This poses challenges in the traditional monolithic applications since these application components are highly cohesive. Attempting to plug in third-party solutions to the monolithic applications results in complex integrations. With microservices, this is not an afterthought. Architecturally, a microservice can be easily replaced by another microservice developed, either in-house or even extended by a microservice from a third party:

A pricing engine in the airline business is complex. Fares for different routes are calculated using complex mathematical formulas known as pricing logic. Airlines may choose to buy a pricing engine from the market instead of building the product in-house. In the monolithic architecture, **Pricing** is a function of **Fares** and **Booking**. In most cases, Pricing, Fares, and Bookings are hardwired, making it almost impossible to detach.

In a well-designed microservices system, Booking, Fares, and Pricing will be independent microservices. Replacing the Pricing microservice will have only a minimal impact on any other services, as they are all loosely coupled and independent. Today, it could be a third-party service, tomorrow, it could be easily substituted by another third-party service or another home grown service.

Enables to build organic systems

Microservices help us build systems that are organic in nature. This is significantly important when migrating monolithic systems gradually to microservices.

Organic systems are systems that grow laterally over a period of time by adding more and more functions to it. In practice, applications grow unimaginably large in its lifespan, and, in most cases, the manageability of the application reduces dramatically over that same period of time.

Microservices are all about independently manageable services. This enables us to keep adding more and more services as the need arises, with minimal impact on the existing services. Building such systems do not need huge capital investment. Hence, businesses can keep building as part of their operational expenditure.

A loyalty system in an airline was built years ago, targeting individual passengers. Everything was fine until the airline started offering loyalty benefits to their corporate customers. Corporate customers are individuals grouped under corporations. Since the current system's core data model is flat, targeting individuals, the corporate requirement needs a fundamental change in the core data model, and hence, a huge rework to incorporate this requirement.

As shown in the following diagram, in a microservices-based architecture, customer information would be managed by the Customer microservices, and loyalty by the Loyalty microservice:

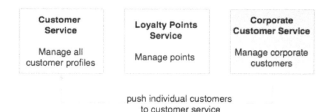

In this situation, it is easy to add a new Corporate Customer microservice to manage corporate customers. When a corporation is registered, individual members will be pushed to the Customer microservices to manage them as usual. The Corporate Customer microservice provides a corporate view by aggregating data from the Customer microservice. It will also provide services to support corporate-specific business rules. With this approach, adding new services will have only a minimal impact on existing services.

Helps managing technology debt

Since microservices are smaller in size and have minimal dependencies, they allow the migration of services that are using end-of-life technologies with minimal cost.

Technology changes are one of the barriers in software development. In many traditional monolithic applications, due to the fast changes in technology, today's next generation applications could easily become legacy, even before releasing to production. Architects and developers tend to add a lot of protection against technology changes by adding layers of abstractions. However, in reality, this approach doesn't solve the issue, but, instead, it results in over-engineered systems. Since technology upgrades are often risky and expensive, with no direct returns for the business, the business may not be happy to invest in reducing the technology debt of the applications.

With microservices, it is possible to change or upgrade technology for each service individually, rather than upgrading an entire application.

Upgrading an application with, for instance, five million lines written on **EJB 1.1** and Hibernate to Spring, **JPA**, and REST services is almost like rewriting the entire application. In the microservices world, this could be done incrementally.

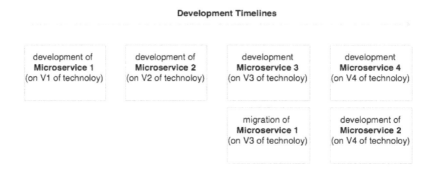

As shown in the preceding diagram, while older versions of the services are running on old versions of technologies, new service developments can leverage the latest technologies. The cost of migrating microservices with end-of-life technologies will be considerably less compared to enhancing monolithic applications.

Allowing co-existence of different versions

Since microservices package the service runtime environment along with the service itself, it enables multiple versions of the service to coexist in the same environment.

There will be situations where we will have to run multiple versions of the same service at the same time. Zero downtime promote, where one has to gracefully switch over from one version to another, is one example of such a scenario, as there will be a time window where both services will have to be up and running simultaneously. With monolithic applications, this is a complex procedure, since upgrading new services in one node of the cluster is cumbersome as, for instance, this could lead to class loading issues. A Canary release, where a new version is only released to a few users to validate the new service, is another example where multiple versions of the services have to coexist.

With microservices, both these scenarios are easily manageable. Since each microservice uses independent environments, including the service listeners such as embedded Tomcat or Jetty, multiple versions can be released and gracefully transitioned without many issues. Consumers, when looking up services, look for specific versions of services. For example, in a canary release, a new user interface is released to user A. When user A sends a request to the microservice, it looks up the canary release version, whereas all other users will continue to look up the last production version.

Care needs to be taken at database level to ensure that the database design is always backward compatible to avoid breaking changes.

As shown in the following diagram, version V01 and V02 of the Customer service can coexist as they are not interfering with each other, given their respective deployment environment:

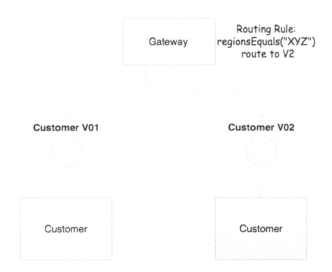

Routing rules can be set at the gateway to divert traffic to specific instances, as shown in the diagram. Alternatively, clients can request specific versions as a part of the request itself. In the diagram, the gateway selects the version based on the region from which the request originated.

Supporting building self-organizing systems

Microservices help us build self-organizing systems. A self-organizing system supporting automated deployment will be resilient and exhibits self-healing and self-learning capabilities.

In a well-architected microservice system, services are unaware of other services. It accepts a message from a selected queue and processes the message. At the end of the process, it may send out another message that triggers other services. This allows us to drop any service into the ecosystem without analyzing the impact on the overall system. Based on the input and output, the service will self-organize into the ecosystem. No additional code changes or service orchestration is required. There is no central brain to control and coordinate the processes.

Imagine an existing notification service that listens to an INPUT queue and sends notifications to a **Simple Mail Transfer Protocol** (**SMTP**) server as follows:

If later, a personalization engine needs to be introduced to personalize messages before sending it to the customer, the personalization engine is responsible for changing the language of the message to the customer's native language.

The updated service linkage is shown as follows:

With microservices, a new personalization service will be created to do this job. The input queue will be configured as INPUT in an external configuration server. The personalization service will pick up the messages from the INPUT queue (earlier, this was used by the notification service), and send the messages to the OUTPUT queue after completing the process. The notification service's input queue will then send to OUTPUT. From the very next moment onward, the system automatically adopts this new message flow.

Supporting event-driven architecture

Microservices enable us to develop transparent software systems. Traditional systems communicate with each other through native protocols and hence behave like a black-box application. Business events and system events, unless published explicitly, are hard to understand and analyze. Modern applications require data for business analysis, to understand dynamic system behaviors, and analyze market trends, and they also need to respond to real-time events. Events are useful mechanisms for data extraction.

A well-architected microservice always works with events for both input and output. These events can be tapped by any services. Once extracted, events can be used for a variety of use cases.

For example, businesses want to see the velocity of orders categorized by the product type in real-time. In a monolithic system, we will need to think about how to extract these events, which may impose changes in the system.

The following diagram shows the addition of **New Event Aggregation Service** without impacting existing services:

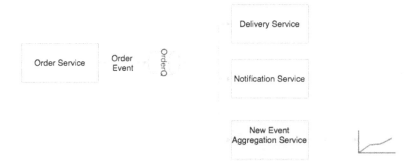

In the microservices world, **Order Event** is already published whenever an order is created. This means that it is just a matter of adding a new service to subscribe to the same topic, extract the event, perform the requested aggregations, and push another event for the dashboard to consume.

Enables DevOps

Microservices are one of the key enablers of DevOps. DevOps is widely adopted as a practice in many enterprises, primarily to increase the speed of delivery and agility. Successful adoption of DevOps requires cultural changes and process changes, as well as architectural changes. It advocates to have agile development, high velocity release cycles, automatic testing, automatic infrastructure provisioning, and automated deployment. Automating all these processes is extremely hard to achieve with traditional monolithic applications. Microservices are not the ultimate answer, but microservices are at the center stage in many DevOps implementations. Many DevOps tools and techniques are also evolving around the use of microservices.

Considering a monolithic application takes hours to complete a full build and twenty to thirty minutes to start the application, one can see that this kind of application is not ideal for DevOps automation. It is hard to automate continuous integration on every commit. Since large monolithic applications are not automation friendly, continuous testing and deployments are also hard to achieve.

On the other hand, small footprint microservices are more automation-friendly, and, therefore, they can more easily support these requirements.

Microservices also enables smaller, focused agile teams for development. Teams will be organized based on the boundaries of microservices.

Summary

In this chapter, we learned about the fundamentals of microservices with the help of a few examples.

We explored the evolution of microservices from traditional monolithic applications. We examined some of the principles and mind shift required for modern application architectures. We also looked at some of the common characteristics repeatedly seen in most of the successful microservices implementations. Finally, we also learned the benefits of microservices.

In the next chapter, we will analyze the link between microservices and a few other architecture styles. We will also examine common microservice use cases.

2
Related Architecture Styles and Use Cases

Microservices are on top of the hype at this point. At the same time, there are noises around certain other architecture styles, for instance, serverless architecture. Which one is good? Are they competing against each other? What are the appropriate scenarios and the best ways to leverage microservices? These are the obvious questions raised by many developers.

In this chapter, we will analyze various other architecture styles and establish the similarities and relationships between microservices and other buzz words such as **Service Oriented Architecture (SOA)**, **Twelve-Factor Apps**, **serverless computing**, **Lambda architectures**, **DevOps**, **Cloud**, **Containers**, **and Reactive Microservices**. Twelve-Factor Apps defines a set of software engineering principles to develop applications targeting cloud. We will also analyze typical use cases of microservices and review some of the popular frameworks available for the rapid development of microservices.

By the end of this chapter, you will have learned about the following:

- Relationship of microservices with SOA and Twelve-Factor Apps
- Link to serverless computing and Lambda architecture style used in the context of Big Data, **cognitive computing**, and the **Internet of Things (IoT)**
- Supporting architecture elements such as Cloud, Containers, and DevOps
- Reactive Microservices
- Typical use cases of microservices architecture
- A few popular microservices frameworks

Service-Oriented Architecture (SOA)

SOA and microservices follow similar concepts. In the `Chapter 1`, *Demystifying Microservices*, we saw that microservices are evolved from SOA and many service characteristics are common in both approaches.

However, are they the same or are they different?

Since microservices are evolved from SOA, many characteristics of microservices are similar to SOA. Let's first examine the definition of SOA.

> The Open Group definition of SOA (`http://www.opengroup.org/soa/sou rce-book/soa/p1.htm`) is as follows:
>
> *SOA is an architectural style that supports service-orientation. Service-orientation is a way of thinking in terms of services and service-based development and the outcomes of services.*

> *A service:*
>
> - *Is a logical representation of a repeatable business activity that has a specified outcome (e.g., check customer credit, provide weather data, consolidate drilling reports)*
> - *Is self-contained*
> - *May be composed of other services*
> - *Is a "black box" to consumers of the service*

We have learned similar aspects in microservices as well. *So, in what way are microservices different?* The answer is--it depends.

The answer to the previous question could be yes or no, depending on the organization and its adoption of SOA. SOA is a broader term, and different organizations approached SOA differently to solve different organizational problems. The difference between microservices and SOA is based on the way an organization approaches SOA.

In order to get clarity, a few scenarios will be examined in the following section.

Service-oriented integration

Service-oriented integration refers to a service-based integration approach used by many organizations:

Many organizations would have used SOA primarily to solve their integration complexities, also known as integration spaghetti. Generally, this is termed as **Service-Oriented Integration** (**SOI**). In such cases, applications communicate with each other through a common integration layer using standard protocols and message formats, such as SOAP/XML based web services over HTTP or **Java Message Service** (**JMS**). These types of organizations focus on **Enterprise Integration Patterns** (**EIP**) to model their integration requirements. This approach strongly relies on heavyweight **Enterprise Service Bus** (**ESB**), such as TIBCO BusinessWorks, WebSphere ESB, Oracle ESB, and the likes. Most of the ESB vendors also packed a set of related products, such as Rules Engines, Business Process Management Engines, and so on, as an SOA suite. Such organization's integrations are deeply rooted into these products. They either write heavy orchestration logic in the ESB layer or business logic itself in the service bus. In both cases, all enterprise services are deployed and accessed via the ESB. These services are managed through an enterprise governance model. For such organizations, microservices is altogether different from SOA.

Legacy modernization

SOA is also used to build service layers on top of legacy applications:

Another category of organizations would have used SOA in transformation projects or legacy modernization projects. In such cases, the services are built and deployed in the ESB connecting to backend systems using ESB adapters. For these organizations, microservices are different from SOA.

Service-oriented application

Some organizations would have adopted SOA at an application level:

In this approach, lightweight integration frameworks, such as **Apache Camel** or **Spring Integration**, are embedded within applications to handle service-related cross-cutting capabilities, such as protocol mediation, parallel execution, orchestration, and service integration. Since some of the lightweight integration frameworks had native Java object support, such applications would have even used native **Plain Old Java Objects** (**POJO**) services for integration and data exchange between services. As a result, all services have to be packaged as one monolithic web archive. Such organizations could see microservices as the next logical step of their SOA.

Monolithic migration using SOA

The following diagram shows a monolithic application, broken down into three micro applications:

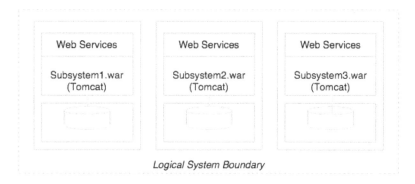

Logical System Boundary

The last possibility is transforming a monolithic application into smaller units after hitting the breaking point with the monolithic system. They would have broken the application into smaller, physically deployable subsystems, similar to the **Y-axis scaling** approach explained earlier, and deployed them as web archives on web servers, or as jars deployed on some homegrown containers. These subsystems as service would have used web services or other lightweight protocols to exchange data between services. They would have also used SOA and service-design principles to achieve this. For such organizations, they may tend to think that microservices are the same old wine in a new bottle.

Twelve-Factor Apps

Cloud computing is one of the most rapidly evolving technologies. It promises many benefits, such as cost advantage, speed, agility, flexibility, and elasticity. There are many cloud providers offering different services. They are lowering the cost models to make it more attractive to the enterprises. Different cloud providers, such as AWS, Microsoft, Rackspace, IBM, Google, and so on, use different tools, technologies, and services. On the other hand, enterprises are aware of this evolving battlefield and, therefore, they are looking for options for de-risking from lockdown to a single vendor.

Many organizations do a lift and shift of their applications to cloud. In such cases, the applications may not realize all benefits promised by the cloud platforms. Some applications need to undergo an overhaul, whereas some may need minor tweaking before moving to the cloud. This is, by and large, depends upon how the application is architectured and developed.

For example, if the application has its production database server URLs hardcoded as a part of the applications war, this needs to be modified before moving the application to cloud. In the cloud, the infrastructure is transparent to the application and, especially, the physical IP addresses cannot be assumed.

How do we ensure that an application, or even microservices, can run seamlessly across multiple cloud providers and take advantages of cloud services such as elasticity?

It is important to follow certain principles while developing cloud-native applications.

Cloud native is a term used to develop applications that can work efficiently in a cloud environment, and understand and utilize cloud behaviors, such as elasticity, utilization-based charging, fail aware, and so on.

Twelve-Factor App, forwarded by Heroku, is a methodology describing characteristics expected from a modern cloud-ready application. These twelve factors are equally applicable for microservices as well. Hence, it is important to understand the Twelve-Factors.

Single code base

The code base principle advices that each application should have a single code base. There can be multiple instances of deployment of the same code base, such as development, testing, or production. The code is typically managed in a source-control system such as Git, Subversion, and so on:

Extending the same philosophy for microservices, each microservice should have its own code base, and this code base is not shared with any other microservice. It also means that one microservice will have exactly one code base.

Bundle dependencies

As per this principle, all applications should bundle their dependencies along with the application bundle. With build tools such as **Maven** and **Gradle**, we explicitly manage dependencies in a **Project Object Model** (**POM**) or gradle file, and link them using a central build artifact repository such as **Nexus** or **Archiva**. This will ensure that the versions are managed correctly. The final executables will be packaged as a war file or an executable jar file embedding all dependencies:

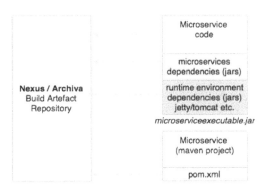

In the context of microservices, this is one of the fundamental principles to be followed. Each microservices should bundle all required dependencies and execution libraries, such as HTTP listener and more, in the final executable bundle.

Externalizing configurations

The Externalize configurations principle gives you an advice to externalize all configuration parameters from the code. An application's configuration parameters vary between environments such as support email IDs or URL of an external system, username, passwords, queue name, and more. These will be different for development, testing, and production. All service configurations should be externalized:

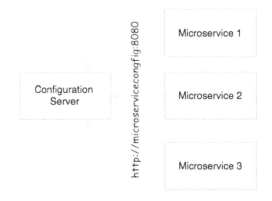

The same principle is obvious for microservices as well. Microservices configuration parameters should be loaded from an external source. This will also help you automate the release and deployment process as the only change between these environments are the configuration parameters.

Backing services are addressable

All backing services should be accessible through an addressable URL. All services need to talk to some external resources during the life cycle of their execution. For example, they could be listening to or sending messages to a messaging system, sending an email, or persisting data to a database. All these services should be reachable through a URL without complex communication requirements:

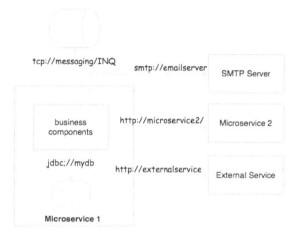

In the microservices world, microservices can either talk to a messaging system to send or receive messages, or they can accept or send messages to another service API. In a regular case, these are either HTTP endpoints using REST and JSON or TCP or HTTP-based messaging endpoints.

Isolation between build, release, and run

This principle advocates strong isolation between the build stage, the release stage, and the run stage. The build stage refers to compiling and producing binaries by including all assets required. The release stage refers to combining binaries with environment-specific configuration parameters. The run stage refers to running applications on a specific execution environment. The pipeline is unidirectional. Hence, it is not possible to propagate changes from run stages back to the build stage. Essentially, it also means that it is not recommended to do specific builds for production; rather, it has to go through the pipeline:

In microservices, the build will create executable jar files, including the service runtime, such as the HTTP listener. During the release phase, these executables will be combined with release configurations, such as production URLs, and so on, and create a release version, most probably as a container like **Docker**. In the run stage, these containers will be deployed on production via a container scheduler.

Stateless, shared nothing processes

This principle suggests that processes should be stateless and share nothing. If the application is stateless, then it is fault tolerant, and can be scaled out easily.

All microservices should be designed as stateless functions. If there is any requirement to store a state, it should be done with a backing database or in an in-memory cache.

Expose services through port bindings

A Twelve-Factor App is expected to be self-contained or standalone. Traditionally, applications are deployed into a server--a web server or an application server, such as Apache Tomcat or JBoss, respectively. A Twelve-Factor App ideally does not relay on an external web server. A HTTP listener, such as Tomcat, **Jetty**, and more, has to be embedded in the service or application itself.

Port binding is one of the fundamental requirements for microservices to be autonomous and self-contained. Microservice embeds the service listeners as a part of the service itself.

Concurrency for scale out

The concurrency for scale out principle states that processes should be designed to scale out by replicating the processes. This is in addition to the use of threads within the process.

In the microservices world, services are designed for a scale out rather than scale up. The X-axis scaling technique is primarily used for scaling a service by spinning up another identical service instance. The services can be elastically scaled or shrunk, based on the traffic flow. Furthermore, microservices may make use of parallel processing and concurrency frameworks to further speed up or scale up the transaction processing.

Disposability, with minimal overhead

The disposability with minimal overhead principle advocates to build applications with minimal startup and shutdown times, and with a graceful shutdown support. In an automated deployment environment, we should be able to bring up or bring down instances as quickly as possible. If the application's startup or shutdown takes considerable time, it will have an adverse effect on automation. The startup time is proportionally related to the size of the application. In a cloud environment targeting auto scaling, we should be able to spin up a new instance quickly. This is also applicable when promoting new versions of services.

In the microservices context, in order to achieve full automation, it is extremely important to keep the size of the application as thin as possible, with minimal startup and shutdown times. Microservices should also consider lazy loading of objects and data.

Development, production parity

The development, production parity principle states the importance of keeping the development and production environments as identical as possible. For example, let's consider an application with multiple services or processes, such as a job scheduler service, cache services, or one or more application services. In a development environment, we tend to run all of them on a single machine. Whereas, in production, we will facilitate independent machines to run each of these processes. This is primarily to manage cost of the infrastructure. The downside is that, if production fails, there is no identical environment to reproduce and fix the issues.

This principle is not only valid for microservices, but it is also applicable to any application development.

Externalizing logs

A Twelve-Factor App never attempts to store or ship log files. In a cloud, it is better to avoid local I/Os or file systems. If the I/Os are not fast enough in a given infrastructure, they could create a bottleneck. The solution to this is to use a centralized logging framework. **Splunk**, **greylog**, **Logstash**, **Logplex**, **Loggly** are some examples of log shipping and analysis tools. The recommended approach is to ship logs to a central repository by tapping the logback appenders and write to one of the shipper's endpoints.

In a microservices ecosystem, this is very important, as we are breaking a system into a number of smaller services, which could result in decentralized logging. If they store logs in a local storage, it would be extremely difficult to correlate logs between services:

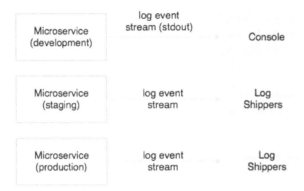

In development, microservice may direct the log stream to **stdout**, whereas, in production, these streams will be captured by the log shippers and sent to a central log service for storage and analysis.

Package admin processes

Apart from application requests, most of the applications provision for admin tasks. This principle advices you to target the same release and an identical environment as the long running processes runs to perform these activities. Admin code should also be packaged along with the application code.

This principle is not only valid for microservices, but it is also applicable to any application development.

Serverless computing

Serverless computing architecture or **Functions as a Service** (**FaaS**) has gained quite a bit of popularity these days. In serverless computing, developers need not worry about application servers, virtual machines, Containers, infrastructure, scalability, and other quality of services. Instead, developers write functions and drop those functions into an already running computing infrastructure. Serverless computing improves faster software deliveries as it eliminates the provisioning and management part of the infrastructure required by microservices. Sometimes, this is even referred to as **NoOps**.

FaaS platforms support multiple language runtimes, such as Java, Python, Go, and so on. There are many serverless computing platforms and frameworks available. Moreover, this space is still evolving. **AWS Lambda**, **IBM OpenWhisk**, **Azure Functions**, **Google Cloud Functions** are some of the popular managed infrastructures for serverless computing. **Red Hat Funktion** is another serverless computing platform on top of **Kubernetes**, which can be deployed on any cloud or on premise. **IronFunctions** is one of the recent entrants--a cloud-agnostic, serverless computing platform. There are other serverless computing platforms, such as Webtask for web-related functions. **BrightWork** is another serverless computing platform for JavaScript applications that offers minimal vendor locking.

There are many other frameworks intended to simplify AWS Lambda development and deployment supporting different languages. **Apex**, **Serverless**, **Lambda Framework for Java**, **Chalice for Python**, **Claudia for Node JS**, **Sparta for Go**, and **Gordon** are some of the popular frameworks in this category.

Serverless computing is closely related to microservices. In other words, microservices are the basis for serverless computing. There are a number of characteristics shared by both, serverless computing as well as microservices. Similar to microservices, functions generally perform one task at a time, are isolated in nature, and communicate through designated APIs that are either event-based or HTTP. Also, functions have smaller footprints like microservices. It is safe to say that functions follow microservices-based architecture.

The following diagram shows a serverless computing scenario based on AWS Lambda:

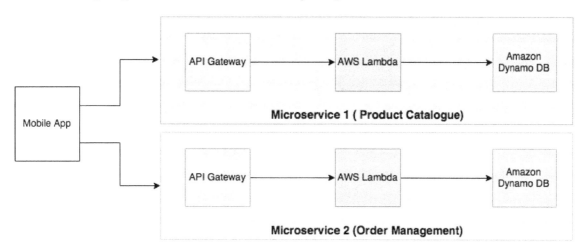

In this scenario, each microservice will be developed as a separate AWS Lambda function and independently wired through an API gateway for HTTP-based communication. In this case, each microservice holds its own data in an Amazon DynamoDB.

Generally, the FaaS billing model is truly based on the **pay as you use** model, as opposed to pay for what is reserved model followed in case of virtual machines or EC2 instances. Moreover, developers need not worry about passivating images when they are no longer used. When there are only a few transactions, just enough computing power will be charged. As the load increases, more resources will be automatically allocated. This makes serverless computing an attractive model for many enterprises.

The new style of microservices use cases such as big data, cognitive computing, IoT, and bots, which are perfect candidates for serverless computing. More about these use cases is explained in the next section.

It is also important to note that the disadvantage of serverless computing is its strong vendor locking. This space is still getting matured, and, perhaps, we will see more tooling in this space to reduce these gaps. In the future, we will also see a large number of services available in the market place that can be utilized by microservice developers when developing on serverless computing platforms. Serverless computing, together with microservices architecture, is definitely a promising choice for developers.

Lambda architecture

There are new styles of microservices use cases in the context of big data, cognitive computing, bots, and IoT:

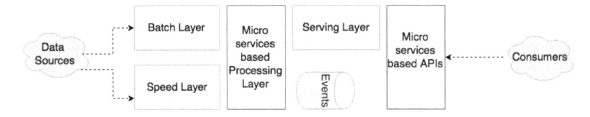

The preceding diagram shows a simplified **Lambda architecture** commonly used in the context of big data, cognitive, and IoTs. As you can see in the diagram, microservices play a critical role in the architecture. The batch layer process data, and store typically in a **Hadoop Distributed File System** (**HDFS**) file system. Microservices are written on top of this batch layer process data and build serving layer. Since microservices are independent, when they encounter new demands, it is easy to add those implementations as microservices.

Speed-layer microservices are primarily reactive microservices for stream processing. These microservices accept a stream of data, apply logic, and then respond with another set of events. Similarly, microservices are also used for exposing data services on top of the serving layer.

The following are different variations of the preceding architecture:

- **Cognitive computing** scenarios, such as integrating an optimization service, forecasting service, intelligent price calculation service, prediction service, offer service, recommendation service, and more, are good candidates for microservices. These are independent stateless computing units that accepts certain data, applies algorithms, and returns the results. These are cognitive computing microservices run on top of either speed layer or batch layer. Platforms such as Algorithmia uses microservices-based architecture.

- **Big Data** processing services that run on top of big data platforms to provide answer sets is another popular use case. These services connect to the big data platform's read-relevant data, process those records, and provide necessary answers. These services typically run on top of the batch layer. Platforms such as **MapR** embrace microservices.

- **Bots** that are conversational in nature use the microservices architecture. Each service is independent and executes one function. This can be treated as either API service on top of the serving layer or stream processing services on top of the speed layer. Bots platforms, such as the Azure bot service, leverages the microservices architecture.

- **IoT** scenarios such as machine or sensor data stream processing utilize microservices to process data. These kinds of services run on top of the speed layer. Industrial internet platforms such as Predix are based on the microservices philosophy.

DevOps, Cloud, and Containers

The trios Cloud (more specifically, Containers), Microservices and **DevOps**, are targeting a set of common objectives--speed of delivery, business value, and cost benefits. All three can stay evolved independently, but they complement each other to achieve the desired common goals. Organizations embarking on any of these naturally tend to consider the others as they are closely linked together:

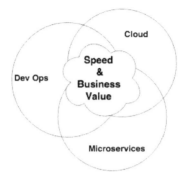

Many organizations start their journey with DevOps as an organizational practice to achieve high velocity release cycles, but eventually move to microservices architecture and cloud. However, it is not mandatory to have microservices and Cloud to support DevOps. However, automating release cycles of large monolithic applications does not make much sense, and, in many cases, it would be impossible to achieve. In such scenarios, microservices architecture and Cloud will be handy when implementing DevOps.

If we flip the coin, Cloud does not need a microservices architecture to achieve its benefits. However, to effectively implement microservices, both Cloud and DevOps are essential.

In summary, if the objective of an organization is to achieve speed of delivery and quality in a cost-effective way, the trio together can bring tremendous success.

DevOps as the practice and process for microservices

Microservice is an architecture style that enables quick delivery. However, microservices cannot provide the desired benefits by itself. A microservices-based project with a delivery cycle of six months does not give the targeted speed of delivery or business agility. Microservices need a set of supporting delivery practices and processes to effectively achieve their goal.

DevOps is the ideal candidate as the underpinning process and practices for microservice delivery. It processes and practices gel well with the microservices architecture philosophies.

Cloud and Containers as the self-service infrastructure for microservices

The main driver for cloud is to improve agility and reduce cost. By reducing the time to provision the infrastructure, the speed of delivery can be increased. By optimally utilizing the infrastructure, one can bring down the cost. Therefore, cloud directly helps you achieve both speed of delivery and cost.

Without having a cloud infrastructure with the cluster management software, it would be hard to control the infrastructure cost when deploying microservices. Hence, the cloud with self-service capabilities is essential for microservices to achieve their full potential benefits. In a microservices context, the cloud not only helps you abstract the physical infrastructure, but also provides software APIs for dynamic provisioning and automatic deployments. This is referred to as **infrastructure as code** or **software defined infrastructure**.

Containers further provide benefits when dealing with DevOps and microservices. They provide better manageability and a cost-effective way of handling large volumes of deployments. Furthermore, container services and container orchestration tools helped you manage infrastructures.

Reactive microservices

The reactive programming paradigm is an effective way to build scalable, fault-tolerant applications. The reactive manifesto defines basic philosophy of reactive programming.

 Read more about the reactive manifesto here:
http://www.reactivemanifesto.org

By combining the reactive programming principles together with the microservices architecture, developers can build low latency high throughput scalable applications.

Microservices are typically designed around business capabilities. Ideally, well-designed microservices will exhibit minimal dependencies between microservices. However, in reality, when microservices are expected to deliver same capabilities delivered by monolithic applications, many microservices have to work in collaboration. Dividing services based on business capabilities will not solve all issues. Isolation and communication between services are also equally important. Even though microservices are often designed around business capabilities, wiring them with synchronous calls can form hard dependencies between them. As a result, organizations may not realize the full benefits of microservices. Distributed systems with strong dependencies between them have its own overheads and are hard to manage. For example, if an upgrade is required for one of the microservices, it can seriously impact other dependent services. Hence, adopting reactive style is important for successful microservices implementations.

Let's examine reactive microservices a bit more. There are four pillars when dealing with reactive programming. These attributes are **resilient**, **responsive**, **message based**, and **elastic**. Resilient and responsive are closely linked to isolation. Isolation is the foundation for both reactive programming as well as microservices. Each microservice is autonomous and is the building block of a larger system. By and large, these microservices are isolated from the rest of its functional components by drawing boundaries around business functions. By doing so, failures of one service can be well isolated from the others. In case of failures, it should not cause issues to its downstream services. Either a fallback service or a replica of the same service will takeover its responsibility temporarily. By introducing isolation, each isolated components can be scaled, managed, and monitored independently.

Even though isolation is in place, if the communication or dependencies between services are modeled as synchronous blocking RPC calls, then failures cannot be fully isolated. Hence, it is extremely important to design communications between services in a reactive style by using asynchronous non-blocking calls:

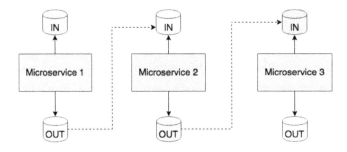

As shown in the preceding diagram, in a reactive system, each microservice will listen to an event. The service reacts upon receiving an input event. The service then starts processing the event and sends out another response event. The microservice itself is not aware of any other services running in the ecosystem. In this example, **Microservice 1** does not have any knowledge of **Microservice 2** and **Microservice 3**. Choreography can be achieved by connecting an output queue of one service to the input queue of another service, as shown in the diagram.

Based on the velocity of events, services can automatically scale up by spinning up replicas of instances. For example, in a reactive style order management system, as soon as an order is placed, the system will send out an **Order Event**. There could be many microservices listening to an **Order Event.** Upon consuming this event, they perform various things. This design also allows developers to keep adding more and more reactive routines as need arises.

The flow control or choreography in case of reactive microservices will be taken care of automatically, as shown earlier in the diagram. There is no central command and control. Instead, messages and input and output contracts of microservices itself will establish flow. Changing the message flow is easy to achieve by rewiring input and output queues.

 The **Promise theory** proposed by Mark Burgess in 2004 has so much relevance in this situation. The Promise theory defines an autonomous collaboration model for systems or entities to interact in a distributed environment using voluntary cooperation. The theory claims that promise-based agents can reproduce the same behavior exhibited by traditional command and control systems that follows the obligation model. Reactive microservices are inline with the Promise theory, in which, each service is independent and can collaborate in a completely autonomous manner. **Swarm Intelligence** is one of these formal architecture mechanisms, increasingly applied in the modern artificial intelligent systems for building highly scalable intelligence routines.

A highly scalable and reliable message system is the single most important component in a reactive microservices ecosystem. **QBit**, **Spring Reactive**, **RxJava**, and **RxJS** are some of the frameworks and libraries that help you build reactive microservices. Spring 5 has inbuilt support to develop reactive web applications. **Spring Cloud Streams** are good choice to build truly reactive microservices using Spring Framework.

A reactive microservice-based order management system

Let's examine another microservices example: an online retail web site. In this case, we will focus more on the backend services, such as the order event generated when the customer places an order through the website:

This microservices system is completely designed based on reactive programming practices.

When an event is published, a number of microservices are ready to kick start upon receiving the event. Each one of them is independent and is not relying on other microservices. The advantage of this model is that we can keep adding or replacing microservices to achieve specific needs.

In the preceding diagram, there are eight microservices shown. The following activities take place on arrival of an **OrderEvent**:

- **OrderService** kicks off when an **OrderEvent** is received. **OrderService** creates an order and saves details to its own database.
- If the order is successfully saved, an **OrderSuccessfulEvent** is created by **OrderService** and published.
- A series of actions will take place when **OrderSuccessfulEvent** arrives.
- **DeliveryService** accepts the event and places a **DeliveryRecord** to deliver the order to the customer. This in turn generates **DeliveryEvent** and publishes the event.

- The **TruckingService** picks up the **DeliveryEvent** and processes it. For instance, **TruckingService** creates a trucking plan.
- **CustomerNotificationService** sends a notification to the customer informing the customer that an order is placed.
- **InventoryCacheService** updates the inventory cache with the available product count.
- **StockReorderService** checks whether the stock limits are adequate and generates **ReplenishEvent** if required.
- **CustomerPointsService** recalculates the customer's loyalty points based on this purchase.
- **CustomerAccountService** updates the order history in the customer account.

In this approach, each service is responsible for only one function. Services accept and generate events. Each service is independent and is not aware of its neighborhoods. Hence, the neighborhood can organically grow as mentioned in the **honeycomb analogy**. New services could be added as and when necessary. Adding a new service does not impact any of the existing service.

Microservice use cases

Microservice is not a silver bullet, and it will not solve all the architectural challenges of today's world. There is no hard and fast rule, or a rigid guideline on when to use microservices.

Microservices may not fit in each and every use case. The success of microservices largely depends on the selection of use cases. The first and the foremost activity is to do a litmus test of the use case against the microservices benefits. The litmus test must cover all microservices benefits we had discussed earlier in this chapter. For a given use case, if there are no quantifiable benefits, or if the cost is outweighing the benefits, then the use case may not be the right choice for microservices.

Let's discuss some commonly used scenarios that are suitable candidates for a microservice architecture:

- Migrating a monolithic application due to improvements required in scalability, manageability, agility, or speed of delivery. Another similar scenario is rewriting an end-of-life heavily-used legacy application. In both cases, microservices presents an opportunity. Using a microservices architecture, it is possible to replatform the legacy application by slowly transforming functions to microservices. There are benefits in this approach. There is no humongous upfront investment required, no major disruption to business, and there are no severe business risks. Since the service dependencies are known, the microservices dependencies can be well managed.

- In many cases, we build headless business applications or business services that are autonomous in nature. For instance, payment service, login service, flight search service, customer profile service, notification service, and more. These are normally reused across multiple channels, and, hence, are good candidates for building them as microservices.

- There could be micro or macro applications that serves a single purpose and performs a single responsibility. A simple time-tracking application is an example of this category. All it does is capture time, duration, and the task performed. Common use enterprise applications are also candidates for microservices.

- Backend services of a well architected, responsive, client side MVC web application (**Backend as a Service** (**BaaS**)). In most of these scenarios, data could be coming from multiple logically different data sources, as described in the *Fly By Points* example mentioned in `Chapter 1`, *Demystifying Microservices*.

- Highly agile applications, applications demanding speed of delivery or time to market, innovation pilots, applications selected for DevOps, System of Innovation type of applications, and so on, could also be considered as potential candidates for microservices architecture.

- Applications that we could anticipate getting benefits from microservices, such as polyglot requirements; applications that require **Command Query Responsibility Segregation** (**CQRS**); and so on, are also potential candidates of microservices architecture.

- Independent technical services and utility services, such as communication service, encryption service, authentication services and so on, are also good candidates for microservices.

If the use case falls into any of these categories, they are potential candidates for microservices architecture. There are a few scenarios that we should consider avoiding in microservices:

- If the organization policies are forced to use centrally-managed heavyweight components, such as ESBs, to host the business logic, or if the organization has any other policies that are hindering the fundamental principles of microservices, then microservices are not the right solution, unless the organizational process is relaxed.
- If the organizations culture, processes, and more are based on traditional waterfall delivery model, lengthy release cycles, matrix teams, manual deployments and cumbersome release processes, no infrastructure provisioning, and more, then microservices may not be the right fit. This is underpinned by the **Conway's law**. The Conway's law states that there is a strong link between organizational structure and the software they create.

 Read more about the conveys law here:
`http://www.melconway.com/Home/Conways_Law.html`

Microservices early adopters - Is there a common theme?

Many organizations had already successfully embarked on their journey to the microservices world. In this section, we will examine some of the front runners on the microservices space to analyze why they did what they did, and how they did it? The following is a curated list of organizations adopted microservices, based on the information available on the internet:

- **Netflix** (`www.netflix.com`): Netflix, an international, on-demand, media streaming company, is a pioneer in the microservices space. Netflix transformed their large pool of developers developing traditional monolithic code to smaller development teams producing microservices. These microservices work together to stream digital media to millions of Netflix customers. At Netflix, engineers started with monolithic architecture, went through the pain, and then broke the application into smaller units that are loosely coupled and aligned to business capability.

- **Uber** (www.uber.com): Uber, an international transportation network company, was started in 2008 with a monolithic architecture with single codebase. All services were embedded into the monolithic application. When Uber expanded their business from one city to multiple cities, challenges started. Uber then moved to SOA-based architecture by breaking the system into smaller independent units. Each module was given to different teams, empowered to choose their language, framework, and database. Uber has many microservices deployed in their ecosystem using RPC and REST.

- **Airbnb** (www.airbnb.com): Airbnb, a world leader providing trusted marketplace for accommodations, started with a monolithic application that performed all required functions of the business. It faced scalability issues with increased traffic. A single codebase became too complicated to manage, resulting in poor separation of concerns, and running into performance issues. Airbnb broke their monolithic application into smaller pieces, with separate codebases, running on separate machines, with separate deployment cycles. Airbnb has developed their own microservices or SOA ecosystem around these services.

- **Orbitz** (www.orbitz.com): Orbitz, an online travel portal, started with a monolithic architecture in the 2000s with a web layer, a business layer, and a database layer. As Orbitz expanded their business, they faced manageability and scalability issues with the monolithic-tiered architecture. Orbitz had then gone through continuous architecture changes. Later, Orbitz broke down their monolithic application in to many smaller applications.

- **eBay** (www.ebay.com): eBay, one of the largest online retailers, started in the late 90s with a monolithic Perl application with **FreeBSD** as its database. eBay went through scaling issues as the business grew. It was consistently invested on improving architecture. In the mid 2000s, eBay moved to smaller decomposed systems based on Java and web services. They employed database partitions and functional segregation to meet the required scalability.

- **Amazon** (www.amazon.com): Amazon, one of the largest online retailer's website in 2001 was running on a big monolith application written on C++. The well-architected monolithic application was based on tiered architecture with many modular components. However, all these components were tightly coupled. As a result, Amazon was not able to speed up their development cycle by splitting teams into smaller groups. Amazon then separated out code as independent functional services wrapped with web services, and eventually advanced to microservices.

- **Gilt** (www.gilt.com): Gilt, an online shopping website, started in 2007 with a tiered monolithic Rails application with Postgres database at the back. Just like many other applications, as traffic volumes increased, this web application was not able to provide the required resiliency. Gilt went through an architecture overhaul by introducing Java and polyglot persistence. Later, Gilts moved to many smaller applications using microservices concept.
- **Twitter** (www.twitter.com): Twitter, one of the largest social websites, started with a three-tiered monolithic rails application in the mid 2000s. Later, when Twitter experienced growth in the user base, it went through an architecture refactoring cycle. With that refactoring, Twitter moved away from a typical web application to an API-based event-driven core. Twitter is using Scala and Java to develop microservices with polyglot persistence.
- **Nike** (www.nike.com): Nike, the world leader in apparels and footwear, transformed their monolithic applications to microservices. Like many other organizations, Nike was running with age old legacy applications that are hardly stable. In their journey, Nike moved to heavyweight commercial products with an objective to stabilize legacy applications, but ended up in monolithic applications that are expensive to scale, have long release cycles, and require too much manual work to deploy and manage applications. Later, Nike moved to microservices-based architecture, which brought down the development cycle considerably.

Monolithic migration as the common use case

When we analyze the preceding enterprises, there is one common theme. All these enterprises started with monolithic applications and transitioned to microservices architecture by applying learning and pain points from their previous editions.

Even today, many start-ups are starting with monolith as it is easy to start, conceptualize, and then slowly move them to microservices when the demand arises. Monolithic to microservices migration scenarios have an added advantage that we have all information upfront, readily available for refactoring.

Although it is a monolithic transformation for all of those enterprises, the catalysts were different for different organizations. Some of the common motivations are lack of scalability, long development cycles, process automation, manageability, and changes in business models.

While monolithic migrations are no brainers, there are opportunities to build ground-up microservices. More than building ground-up systems, look for an opportunity to build smaller services that are quick wins for the business. For example, adding a trucking service to an airline's end-to-end cargo management system, or adding a customer scoring service to a retailer's loyalty system. These could be implemented as independent microservices exchanging messages with their respective monolithic applications.

Another point is that many of the organizations are using microservices only for their business' critical and customer engagement applications, leaving the rest of their legacy monolithic applications to take its own trajectory.

Another important observation is that most of the organizations examined previously are at different levels of maturity in their microservices journey. When eBay transitioned from the monolithic application in the early 2000s, they functionally split the application into smaller, independent, deployable units. These logically divided units are wrapped with web services. While single responsibility and autonomy are their underpinning principles, the architectures are limited to the technologies and tools available at that point in time. Organizations such as Netflix and Airbnb built capabilities of their own to solve specific challenges they faced. To summarize, all of them are not truly microservices, but are small, business-aligned services following the same characteristics.

There is no state called definite or ultimate microservices. It is a journey, and it is evolving and maturing day by day. The mantra for architects and developers is the replaceability principle--build an architecture that maximizes the ability to replace its parts and minimizes the cost of replacing its parts. The bottom line is that enterprises shouldn't attempt to develop microservices by just following the hype.

Microservice frameworks

Microservices are already in the main stream. When developing microservices, there are some cross-cutting concerns that need to be implemented, such as externalized logging, tracing, embedded HTTP listener, health checks, and so on. As a result, significant efforts will go into developing these cross-cutting concerns. Microservices frameworks are emerged in this space to fill these gaps.

There are many microservices frameworks available apart from those that are mentioned specifically under the serverless computing. The capabilities vary between these microservice frameworks. Hence, it is important to choose the right framework for development.

Spring Boot, **Dropwizard**, and **Wildfly Swarm** are popular enterprise-grade HTTP/REST implementations for the development of microservices. However, these frameworks only provide minimalistic support for large-scale microservices development. Spring Boot, together with **Spring Cloud**, offers sophisticated support for microservices. **Spring Framework 5** introduced the reactive web framework. Combining Spring Boot and Spring Framework 5 reactive is a good choice for reactive style microservices. Alternatively, **Spring Streams** can also be used for the microservices development.

The following is a curated list of other microservices frameworks:

- Lightbend's **Lagom** (`www.lightbend.com/lagom`) is a full-fledged, sophisticated, and popular microservices framework for Java and Scala.
- WSO2 **Microservices For Java - MSF4J** (`github.com/wso2/msf4j`) is a lightweight, high performance microservices framework.
- **Spark** (`sparkjava.com`) is a micro framework to develop REST services.
- **Seneca** (`senecajs.org`) is a microservices toolkit for Node JS in a fast and easy way similar to Spark.
- **Vert.x** (`vertx.io`) is a polyglot microservices toolkit to build reactive microservices quickly.
- **Restlet** (`restlet.com`) is a framework used to develop REST-based APIs in a quick and efficient way.
- **Payra-micro** (`payara.fish`) is used to develop web applications (war files) and run them on a standalone mode. Payra is based on Glass Fish.
- **Jooby** (`jooby.org`) is another micro-web framework that can be used to develop REST-based APIs.
- **Go-fasthttp** (`github.com/valyala/fasthttp`) is a high performance HTTP package for Go, useful to build REST services.
- **JavaLite** (`javalite.io`) is a framework to develop applications with HTTP endpoints.
- **Mantl** (`mantl.io`) is open source microservices framework come from Cisco for the microservice development and deployments.
- **Fabric8** (`fabric8.io`) is an integrated microservices development platform on top of Kubernetes, backed by Red Hat.
- **Hook.io** (`hook.io`) is another microservices deployment platform.
- **Vamp** (`vamp.io`) is an open source self-hosted platform to manage microservices that relies on container technologies.
- **Go Kit** (`github.com/go-kit/kit`) is a standard library for microservices using the Go language.
- **Micro** (`github.com/micro/micro`) is a microservice toolkit for Go language.

- **Lumen** (lumen.laravel.com) is a lightweight, fast micro-framework.
- **Restx** (restx.io) is a lightweight, REST development framework.
- **Gizmo** (github.com/NYTimes/gizmo) is a reactive microservices framework for Go.
- **Azure service fabric** (azure.microsoft.com/en-us/services/service-fabric/) has also emerged as a microservice development platform.

This list does not end here. There are many more in this category, such as Kontena, Gilliam, Magnetic, Eventuate, LSQ, and Stellient, which are some of the platforms supporting microservices.

The rest of this book will focus on building microservices using Spring Framework projects.

Summary

In this chapter, we learned about the relationship of the microservices architecture with a few other popular architecture styles.

We started with microservices relationships with SOA and Twelve-Factor Apps. We also examined the link between the microservices architecture and other architectures, such as serverless computing architecture and Lambda Architecture. We also learned the advantages of using microservices together with cloud and DevOps. We then analyzed examples of a few enterprises from different industries that successfully adopted microservices and their use cases. Finally, we reviewed some of the microservices frameworks evolved over a period of time.

In the next chapter, we will develop a few sample microservices to bring more clarity to our learnings in this chapter.

3
Building Microservices with Spring Boot

Developing microservices is not so tedious anymore--thanks to the powerful Spring Boot framework. Spring Boot is a framework for developing production-ready microservices in Java.

This chapter will move from the microservices theory explained in the previous chapters to hands-on practice by reviewing code samples. Here, we will introduce the Spring Boot framework, and explain how Spring Boot can help building RESTful microservices inline with the principles and characteristics discussed in the previous chapter. Finally, some of the features offered by Spring Boot for making the microservices production ready will be reviewed.

At the end of this chapter, you will have learned about the following:

- Setting up the latest Spring development environment
- Developing RESTful services using Spring Framework 5 and Spring Boot
- Building reactive microservices using Spring WebFlux and Spring Messaging
- Securing microservices using Spring Security and OAuth2
- Implementing cross-origin microservices
- Documenting Spring Boot microservices using Swagger
- Spring Boot Actuator for building production-ready microservices

Setting up a development environment

To crystalize microservices' concepts, a couple of microservices will be built. For that, it is assumed that the following components are installed:

- **JDK 1.8** (http://www.oracle.com/technetwork/java/javase/downloads/jdk8-downloads-2133151.html)
- **Spring Tool Suite 3.8.2** (**STS**) (https://spring.io/tools/sts/all)
- **Maven 3.3.1** (https://maven.apache.org/download.cgi)

Alternately, other IDEs like **IntelliJ IDEA/NetBeans/Eclipse** could be used. Similarly, alternate build tools like **Gradle** can be used. It is assumed that Maven repository, class path, and other path variables are set properly for running STS and Maven projects.

This chapter is based on the following versions of Spring libraries:

- Spring Framework 5.0.0.RC1
- Spring Boot 2.0.0. M1

The focus of this chapter is not to explore the full features of Spring Boot, but to understand some of the essential and important features of Spring Boot, required when building microservices.

Spring Boot for building RESTful microservices

Spring Boot is a utility framework from the Spring team for bootstrapping Spring-based applications and microservices quickly and easily. The framework uses an opinionated approach over configurations for decision making, thereby reducing the effort required on writing a lot of boilerplate code and configurations. Using the 80-20 principle, developers should be able to kick start a variety of Spring applications with many default values. Spring Boot further presents opportunities to the developers for customizing applications by overriding auto-configured values.

Spring Boot not only increases the speed of development, but also provides a set of production-ready ops features such as health checks and metrics collections. Since Spring Boot masks many configuration parameters and abstracts many lower level implementations, it minimizes the chances of errors to a certain extent. Spring Boot recognizes the nature of the application based on the libraries available in the classpath, and runs the auto-configuration classes packaged in those libraries.

Often, many developers mistakenly see Spring Boot as a code generator, but, in reality, it is not. Spring Boot only auto-configures build files, for example, pom files in the case of Maven. It also sets properties, such as data source properties, based on certain opinionated defaults.

Consider the following dependencies in the file pom.xml:

```
<dependency>
  <groupId>org.springframework.boot</groupId>
  <artifactId>spring-boot-starter-data-jpa</artifactId>
</dependency>

<dependency>
  <groupId>org.hsqldb</groupId>
  <artifactId>hsqldb</artifactId>
  <scope>runtime</scope>
</dependency>
```

For instance, in the preceding case, Spring Boot understands that the project is set to use the Spring Data JPA and HSQL database. It automatically configures the driver class and other connection parameters.

One of the great outcomes of Spring Boot is that it almost eliminates the need to have traditional XML configurations. Spring Boot also enables microservices development by packaging all the required runtime dependencies into a fat executable jar.

Getting started with Spring Boot

These are the different ways in which Spring Boot-based application development can be started:

- By using **Spring Boot CLI** as a command-line tool
- By using IDEs like **Spring Tool Suite** (**STS**), which provide Spring Boot, supported out of the box

- By using the **Spring Initializr** project at http://start.spring.io
- By using **SDKMAN! (The Software Development Kit Manager)** from http://sdkman.io

The first three options will be explored in this chapter, developing a variety of example services.

Developing a Spring Boot microservice

The easiest way to develop and demonstrate Spring Boot's capabilities is by using the Spring Boot CLI, a command-line tool.

The following are the steps to set up and run Spring Boot CLI:

1. Install the Spring Boot command-line tool by downloading the spring-boot-cli-2.0.0.BUILD-M1-bin.zip file from the following location URL: https://repo.spring.io/milestone/org/springframework/boot/spring-boot-cli/2.0.0.M1/

2. Unzip the file into a directory of choice. Open a terminal window, and change the terminal prompt to the bin folder.

> Ensure that the /bin folder is added to the system path so that Spring Boot can be run from any location. Otherwise, execute from the bin folder by using the command ./spring.

3. Verify the installation with the following command. If successful, the Spring CLI version will be printed on the console as shown:

   ```
   $spring --version
   Spring CLI v2.0.0.M1
   ```

4. As the next step, a quick REST service will be developed in groovy, which is supported out of the box in Spring Boot. To do so, copy and paste the following code using any editor of choice, and save it as myfirstapp.groovy into any folder:

   ```
   @RestController
   class HelloworldController {
     @RequestMapping("/")
     String sayHello(){
   ```

```
        return "Hello World!"
    }
}
```

5. In order to run this groovy application, go to the folder where
   `myfirstapp.groovy` is saved, and execute the following command. The last few
   lines of the server startup log will be as shown in the following command
   snippet:

```
$spring run myfirstapp.groovy
2016-12-16 13:04:33.208  INFO 29126 --- [ runner-0]
s.b.c.e.t.TomcatEmbeddedServletContainer : Tomcat started on
port(s):
8080 (http)
2016-12-16 13:04:33.214  INFO 29126 --- [ runner-0]
o.s.boot.SpringApplication : Started application in 4.03
seconds (JVM running for 104.276)
```

6. Open a browser window, and point the URL to `http://localhost:8080`; the
   browser will display the following message:

```
Hello World!
```

There is no war file created and no Tomcat server was running. Spring Boot automatically
picked up Tomcat as the web server, and embedded it into the application. This is a very
basic, minimal microservice. The `@RestController`, used in the previous code, will be
examined in detail in the next example.

Developing our first Spring Boot microservice

In this section, we will demonstrate how to develop a Java-based REST/JSON Spring Boot
service using STS.

The full source code of this example is available as the
`chapter3.Bootrest` project in the code files of this book under the
following Git repository: `https://github.com/rajeshrv/Spring5Micros
ervice`

1. Open STS, right-click in **Project Explorer** window, select **New Project**, then select `Spring Starter Project` as shown in the following screenshot. Then click on **Next**:

2. The `Spring Starter Project` is a basic template wizard, which provides a selection of a number of other starter libraries.

3. Type the project name as `chapter3.bootrest`, or any other name of your choice. It is important to choose the packaging as Jar. In traditional web applications, a war file is created, and then deployed into a servlet container, whereas, Spring Boot packages all the dependencies into a self-contained, autonomous jar with an embedded HTTP listener.

4. Select **Java Version** as **1.8**. Java 1.8 is recommended for Spring 5 applications. Change other Maven properties such as **Group, Artifact**, and **Package** as shown in the following screenshot:

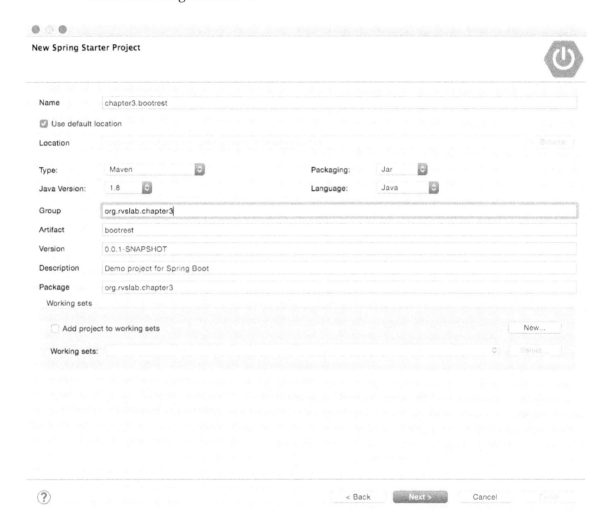

5. Once completed, click on **Next**.

6. The wizard will show the library options. In this case, since we are developing REST services, select **Web** under **Web**. This is an interesting step, which tells Spring Boot that a Spring MVC web application is being developed so that spring boot can include the necessary libraries, including Tomcat, as the HTTP listener and other configurations as required:

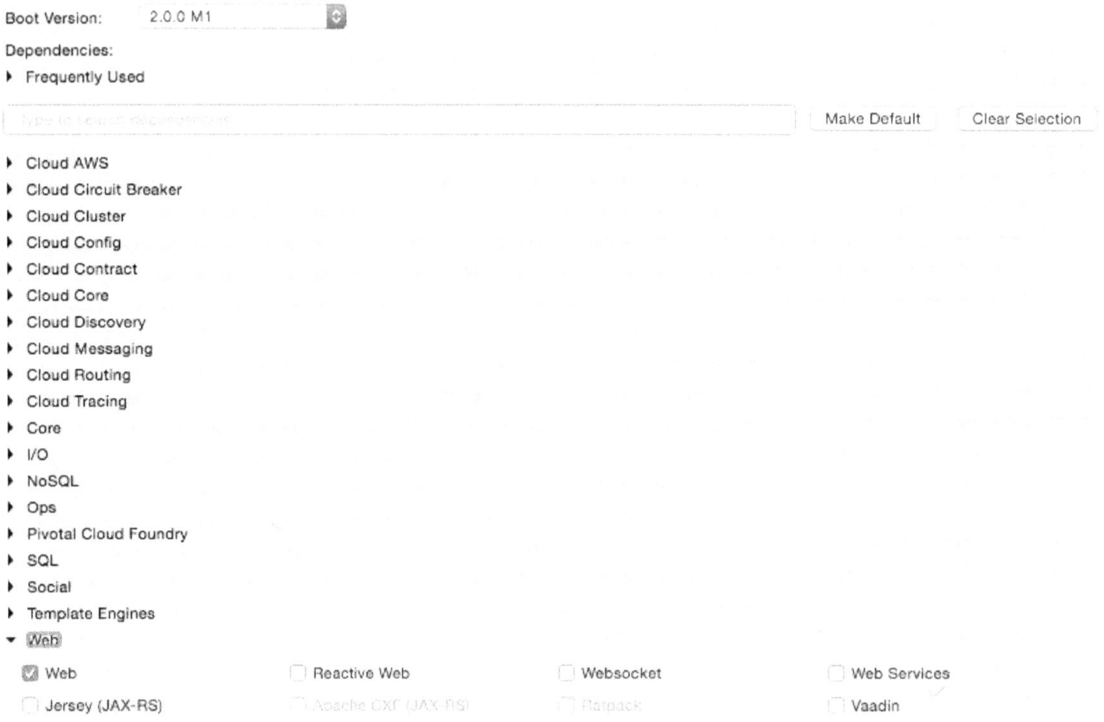

Boot Version: 2.0.0 M1

Dependencies:

▸ Frequently Used

Type to search dependencies		Make Default	Clear Selection

▸ Cloud AWS
▸ Cloud Circuit Breaker
▸ Cloud Cluster
▸ Cloud Config
▸ Cloud Contract
▸ Cloud Core
▸ Cloud Discovery
▸ Cloud Messaging
▸ Cloud Routing
▸ Cloud Tracing
▸ Core
▸ I/O
▸ NoSQL
▸ Ops
▸ Pivotal Cloud Foundry
▸ SQL
▸ Social
▸ Template Engines
▾ Web

☑ Web	☐ Reactive Web	☐ Websocket	☐ Web Services
☐ Jersey (JAX-RS)	☐ Apache CXF (JAX-RS)	☐ Ratpack	☐ Vaadin

7. Click on **Finish**.

8. This will generate a project named `chapter3.bootrest` in **STS Project Explorer**:

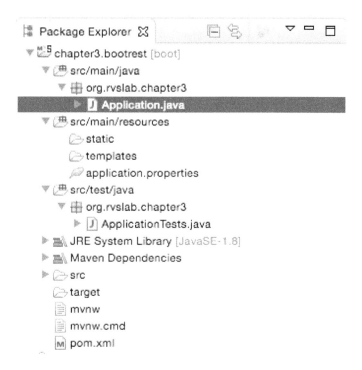

9. Let us examine the `pom` file. The parent element is one of the interesting aspects in `pom.xml`:

```
<parent>
  <groupId>org.springframework.boot</groupId>
  <artifactId>spring-boot-starter-parent</artifactId>
  <version>2.0.0.M1</version>
</parent>
```

`Spring-boot-starter-parent` is a **bill-of-materials** (**BOM**), a pattern used by Maven's dependency management. The BOM is a special kind of pom used for managing different library versions required for a project. The advantage of using the `spring-boot-starter-parent` pom is that developers need not worry about finding the right, compatible versions of different libraries such as Spring, Jersey, Junit, Logback, Hibernate, Jackson, and more.

The starter pom has a list of Boot dependencies, sensible resource filtering, and sensible plug-in configurations required for the Maven builds.

Refer to the following link to see the different dependencies provided in the starter parent (version 2.0.0). All these dependencies can be overridden if required: `https://github.com/spring-projects/spring-boot/blob /a9503abb94b203a717527b81a94dc9d3cb4b1afa/spring-boot-dependenc ies/pom.xml`

The starter pom itself does not add jar dependencies to the project. Instead, it only adds library versions. Subsequently, when dependencies are added to `pom.xml`, they refer to the library versions from this `pom.xml`. Some of the properties are as shown next:

```
<activemq.version>5.14.5</activemq.version>
<commons-collections.version>3.2.2
</commons-collections.version>
<hibernate.version>5.2.10.Final</hibernate.version>
<jackson.version>2.9.0.pr3</jackson.version>
<mssql-jdbc.version>6.1.0.jre8</mssql-jdbc.version>
<spring.version>5.0.0.RC1</spring.version>
<spring-amqp.version>2.0.0.M4</spring-amqp.version>
<spring-security.version>5.0.0.M1</spring-security.version>
<thymeleaf.version>3.0.6.RELEASE</thymeleaf.version>
<tomcat.version>8.5.15</tomcat.version>
```

Reviewing the dependency section of our `pom.xml`, one can see that this is a clean and neat `pom` file with only two dependencies:

```
<dependencies>
  <dependency>
    <groupId>org.springframework.boot</groupId>
    <artifactId>spring-boot-starter-web</artifactId>
  </dependency>
  <dependency>
    <groupId>org.springframework.boot</groupId>
    <artifactId>spring-boot-starter-test</artifactId>
    <scope>test</scope>
  </dependency>
</dependencies>
```

Since **Web** is selected, `spring-boot-starter-web` adds all dependencies required for a Spring MVC project. It also includes dependencies to Tomcat as an embedded HTTP listener. This provides an effective way to get all the dependencies required as a single bundle. Individual dependencies could be replaced with other libraries, such as replacing Tomcat with Jetty.

Similar to web, Spring Boot also comes up with a number of `spring-boot-starter-*` libraries, such as amqp, aop, batch, data-jpa, thymeleaf, and so on.

The last thing to be reviewed in the file `pom.xml` is the Java 8 property as shown here:

```
<java.version>1.8</java.version>
```

By default, the parent pom adds Java 6. It is recommended to override the Java version to 8 for Spring 5.

10. Let us now examine `Application.java`. Spring Boot, by default, generated a class `org.rvslab.chapter3.Application.java` under `src/main/java` for bootstrapping:

```
@SpringBootApplication
public class Application {
    public static void main(String[] args) {
        SpringApplication.run(Application.class, args);
    }
}
```

There is only a main method in the application, which will be invoked at startup, as per the Java convention. The main method bootstraps the Spring Boot application by calling the run method on `SpringApplication`. `Application.class` is passed as a parameter to tell Spring Boot that this is the primary component.

More importantly, the magic is done by the `@SpringBootApplication` annotation. `@SpringBootApplication` is a top-level annotation, which encapsulates three other annotations, as shown in the following code snippet:

```
@Configuration
@EnableAutoConfiguration
@ComponentScan
public class Application {
```

The `@Configuration` annotation hints that the contained class declares one or more `@Bean` definitions. `@Configuration` is meta-annotated with `@Component`, therefore, they are candidates for component scanning.

`@EnableAutoConfiguration` tells Spring Boot to automatically configure the Spring application based on the dependencies available in the class path.

11. Let us examine `application.properties`--a default `application.properties` file is placed under `src/main/resources`. It is an important file for configuring any required properties for the Spring Boot application. At the moment, this file is kept empty, and will be revisited with some test cases later in this chapter.

12. Let us examine `ApplicationTests.java` under `src/test/java`. This is a placeholder for writing test cases against the Spring Boot application.

13. As the next step, add a REST endpoint. Let us edit `Application.java` under `src/main/java`, and add a RESTful service implementation. The RESTful service is exactly the same as what was done in the previous project. Append the following code at the end of the `Application.java` file:

```
@RestController
class GreetingController{
  @GetMapping("/")
  Greet greet(){
    return new Greet("Hello World!");
  }
}
class Greet{
  private String message;
  public Greet() {}
  public Greet(String message){
    this.message = message;
  }
  //add getter and setter
}
```

14. To run, go to **Run As | Spring Boot App**. Tomcat will be started on the `8080` port:

```
rvslab:chapter3.bootrest rajeshrv$ java -jar target/bootrest-0.0.1-SNAPSHOT.jar
```

```
:: Spring Boot ::       (v2.0.0.M1)
2017-06-04 12:06:59.503  INFO 3909 --- [           main] org.rvslab.chapter3.Application          : Starting Application v0.0.1-S
NAPSHOT on rvslab.local with PID 3909 (/Users/rajeshrv/work/spring5bookprefinal/chapter3/chapter3.bootrest/target/bootrest-0.0.1-
SNAPSHOT.jar started by rajeshrv in /Users/rajeshrv/work/spring5bookprefinal/chapter3/chapter3.bootrest)
```

15. We can notice the following things from the log:
    - Spring Boot gets its own process ID (in this case, `3909`)
    - Spring Boot automatically starts the Tomcat server at the local host, port `8080`
    - Next, open a browser and point to `http://localhost:8080`. This will show the JSON response as follows:

`{"message":"Hello World!"}`

The key difference between the legacy service and this one is that the Spring Boot service is self-contained. To make this clearer, run the Spring Boot application outside STS.

Open a terminal window, go to the project folder, and run Maven as follows:

```
$ maven install
```

This preceding command will generate a fat jar under the target folder of the project. Running the application from the command line shows the following:

```
$java -jar target/bootrest-0.0.1-SNAPSHOT.jar
```

As one can see, `bootrest-0.0.1-SNAPSHOT.jar` is self-contained, and could be run as a standalone application. At this point, the jar is as thin as 14 MB. Even though the application is not more than just a *hello world*, the spring boot service just developed practically follows the principles of microservices.

Testing Spring Boot microservice

There are multiple ways to test REST/JSON Spring Boot microservices. The easiest way is to use a web browser or a curl command pointing to the URL, like this:

```
curl localhost:8080
```

There are number of tools available for testing RESTful services such as Postman, Advanced Rest Client, SOAP UI, Paw, and more.

In this example, for testing the service, the default test class generated by Spring Boot will be used. Adding a new test case to `ApplicatonTests.java` results in this:

```
@RunWith(SpringRunner.class)
@SpringBootTest(webEnvironment = WebEnvironment.RANDOM_PORT)
public class ApplicationTests {
  @Autowired
  private TestRestTemplate restTemplate;
  @Test
  public void testSpringBootApp() throws JsonProcessingException,
  IOException {
    String body = restTemplate.getForObject("/", String.class);
    assertThat(new ObjectMapper().readTree(body)
      .get("message")
      .textValue())
      .isEqualTo("Hello World!");
  }
}
```

Note that `@SpringBootTest` is a simple annotation for testing Spring Boot applications, which enables Spring Boot features during test execution. `webEnvironment=WebEnvironment.RANDOM_PORT` property directs the Spring Boot application to bind to a random port. This will be handy when running many Spring Boot services as part of a regression test. Also note that `TestRestTemplate` is being used for calling the RESTful service. `TestRestTemplate` is a utility class, which abstracts the lower-level details of the HTTP client, and also automatically discovers the actual port used by Spring Boot.

To test this, open a terminal window, go to the project folder, and run `mvn install`.

HATEOAS-enabled Spring Boot microservice

In the next example, **Spring Initializr** will be used to create a Spring Boot project. Spring Initializr is a drop-in replacement for the STS project wizard, and provides a web UI for configuring and generating a Spring Boot project. One of the advantages of the Spring Initializr is that it can generate a project through the website, which can then be imported into any IDE.

In this example, the concept of **HyperMedia As The Engine Of Application State** (**HATEOAS**) for REST-based services and the **Hypertext Application Language** (**HAL**) browser will be examined.

HATEOAS is useful for building conversational style microservices which exhibit strong affinity between UI and its backend services.

HATEOAS is a REST service pattern in which navigation links are provided as part of the payload metadata. The client application determines the state, and follows the transition URLs provided as part of the state. This methodology is particularly useful in responsive mobile and web applications where the client downloads additional data based on user navigation patterns.

The HAL browser is a handy API browser for hal+json data. HAL is a format based on JSON, which establishes conventions for representing hyperlinks between resources. HAL helps APIs to be more explorable and discoverable.

 The full source code of this example is available as the `chapter3.boothateoas` project in the code files of this book under the following Git repository: `https://github.com/rajeshrv/Spring5Micros ervice`

Here are the concrete steps for developing a HATEOAS sample using Spring Initilizr:

1. In order to use Spring Initilizr, go to `https://start.spring.io`:

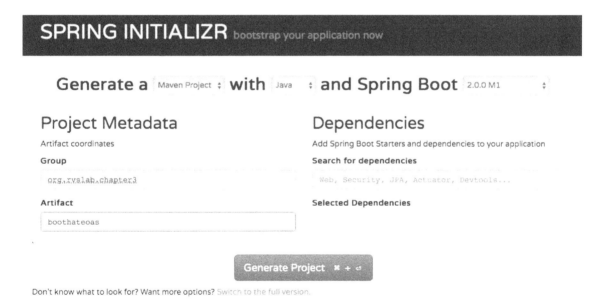

2. Fill the details such as **Maven Project**, Spring Boot version, **Group**, and **Artifact**, as shown in the preceding screenshot, and click on **Switch to the full** version below the **Generate Projects** button. Select **Web**, **HATEOAS**, and **Rest Repositories HAL Browser**. Make sure the Java version is 8, and the package type is selected as Jar, as shown in the following screenshot:

3. Once selected, hit the **Generate Project** button. This will generate a Maven project, and download the project as a zip file into the download directory of the browser.
4. Unzip the file, and save it to a directory of your choice.

5. Open STS, go to the **File** menu, and click on **Import**:

6. Navigate to Maven | Existing Maven Projects, then click on **Next**.

7. Click on browse next to the root directory, and select the unzipped folder. Click on **Finish**. This will load the generated Maven project in **STS Project Explorer**.

8. Edit `BoothateoasApplication.java` to add a new REST endpoint as follows:

```
@RequestMapping("/greeting")
@ResponseBody
public HttpEntity<Greet> greeting(@RequestParam(value = "name",
  required = false, defaultValue = "HATEOAS") String name) {
  Greet greet = new Greet("Hello " + name);
  greet.add(linkTo(methodOn(GreetingController.class)
    .greeting(name)).withSelfRel());
  return new ResponseEntity<Greet>(greet, HttpStatus.OK);
}
```

9. Note that this is the same `GreetingController` class as in the previous example. But a method named greeting was added this time. In this new method, an additional optional request parameter is defined and defaulted to HATEOAS. The following code adds a link to the resulting JSON--in this case, it adds the link to the same API.

10. The following code adds a self-reference web link to the Greet object: `"href"`: `"http://localhost:8080/greeting?name=HATEOAS"`:

```
greet.add(linkTo(methodOn(
  GreetingController.class).greeting(name)).withSelfRel());
```

In order to do this, we need to extend the `Greet` class from `ResourceSupport` as shown in following code. The rest of the code remains the same:

```
class Greet extends ResourceSupport{
```

11. `Add` is a method on `ResourceSupport`. The `linkTo` and `methodOn` are static methods of `ControllerLinkBuilder`, a utility class for creating links on controller classes. The `methodOn` method does a dummy method invocation, and `linkTo` creates a link to the controller class. In this case, we use `withSelfRel` to point it to self.

12. This will essentially produce a link, `/greeting?name=HATEOAS`, by default. A client can read the link, and initiate another call.

13. Run as Spring Boot App. Once the server startup is completed, point the browser to `http://localhost:8080`.

14. This will open the HAL browser window. In the **Explorer** field, type `/greeting?name=World!`, and click on the **Go** button. If everything is fine, the response details will be seen in the HAL browser as shown in the following screenshot:

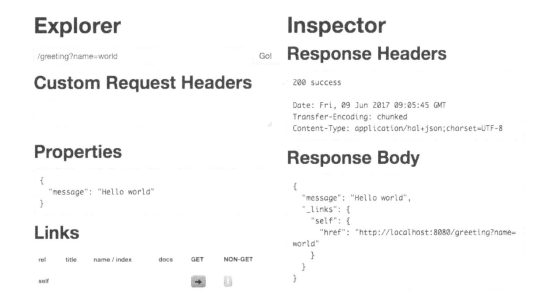

As shown in the preceding screenshot, the **Response Body** has the result with a link, `href`, which points back to the same service. This is because we pointed the reference to itself. Also, review the **Links** section. The little green box against self is the navigable link.

It does not make much sense in this simple example, but this could be handy in larger applications with many related entities. Using the links provided, the client can easily navigate back and forth between these entities with ease.

Reactive Spring Boot microservices

Reactive microservices mentioned in `Chapter 2`, *Related Architecture Styles and Use cases*, basically highlight the need of asynchronously integrating microservices in an ecosystem. Even though external service calls primarily get benefits from reactive style programming, reactive principles are useful in any software development, as it improves resource efficiency and scalability characteristics. Therefore, it is important build microservices using reactive programming principles.

There are two ways we can implement reactive microservices. The first approach is to use the Spring **WebFlux** in the Spring Framework 5. This approach uses reactive style web server for microservices. The second approach is to use a messaging server such as RabbitMQ for asynchronous interaction between microservices. In this chapter, we will explore both the options mentioned here.

Reactive microservices using Spring WebFlux

Reactive programming in Java is based on the **Reactive Streams** specification. Reactive stream specification defines the semantics for asynchronous stream processing or flow of events between disparate components in a non-blocking style.

Unlike the standard observer pattern, Reactive Streams allow to maintain sequence, notification on completion, and notification when there is an error with full backpressure support. With backpressure support, a receiver can set terms such as how much data it wants from the publisher. Also, the receiver can start receiving data only when data is ready to be processed. Reactive Streams are particularly useful for handling different thread pools for different components, or in the case of integrating slow and fast components.

 Reactive streams specification is now adopted as part of Java 9 `java.util.concurrent.Flow`. Its semantics are similar to `CompletableFuture` in Java 8 with lambda expressions for collecting results.

Spring Framework 5 integrates reactive programming principles at its core as WebFlux. Spring 5 WebFlux is based on Reactive Streams specification. Under the hood, Spring's Web Reactive Framework uses the Reactor project (`https://projectreactor.io`) for implementing reactive programming. Reactor is an implementation of Reactive Streams specification. With Spring Framework, developers can also choose to use RxJava instead of Reactor.

In this section, we will see how to build Reactive Spring Boot microservices using Spring 5 WebFlux libraries. These libraries help developers to create asynchronous, non-blocking HTTP servers with full backpressure support, without coding callback methods. Note that it is not a one-size-fits solution in all cases and, if not used property, this can backfire on the quality of services. Also, developers need to be sure that the downstream components support full reactive programming.

In order to get full power of reactive programming, reactive constructs should be used end-to-end from client, endpoint, and to the repository. That means, if a slow client accesses a reactive server, then the data read operations in the repository can slow down to match the slowness of the client.

 At the time of writing this book, Spring Data Kay M1 supports reactive drivers for Mongo DB, Apache Cassandra, and Redis. The reactive CRUD repository, `ReactiveCrudRepository`, is a handy interface for implementing reactive repositories.

Spring WebFlux supports two options for implementing Spring Boot applications. The first approach is annotation based with `@Controller` and the other annotations generally used with Spring Boot. The second approach is functional programming Java 8 lambda style coding.

Let us build a sample using the annotation style reactive programming using WebFlux.

 The full source code of this example is available as the `chapter3.webflux` project in the code files of this book under the following Git repository: `https://github.com/rajeshrv/Spring5Microservice`

Follow these steps to build a reactive Spring Boot application:

1. Go to `https://start.spring.io`, and generate a new Spring Boot project.

2. Select **Reactive Web** under the **Web** section:

3. Generate project, and import the newly generated project into STS.
4. Examine `pom.xml`; there is only one difference. Instead of `spring-boot-starter-web`, this project uses `spring-boot-starter-webflux` in the dependency section. Following is the dependency to Spring Webflux:

```
<dependency>
    <groupId>org.springframework.boot</groupId>
    <artifactId>spring-boot-starter-webflux</artifactId>
</dependency>
```

5. Add the `GreetingController` and `Greet` classes from `chapter3.bootrest` to the `Application.java` class.
6. Run this project, and test with a browser by pointing to `http://localhost:8080`. You will see the same response.
7. Let us add some Reactive APIs to enable reactive programming to the Boot application. Let us modify `RestController`. Let us add a construct, `Mono`, as follows:

```
@RequestMapping("/")
Mono<Greet> greet(){
    return Mono.just(new Greet("Hello World!"));
}
```

In this case, the response body uses `Mono`, which means that the Greet object will be serialized only when `Mono` is completed in an asynchronous non-blocking mode. Since we have used Mono, this method just creates a single definitive item.

In this case, Mono is used to declare a logic which will get executed as soon as the object is deserialized. You may consider Mono as a placeholder (deferred) for zero or one object with a set of callback methods.

In case of Mono as a parameter to a controller method, the method may be executed even before the serialization gets over. The code in the controller will decide what we want to do with the Mono object. Alternately, we can use **Flux**. Both these constructs will be explained in detail in the next section.

Let us now change the client. Spring 5 reactive introduced `WebClient` and `WebTestClient` as an alternate to `RestTemplate`. `WebClient` is fully support reactive under the hood.

The client-side code is as follows:

```
@RunWith(SpringRunner.class)
@SpringBootTest(webEnvironment = WebEnvironment.DEFINED_PORT)
public class ApplicationTests {
  WebTestClient webClient;
  @Before
  public void setup() {
    webClient = WebTestClient.bindToServer()
      .baseUrl("http://localhost:8080").build();
  }

  @Test
  public void testWebFluxEndpoint() throws Exception {
    webClient.get().uri("/")
      .accept(MediaType.APPLICATION_JSON)
      .exchange()
      .expectStatus().isOk()
      .expectBody(Greet.class).returnResult()
      .getResponseBody().getMessage().equals("Hello World!");
  }
}
```

`WebTestClient` is a purpose build class for testing WebFlux server. `WebClient`, another client class similar to `RestTemplate` is more handy when invoking WebFlux from a non-testing client. The preceding test code first creates a `WebTestClient` with the server URL. Then it executes a get method on the / URL, and verifies it against the existing result.

8. Run the test from the command prompt using `mvn install`. You will not notice any difference in functionality, but the execution model has changed under the hood.

Understanding Reactive Streams

Let us understand the Reactive Streams specification. Reactive Streams has just four interfaces, which are explained as follows:

Publisher

A `Publisher` holds the source of data, and then publishes data elements as per the request from a subscriber. A `Subscriber` can then attach a subscription on the `Publisher`. Note that the `subscribe` method is just a registration method, and will not return any result:

```
public interface Publisher<T> {
  public void subscribe(Subscriber<? super T> s);
}
```

Subscriber

`Subscriber` subscribes to a `Publisher` for consuming streams of data. It defines a set of callback methods, which will be called upon those events. Complete is when everything is done and success. Note, that all these are callback registrations, and the methods themselves do not respond with any data:

```
public interface Subscriber<T> {
  public void onSubscribe(Subscription s);
  public void onNext(T t);
  public void onError(Throwable t);
  public void onComplete();
}
```

Subscription

A `Subscription` is shared by exactly one `Publisher` and one `Subscriber` for the purpose of mediating data exchange between this pair. Data exchange happens when the subscriber calls `request`. `cancel` is used basically to stop the subscription as seen in this example:

```
public interface Subscription {
  public void request(long n);
  public void cancel();
}
```

Processor

A `Processor` represents a processing stage--which is both a `Subscriber` and a `Publisher`, and **MUST** obey the contracts of both. A of can be chained by connecting a `Publisher` and `Subscriber`:

```
public interface Processor<T, R> extends Subscriber<T>,
   Publisher<R> {
}
```

Reactor has two implementations for `Publisher`--**Flux** and **Mono**. Flux can emit 0...N events, whereas, Mono is for a single event (0...1). Flux is required when many data elements or a list of values is transmitted as Streams.

Reactive microservices using Spring Boot and RabbitMQ

In an ideal case, all microservice interactions are expected to happen asynchronously using publish subscribe semantics. Spring Boot provides a hassle-free mechanism to configure messaging solutions:

In this next example, we will create a Spring Boot application with a sender and receiver, both connected through an external queue.

The full source code of this example is available as the `chapter3.bootmessaging` project in the code files of this book under the following Git repository: https://github.com/rajeshrv/Spring5Microservice

Let us follow these steps to create a string boot reactive microservice using RabbitMQ:

1. Create a new project using STS to demonstrate this capability. In this example, instead of selecting **Web**, select **AMQP** under **I/O**:

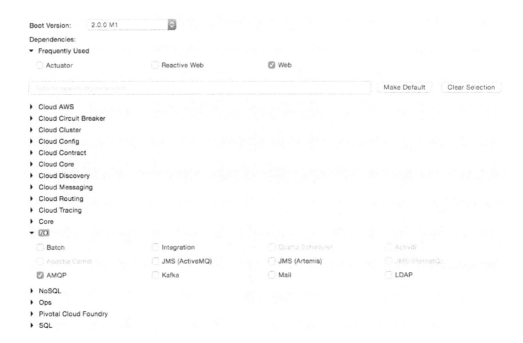

2. RabbitMQ will also be needed for this example. Download and install the latest version of RabbitMQ from `https://www.rabbitmq.com/download.html`. RabbitMQ 3.5.6 is used in this book.

3. Follow the installation steps documented on the site. Once ready, start the RabbitMQ server like this:

```
$ ./rabbitmq-server
```

4. Make the configuration changes to the `application.properties` file to reflect the RabbitMQ configuration. The following configuration uses the default port, username, and password of RabbitMQ:

```
spring.rabbitmq.host=localhost
spring.rabbitmq.port=5672
spring.rabbitmq.username=guest
spring.rabbitmq.password=guest
```

5. Add a message sender component and a queue named `TestQ` of the type `org.springframework.amqp.core.Queue` to `Application.java` under `src/main/java`. The `RabbitMessagingTemplate` template is a convenient way to send messages, and abstracts all the messaging semantics. Spring Boot provides all boilerplate configurations for sending messages:

```
@Component
class Sender {
  @Autowired
  RabbitMessagingTemplate template;

  @Bean
  Queue queue() {
    return new Queue("TestQ", false);
  }
  public void send(String message){
    template.convertAndSend("TestQ", message);
  }
}
```

6. For receiving a message, all that is needed is a `@RabbitListener` annotation. Spring Boot auto-configures all required boilerplate configurations:

```
@Component
class Receiver {
  @RabbitListener(queues = "TestQ")
  public void processMessage(String content) {
    System.out.println(content);
  }
}
```

7. The last piece of this exercise is to wire the sender to our main application, and implement the `CommandLineRunner` interface's run method to initiate the message sending. When the application is initialized, it invokes the run method of the `CommandLineRunner`:

```
@SpringBootApplication
public class Application implements CommandLineRunner{
  @Autowired
  Sender sender;
  public static void main(String[] args) {
    SpringApplication.run(Application.class, args);
  }
  @Override
  public void run(String... args) throws Exception {
    sender.send("Hello Messaging..!!!");
```

```
    }
  }
```

8. Run the application as a Spring Boot application, and verify the output. The following message will be printed on the console:

```
Hello Messaging..!!!
```

Implementing security

It is important to secure the microservices. This will be more significant when there are many microservices communicating with each other. Each service needs to be secured, but at the same time, security shouldn't surface as an overhead. In this section, we will learn some basic measures to secure microservices.

 The full source code of this example is available as the chapter3.security project in the code files of this book under the following Git repository: https://github.com/rajeshrv/Spring5Micros ervice

Perform the following steps for building this example:

- Create a new Spring Starter project, and select **Web** and **Security** (under core)
- Name the project as chapter3.security
- Copy rest endpoint from chapter3.bootrest

Securing a microservice with basic security

Adding basic authentication to Spring Boot is pretty simple. The pom.xml file will have the following dependency. This will include the necessary Spring security library files:

```
<dependency>
  <groupId>org.springframework.boot</groupId>
  <artifactId>spring-boot-starter-security</artifactId>
</dependency>
```

This will, by default, assume that basic security is required for this project. Run the application, and test it with a browser. The browser will ask for the login username and password.

The default basic authentication assumes the . The default password will be printed on the console at startup:

```
Using default security password: a7d08e07-ef5f-4623-b86c-
63054d25baed
```

Alternately, the username and password can be added in `application.properties` as shown next:

```
security.user.name=guest
security.user.password=guest123
```

Securing microservice with OAuth2

In this section, we will see the basic Spring Boot configuration for OAuth2. When a client application requires access to a protected resource, the client sends a request to an authorization server. The authorization server validates the request, and provides an access token. This access token will be validated for every client-to-server request. The request and response sent back and forth depends on the grant type.

 Read more about OAuth and grant types at this link: `http://oauth.net`

The resource owner password credentials grant approach will be used in the following example:

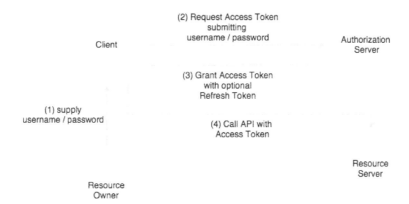

In this case, as shown in the preceding diagram, the resource owner provides the client with a username and password. The client then sends a token request to the authorization server by providing the credentials. The authorization server authorizes the client, and returns an access token. On every subsequent request, the server validates the client token.

To implement OAuth2 in our example, follow these steps:

1. As the first step, update `pom.xml` with oauth2 dependency as follows:

```
<dependency>
  <groupId>org.springframework.security.oauth</groupId>
  <artifactId>spring-security-oauth2</artifactId>
</dependency>

<!-- below dependency is explicitly required when
 testing OAuth2 with Spring Boot 2.0.0.M1 -->
<dependency>
  <groupId>org.springframework.security</groupId>
  <artifactId>spring-security-crypto</artifactId>
  <version>4.2.2.RELEASE</version>
</dependency>
```

2. Next, add two new annotations-- `@EnableAuthorizationServer` --and `@EnableResourceServer` to `Application.java`. The `@EnableAuthorizationServer` annotation creates an authorization server with an in-memory repository to store client tokens and to provide clients with a username, password, client ID, and secret. `@EnableResourceServer` is used to access the tokens. This enables a spring security filter that authenticates via an incoming OAuth2 token.

 In our example, both, authorization server and resource server, are the same. But in practice, these two will be running.

```
@EnableResourceServer
@EnableAuthorizationServer
@SpringBootApplication
public class Application {
```

3. Add the following properties to the `application.properties` file:

```
security.user.name=guest
security.user.password=guest123
security.oauth2.client.client-id: trustedclient
security.oauth2.client.client-secret: trustedclient123
security.oauth2.client.authorized-grant-types:
authorization_code,refresh_token,password
```

4. Add another test case to test OAuth2 as follows:

```
@Test
public void testOAuthService() {
  ResourceOwnerPasswordResourceDetails resource =
    new ResourceOwnerPasswordResourceDetails();
  resource.setUsername("guest");
  resource.setPassword("guest123");
  resource.setAccessTokenUri("http://localhost:8080/oauth
    /token");
  resource.setClientId("trustedclient");
  resource.setClientSecret("trustedclient123");
  resource.setGrantType("password");
  resource.setScope(Arrays.asList(new String[]
    {"read","write","trust"}));
  DefaultOAuth2ClientContext clientContext =
    new DefaultOAuth2ClientContext();
  OAuth2RestTemplate restTemplate =
    new OAuth2RestTemplate(resource, clientContext);

  Greet greet = restTemplate
    .getForObject("http://localhost:8080", Greet.class);
  Assert.assertEquals("Hello World!", greet.getMessage());
}
```

As shown in the preceding code, a special rest template, `OAuth2RestTemplate`, is created by passing the resource details encapsulated in a resource details object. This rest template handles the OAuth2 processes underneath. The access token URI is the endpoint for the token access.

5. Rerun the application using maven install. The first two test cases will fail, and the new one will succeed. This is because the server accepts only OAuth2-enabled requests.

These are quick configurations provided by Spring Boot out of the box, but are not good enough to be production grade. We may need to customize `ResourceServerConfigurer` and `AuthorizationServerConfigurer` to make them production ready. Regardless, the approach remains the same.

Enabling cross origin for microservices interactions

Browsers are generally restricted when client-side web applications running from one origin request data from another origin. Enabling cross origin access is generally termed as **CORS (Cross Origin Resource Sharing)**.

This is particularly important when dealing with microservices, such as when the microservices run on separate domains, and the browser tries to access these microservices from one browser after another:

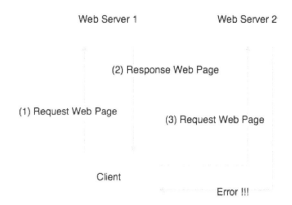

The preceding example showcases how to enable cross origin requests. With microservices, since each service runs with its own origin, it will easily get into the issue of a client-side web application, which consumes data from multiple origins. For instance, a scenario where a browser client accesses customers from the customer microservice, and order history from the order microservices is very common in microservices world.

Spring Boot provides a simple declarative approach for enabling cross origin requests.

The following code example shows how to use a microservice to enable cross origin:

```
@RestController
class GreetingController{
  @CrossOrigin
  @RequestMapping("/")
  Greet greet(){
    return new Greet("Hello World!");
  }
}
```

By default, all origins and headers are accepted. We can further customize the cross origin annotations by giving access to a specific origin as follows. The `@CrossOrigin` annotation enables a method or a class to accept cross origin requests:

```
@CrossOrigin("http://mytrustedorigin.com")
```

Global CORS could be enabled by using the `WebMvcConfigurer` bean, and customizing the `addCorsMappings(CorsRegistry registry)` method.

Spring Boot actuators for microservices instrumentation

The previous sections explored most of the Spring Boot features required for developing a microservices. In this section, we will explore some of the production-ready operational aspects of Spring Boot.

Spring Boot actuators provide an excellent out-of-the-box mechanism for monitoring and managing Spring Boot microservices in production.

 The full source code of this example is available as the `chapter3.bootactuator` project in the code files of this book under the following Git repository: https://github.com/rajeshrv/Spring5Microservice

Create another Spring starter project, and name it as `chapter3.bootactuator.application`; this time, select the **Web**, **HAL browser**, **hateoas,** and **Actuator** dependencies. Similar to `chapter3.bootrest`, add a `GreeterController` endpoint with the greet method. Add `management.security.enabled=false` to the `application.properties` file to grant access to all endpoints.

Do the following to execute the application:

1. Start the application as Spring Boot App.
2. Point the browser to `localhost:8080/application`. This will open the HAL browser. Review the **Links** section.

   A number of links are available under the **Links** section. These are automatically exposed by the Spring Boot actuator:

Links

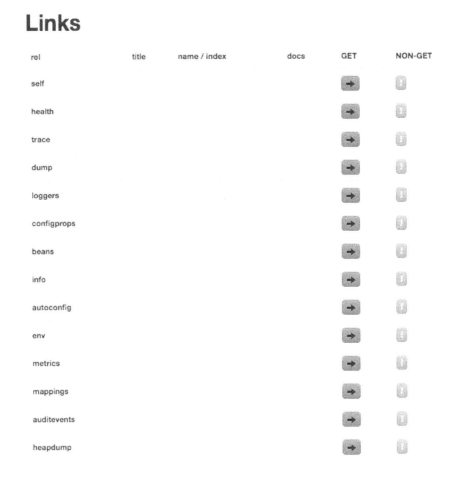

rel	title	name / index	docs	GET	NON-GET
self					
health					
trace					
dump					
loggers					
configprops					
beans					
info					
autoconfig					
env					
metrics					
mappings					
auditevents					
heapdump					

Some of the important links are listed as follows:

- **dump**: Performs a thread dump and displays the result
- **mappings**: Displays a list of all the http request mappings
- **info**: Displays information about the application

- **health**: Displays the health condition of the application
- **autoconfig**: Displays the auto configuration report
- **metrics**: Shows different metrics collected from the application

From the browser, individual endpoints are accessible using
`/application/<endpoint_name>`. For example, to access the `/health` endpoint, point
the browser to `localhost:8080/application/health`.

Monitoring using JConsole

Alternately, we can use the JMX console to see Spring Boot information. Connect to the
remote Spring Boot instance from a jconsole. The Boot information will be shown as
follows:

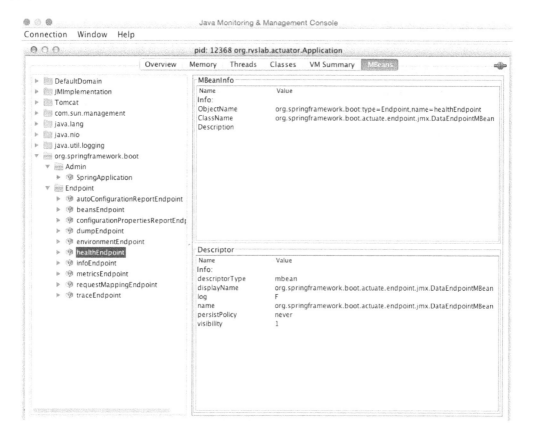

Monitoring using ssh

Spring Boot provides remote access to the Boot application using ssh. The following command connects to the Spring Boot application from a terminal window. The password can be customized by adding the `shell.auth.simple.user.password` property in the `application.properties` file. The updated `application.properties` will look as follows:

```
shell.auth.simple.user.password=admin
```

Use a terminal window to connect to the remote boot application using the following code:

```
$ ssh -p 2000 user@localhost
```

When connected with the preceding command, similar actuator information can be accessed. The following is an example of the metrics information accessed through the CLI:

- **help**: lists all the options available
- **dashboard**: dashboard is one interesting feature, which shows a lot of system-level information

Adding a custom health module

Adding a new custom module to the Spring Boot application is not so complex. For demonstrating this feature, assume that if a service gets more than two transactions in a minute, then the server status will be set as `Out of Service`.

In order to customize this, we have to implement the `HealthIndicator` interface, and override the `health` method. The following code is a quick and dirty implementation to do the job:

```
class TPSCounter {
  LongAdder count;
  int threshold = 2;
  Calendar expiry = null;

  TPSCounter(){
    this.count = new LongAdder();
    this.expiry = Calendar.getInstance();
    this.expiry.add(Calendar.MINUTE, 1);
  }
  boolean isExpired(){
    return Calendar.getInstance().after(expiry);
  }
```

```
    boolean isWeak(){
      return (count.intValue() > threshold);
    }

    void increment(){
      count.increment();
    }
}
```

The preceding code is a simple **Plain Old Java Object** (**POJO**) class, which maintains the transaction counts window. The `isWeak` method checks whether the transaction in a particular window has reached its threshold. `isExpired` checks whether the current window is expired or not. The `increment` method simply increases the counter value.

As the next step, implement our custom health indicator class, `TPSHealth`. This is done by extending `HealthIndicator` as follows:

```
@Component
class TPSHealth implements HealthIndicator {
  TPSCounter counter;
  @Override
  public Health health() {
    boolean health = counter.isWeak();
    if (health) {
      return Health.outOfService()
        .withDetail("Too many requests", "OutofService")
        .build();
    }
    return Health.up().build();
  }

  void updateTx(){
    if(counter == null || counter.isExpired()){
      counter = new TPSCounter();
    }
  counter.increment();
  }
}
```

The `health` method checks whether the counter `isWeak` or not. If it is weak, it marks the instance as out of service.

Finally, we autowire `TPSHealth` into the `GreetingController` class, and then call `health.updateTx()` in the greet method, like this:

```
Greet greet(){
  logger.info("Serving Request....!!!");
  health.updateTx();
  return new Greet("Hello World!");
}
```

Go to the `/application/health` endpoint in the HAL browser, and see the status of the server.

Now open another browser, point to `http://localhost:8080`, and fire the service twice or thrice. Go back to the `/application/health` endpoint, and refresh to see the status. It would have been changed to out of service.

In this example, since there is no action taken other than collecting the health status, new service calls will still go through even though the status is out of service. But in the real world, a program should read the `/application/health` endpoint, and block further requests going to that instance.

Building custom metrics

Just like health, customization of the metrics is also possible. The following example shows how to add a counter service and gauge service, just for demonstration purpose:

```
@Autowired
CounterService counterService;

@Autowired
GaugeService gaugeService;
```

And add the following methods to the `greet` method:

```
this.counterService.increment("greet.txnCount");
this.gaugeService.submit("greet.customgauge", 1.0);
```

Restart the server, and go to `/application/metrics` to see the new gauge and counter added already reflected there.

Documenting microservices

The traditional approach of API documentation is either to write service specification documents or to use static service registries. With a large number of microservices, it would be hard to keep the documentation of APIs in sync.

Microservices can be documented in many ways. This section will explore how microservices can be documented using the popular Swagger framework. In the following examples, we will use `Springfox` libraries for generating REST API documentation. `Springfox` is a set of Java Spring-friendly library.

Create a new `Spring Starter` project, and choose **Web** in the library selection window. Name the project as `chapter3.swagger`.

 The full source code of this example is available as the `chapter3.swagger` project in the code files of this book under the following Git repository:
`https://github.com/rajeshrv/Spring5Microservice`

Since `Springfox` libraries are not part of the Spring suite, edit the `pom.xml` file, and add the `springfox-swagger` library dependencies. Add the following dependencies to the project:

```
<dependency>
  <groupId>io.springfox</groupId>
  <artifactId>springfox-swagger2</artifactId>
  <version>2.6.1</version>
</dependency>

<dependency>
  <groupId>io.springfox</groupId>
  <artifactId>springfox-swagger-ui</artifactId>
  <version>2.6.1</version>
</dependency>
```

Create a REST service similar to the services created earlier, but also add the `@EnableSwagger2` annotation as shown next:

```
@SpringBootApplication
@EnableSwagger2
public class Application {
```

This is all that is required for a basic swagger documentation. Start the application, and point the browser to `http://localhost:8080/swagger-ui.html`. This will open the **swagger** API documentation page, as seen in this screenshot:

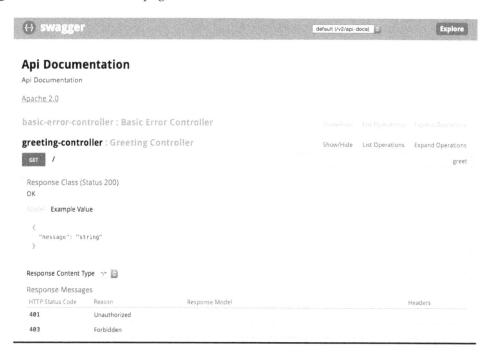

As shown in the preceding screenshot, the Swagger lists out the possible operations on the `GreetingController` class. Click on the **GET** operation. This expands the **GET** row, which provides an option to try out the operation.

Putting it all together - Developing a customer registration microservice example

So far, the examples we have seen are not more than just a simple *hello world*. Putting our learnings together, this section demonstrates an end-to-end customer profile microservice implementation. The customer profile microservices will demonstrate the interaction between different microservices. It will also demonstrate microservices with business logic and primitive data stores.

In this example, two microservices--**Customer Profile Service** and **Customer Notification Service**-- will be developed:

As shown in the preceding diagram, the customer profile microservice exposes methods to create, read, update, and delete a customer, and a registration service for registering a customer. The registration process applies certain business logic, saves the customer profile, and sends a message to the customer notification microservice. The customer notification microservice accepts the message sent by the registration service, and sends an e-mail message to the customer using an SMTP server. Asynchronous messaging is used for integrating customer profile with the customer notification service.

The customer microservices class domain model is shown in the following diagram:

<<RestController>> **CustomerController**	<<Component>> **CustomerComponent**	<<JPA Entity>> **Customer**	<<JpaRepository>> **CustomerRepository**
register : Customer	register : Customer	+ id: Long	findByName: Customer
		+ name: String	
		+ email: String	

The `CustomerController` in the diagram is the REST endpoint, which invokes a component class, `CustomerComponent`. The component class/bean handles all the business logic. `CustomerRepository` is a Spring data JPA repository defined for handling persistence of the Customer entity.

The full source code of this example is available as the `chapter3.bootcustomer` and `chapter3.bootcustomernotification` projects in the code files of this book.

Follow the steps listed next to build this example:

1. Create a new Spring Boot project, and call it `chapter3.bootcustomer` the same way as earlier. Select the checkbox of the following options in the starter module selection screen:

▾ Data
- ☐ JDBC
- ☑ JPA
- ☐ JOOQ
- ☐ MongoDB
- ☐ Cassandra
- ☐ Redis
- ☐ Gemfire
- ☐ Solr
- ☐ Elasticsearch

▾ Database
- ☑ H2
- ☐ HSQLDB
- ☐ Apache Derby
- ☐ MySQL
- ☐ PostgreSQL

▾ I/O
- ☐ Batch
- ☐ Integration
- ☐ Activiti
- ☐ JMS (Artemis)
- ☐ JMS (HornetQ)
- ☑ AMQP
- ☐ Mail

▸ Ops
▸ Social
▸ Template Engines

▾ Web
- ☑ Web
- ☐ Websocket
- ☐ WS
- ☐ Jersey (JAX-RS)
- ☐ Ratpack
- ☐ Vaadin
- ☑ Rest Repositories
- ☑ HATEOAS
- ☑ Rest Repositories HAL Browser
- ☐ Mobile
- ☐ REST Docs

This will create a web project with **JPA**, **Rest Repository**, and **H2** as database. **H2** is a tiny in-memory embedded database with easy-to-demonstrate database features. In the real world, it is recommended to use an appropriate enterprise-grade database. This example uses **JPA** for defining persistence entities and the REST repository for exposing REST-based repository services.

The project structure will look like the following screenshot:

2. Start building the application by adding an entity class named `Customer`. For simplicity, there are only three fields added to the customer entity which are auto-generated--`Id` field, `name`, and `email`:

```
@Entity
class Customer  {
  @Id
  @GeneratedValue(strategy = GenerationType.AUTO)

  private Long id;
  private String name;
  private String email;
```

3. Add a `Repository` class for handling persistence handling of customer. The `CustomerRepository` extends the standard `JpaRepository`. That means, all the CRUD methods and default finder methods are automatically implemented by the Spring Data JPA:

```
@RepositoryRestResource
interface CustomerRespository extends JpaRepository
<Customer,Long>{
  Optional<Customer> findByName(@Param("name") String name);
}
```

In the preceding example, we added a new method, `findByName`, to the `Repository` class, which essentially searches for a customer based on customer name, and returns a `Customer` object if there is a matching name.

`@RepositoryRestResource` enables repository access through RESTful services. This also enables **HATEOAS** and **HAL** by default. Since for CRUD methods there is no additional business logic required, we will leave it as it is, without controller or component classes. Using **HATEOAS** helps us to navigate through the `CustomerRepository` methods effortlessly.

 Note that there is no configuration added anywhere to point to any database. Since **H2** libraries are in the class path, all configurations are done by default by Spring Boot, based on **H2** auto-configuration.

4. Update `Application.java` by adding `CommandLineRunner` to initialize the repository with some customer records, as follows:

```
@SpringBootApplication
public class Application {
  public static void main(String[] args) {
    SpringApplication.run(Application.class, args);
  }
  @Bean
  CommandLineRunner init(CustomerRespository repo) {
    return (evt) ->    {
      repo.save(new Customer("Adam","adam@boot.com"));
      repo.save(new Customer("John","john@boot.com"));
      repo.save(new Customer("Smith","smith@boot.com"));
      repo.save(new Customer("Edgar","edgar@boot.com"));
      repo.save(new Customer("Martin","martin@boot.com"));
      repo.save(new Customer("Tom","tom@boot.com"));
      repo.save(new Customer("Sean","sean@boot.com"))
    };
  }
}
```

`CommandLineRunner`, defined as a bean, indicates that it should run when it is contained in a `SpringApplication`. This will insert six sample customer records to the database at startup.

5. At this point, run the application as Spring Boot App. Open the HAL browser by pointing the browser URL to `http://localhost:8080`.

6. In the **Explorer**, point to `http://localhost:8080/customers` and click on **Go**. This will list all customers in the **Response Body** section of the HAL browser.

7. In the **Explorer** section, enter the following URL, and click on **Go**. This will automatically execute paging and sorting on the repository, and return the result- `-http://localhost:8080/customers?size=2&page=1&sort=name`

   Since the page size is set as two, and first page is requested, it will come back with two records in a sorted order.

8. Review the **Links** section. As shown in the following diagram, it will facilitate navigating first, next, previous, and last. These are done using the HATEOAS links automatically generated by the repository browser:

Links

rel	title	name / index	docs	GET	NON-GET
first				→	
prev				→	
self				→	
next				→	
last				→	
profile				→	
search				→	

9. Also, one can explore the details of a customer by selecting the appropriate link, `http://localhost:8080/customers/2`.

10. As the next step, add a controller class, `CustomerController`, for handling the service endpoints. There is only one endpoint in this class, /register, which is used for registering a customer. If successful, it returns the customer object as the response:

```
@RestController
class CustomerController{
  @Autowired
  CustomerRegistrar customerRegistrar;

  @RequestMapping( path="/register", method =
   RequestMethod.POST)
  Customer register(@RequestBody Customer customer){
    return customerRegistrar.register(customer);
  }
}
```

The `CustomerRegistrar` component is added for handling business logic. In this case, there is only minimal business logic added to the component. In this component class, while registering a customer, we will just check whether the customer name already exists in the database or not. If it does not exist, then a new record should be inserted, otherwise, an error message should be returned:

```
@Component
class CustomerRegistrar {
  CustomerRespository customerRespository;
  @Autowired
  CustomerRegistrar(CustomerRespository customerRespository){
    this.customerRespository = customerRespository;
  }
  // ideally repository will return a Mono object
  public Mono<Customer> register(Customer customer){
    if(customerRespository
      .findByName(customer.getName())
      .isPresent())
      System.out.println("Duplicate Customer.
        No Action required");
    else {
      customerRespository.save(customer);
    }
    return Mono.just(customer);
  }
}
```

11. Restart the Boot application, and test using the HAL browser using the following URL: http://localhost:8080.

12. Point the Explorer field to `http://localhost:8080/customers`. Review the results in the **Links** section:

Links

rel	title	name / index	docs	GET	NON-GET
self				→	
profile				→	Perform non-GET rec
search				→	

13. Click on **NON-GET** against self. This will open a form for creating a new customer.
14. Fill the form and change the action as shown in the preceding screenshot. Click on the **Make Request** button. This will call the register service and register the customer. Try giving a duplicate name to test the negative case as follows:

Create/Update

Customer

Name

World

Email

world@hello.com

Action:

POST

http://localhost:8080/register

Make Request

Let us complete the last part in the example by integrating the customer notification service for notifying the customer. When registration is successful, an e-mail should be sent to the customer by asynchronously calling the customer notification microservice.

Perform the following steps to build the customer notification microservice:

1. First update `CustomerRegistrar` for calling the second service. This is done through messaging. In this case, we inject a `Sender` component for sending a notification to the customer by passing the customer's e-mail address to the sender:

```
@Component
@Lazy
class CustomerRegistrar {
  CustomerRespository customerRespository;
  Sender sender;
  @Autowired
  CustomerRegistrar(CustomerRespository customerRespository,
  Sender sender){
    this.customerRespository = customerRespository;
    this.sender = sender;
  }
  // ideally repository will return a Mono object
  public Mono<Customer> register(Customer customer){
    if(customerRespository.findByName(
      customer.getName()).isPresent())
      System.out.println("Duplicate Customer.
      No Action required");
    else {
      customerRespository.save(customer);
      sender.send(customer.getEmail());
    }
    return Mono.just(customer); //HARD CODED BECOSE THERE
      IS NO REACTIVE REPOSITORY.
  }
}
```

The sender component will be based on RabbitMQ and AMQP. In this example, `RabbitMessagingTemplate` is used as explored in the last messaging example:

```
@Component
@Lazy
class Sender {
  @Autowired
  RabbitMessagingTemplate template;
  @Bean
  Queue queue() {
```

```
      return new Queue("CustomerQ", false);
    }
  public void send(String message){
    template.convertAndSend("CustomerQ", message);
  }
}
```

 `@Lazy` is a useful annotation, which helps to increase the boot startup time. Those beans will be initialized only when the need arises.

2. We will also update the `Application.property` file to include RabbitMQ-related properties:

```
spring.rabbitmq.host=localhost
spring.rabbitmq.port=5672
spring.rabbitmq.username=guest
spring.rabbitmq.password=guest
```

3. We are ready to send the message. For consuming the message and sending emails, we will create a notification service. For this, let us create another Spring Boot service, `chapter3.bootcustomernotification`. Make sure that the AMQP and Mail starter libraries are selected when creating the Spring Boot service. Both AMQP and Mail are under I/O.

The package structure of the `chapter3.bootcustomernotifcation` project is as shown in following screenshot:

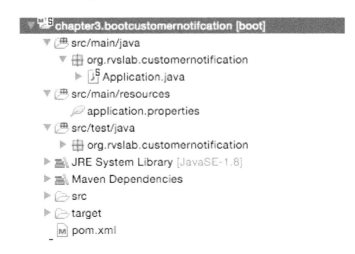

4. Add a `Receiver` class. The `Receiver` class waits for a message on the customer. This will receive a message sent by the Customer Profile service. On the arrival of a message, it sends an email:

```
@Component
class Receiver {
  @Autowired
  Mailer mailer;

  @Bean
  Queue queue() {
    return new Queue("CustomerQ", false);
  }

  @RabbitListener(queues = "CustomerQ")
  public void processMessage(String email)  {
    System.out.println(email);
    mailer.sendMail(email);
  }
}
```

5. Add another component for sending an email to the customer. We use `JavaMailSender` to send the email:

```
@Component
class Mailer  {
  @Autowired
  private  JavaMailSender  javaMailService;

  public void sendMail(String email) {
    SimpleMailMessage mailMessage=new SimpleMailMessage();
    mailMessage.setTo(email);
    mailMessage.setSubject("Registration");
    mailMessage.setText("Successfully Registered");
    javaMailService.send(mailMessage);
  }
}
```

Behind the scene, Spring Boot automatically configures all the parameters required for `JavaMailSender`.

Perform the following steps to test the application:

1. To test SMTP, a test setup for SMTP is required to ensure that the mails are going out. In this example, Fake SMTP will be used.
2. Download the Fake SMTP server from `http://nilhcem.github.io/FakeSMTP`.
3. Once you have downloaded `fakeSMTP-2.0.jar`, run the SMTP server by executing the following command:

```
$ java -jar fakeSMTP-2.0.jar
```

4. This will open a GUI for monitoring email messages. Click on the **Start Server** button next to the listening port text box.
5. Update `Application.properties` with the following configuration parameters to connect to RabbitMQ as well as to the mail server:

```
spring.rabbitmq.host=localhost
spring.rabbitmq.port=5672
spring.rabbitmq.username=guest
spring.rabbitmq.password=guest
spring.mail.host=localhost
spring.mail.port=2525
```

6. We are ready to test our microservices end to end. Start both Spring Boot Apps. Open the browser, and repeat the customer creation steps through the HAL browser. In this case, immediately after submitting the request, we will be able to see the e-mail in the SMTP GUI.

7. Internally, the Customer Profile service asynchronously calls the Customer Notification service, which, in turn, sends the email message to the SMTP server:

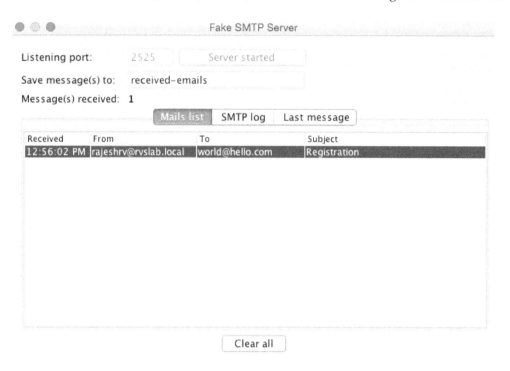

Summary

In this chapter, we learned about Spring Boot, and its key features for building production-ready applications.

We explored the previous generation web applications, and then compared how Spring Boot makes developers' lives easier in developing fully qualified microservices. We also saw HTTP-based and message-based asynchronous reactive microservices. Further, we explored how to achieve some of the key capabilities required for microservices such as security, HATEOAS, cross-origin, and so on, with practical examples. We also saw how the Spring Boot actuators help the operations teams, and also how to customize our needs. Then, documenting microservices APIs was also discussed. We closed the chapter with a complete example that puts together all our learnings.

In the next chapter, we will take a step back, and perform a pragmatic analysis of microservices with the help of practical day-to-day scenarios.

4
Applying Microservices Concepts

Microservices are good, but can also be an evil if they are not properly conceived. Wrong interpretations and design choices could lead to irrecoverable failures.

This chapter will examine the technical challenges around the practical implementations of microservices. It will also provide guidelines around critical design decisions for successful microservice developments. The solutions and patterns for a number of commonly raised concerns around microservices will also be examined.

In this chapter, you will learn about the following:

- Trade-offs between different design choices
- Patterns to be considered when developing microservices
- General guidelines for designing scalable, first-class microservices

Microservice design guidelines

Microservices have gained enormous popularity in recent years. It has evolved as the preferred choice of architects, putting SOA into the backyard. While acknowledging the fact that microservices are a vehicle for developing scalable cloud-native systems, successful microservices need to be carefully designed to avoid catastrophes. Microservices are not the one-size-fits-all, universal solution for all architecture problems.

Generally speaking, microservices are a great choice for building a lightweight, modular, scalable, and distributed system of systems. However, over engineering, wrong use cases, and misinterpretations could easily turn the system into a disaster. While selecting the right use cases is paramount in developing a successful microservice, it is equally important to take the right design decisions by carrying out an appropriate trade-off analysis. A number of factors are to be considered when designing microservices, as detailed in the following sections.

Deciding microservice boundaries

One of the most common questions around microservices is on the size of the service. How big (mini-monolithic) or how small (nano service) can a microservice be, or is there anything like a right-sized service? Does size really matter?

A quick answer could be any of these--*one REST endpoint per microservice,* or *less than 300 lines of code,* or *a component that performs a single responsibility.* But before we pick up any of these answers, there is lot more analysis to be done to understand the boundaries for our services.

 Domain-Driven Design (DDD) defines the concept of a **bounded context**. A bounded context is a subdomain or a subsystem of a larger domain or system, which is responsible for performing a particular function. Read more about DDD at the following site: https://domainlanguage.com/ddd/.

The following diagram is an example of a domain model:

<<bounded context>>
Invoice

<<bounded context>>
Accounting

<<bounded context>>
Billing

Finance Back Office Domain

In a finance back office system, invoice, accounting, billing, and so on represent the different bounded contexts. These bounded contexts are strongly isolated domains that are closely aligned with business capabilities. In the financial domain, the invoices, accounting, and billing are different business capabilities, often handled by different subunits under the finance department.

Bounded context is a good way to determine the boundaries of microservices. Each bounded context could be mapped to a single microservice. In the real world, communication between bounded contexts is typically less coupled, and often, disconnected.

Even though real-world organizational boundaries are the simplest mechanisms to establish a bounded context, this may prove wrong in some cases due to the inherent problems within the organization's structures. For example, a business capability may be delivered through different channels, such as front offices, online, roaming agents, and more. In many organizations, the business units may be organized based on delivery channels rather than the actual underlying business capabilities. In such cases, organization boundaries may not provide accurate service boundaries.

A top-down domain decomposition could be another way to establish the right bounded contexts.

There is no silver bullet to establish microservice boundaries, and often, this is quite challenging. Establishing boundaries is much easier in the scenario of monolithic application to microservice migration, as the service boundaries and dependencies are known from the existing system. On the other hand, the dependencies are hard to establish upfront in a green field microservice development.

The most pragmatic way to design microservice boundaries is to run the scenario at hand through a number of possible options, just like a service litmus test. Keep in mind that there may be multiple conditions matching a given scenario that will lead to a trade-off analysis.

The following scenarios could help in defining the microservice boundaries.

Autonomous functions

If the function under review is autonomous by nature, then it can be taken as a microservice boundary. Autonomous services typically would have fewer dependencies on external functions. They accept input, use its internal logic and data for computation, and return a result. All utility functions, such as an encryption engine or a notification engine, are straightforward candidates.

A delivery service that accepts an order, processes it, and then informs the trucking service is another example of an autonomous service. An online flight search based on cached seat availability information is yet another example of an autonomous function.

Size of the deployable unit

Most of the microservice ecosystems will take advantage of automation, such as automatic integration, delivery, deployment, and scaling. Microservices covering broader functions will result in larger deployment units. Large deployment units pose challenges in automatic file copy, file download, deployment, and startup times. For instance, the size of a service increases with the density of the functions it implements.

A good microservice will ensure that the size of its deployable units remains manageable.

Most appropriate function or sub-domain

It is important to analyze what would be the most useful component to detach from the monolithic application. This is particularly applicable when breaking monolithic applications into microservices. This could be based on parameters such as resource intensiveness, cost of ownership, business benefits, or flexibility.

In a typical hotel booking system, approximately 50-60% of the requests are searches. In this case, moving out the search function could immediately bring in flexibility, business benefits, cost reduction, resource free up, and so on.

Polyglot architecture

One of the key characteristics of microservices is their support for a polyglot architecture. In order to meet different non-functional and functional requirements, components may require different treatments. It could be different architectures, different technologies, different deployment topologies, and more. When components are identified, review them against the requirement for polyglot architectures.

In the hotel booking scenario mentioned earlier, a Booking microservice may need transactional integrity, whereas a Search microservice may not. In this case, the Booking microservice may use an ACID compliance database such as MySQL, whereas, the Search microservice may use an eventual consistent database such as Cassandra.

Selective scaling

Selective scaling is related to the previously discussed polyglot architecture. In this context, all functional modules may not require the same level of scalability. Sometimes, it may be appropriate to determine boundaries based on scalability requirements.

For example, in the hotel booking scenario, the Search microservice has to scale considerably more than many of the other services, such as the Booking microservice or the Notification microservice, due to the higher velocity of search requests. In this case, a separate Search microservice could run on top of an Elasticsearch, or in a memory data grid for better response.

Agile teams and co-development

Microservices enable agile development with small, focused teams developing different parts of the pie. There could be scenarios where parts of the systems are built by different organizations, or even across different geographies, or by teams with varying skill sets. This approach is a common practice, for example, in the manufacturing industries.

In the microservices world, each of these teams builds different microservices and then assembles them together. Though this is not the desired way to break down the system, organizations may end up in such situations. Hence, this approach cannot be completely ruled out.

In an online product search scenario, a service could provide personalized options based on what the customer is looking for. This may require complex machine learning algorithms, and, thus, need a specialist team. In this scenario, this function could be built as a microservice by a separate specialist team.

Single responsibility

In theory, the single responsibility principle could be applied to a method, a class, or a service. However, in the context of microservices, it does not necessarily map to a single service or endpoint. A more practical approach could be to translate the single responsibility into a single business capability, or a single technical capability. As per the single responsibility principle, one responsibility cannot be shared by multiple microservices. Similarly, one microservice should not perform multiple responsibilities.

There could, however, be special cases where a single business capability is divided across multiple services. One such case could be managing the customer profile, where there could be situations where you may use two different microservices for managing reads and writes using a **Command Query Responsibility Segregation** (**CQRS**) approach to achieve some of the quality attributes.

Replicability or changeability

Innovation and speed are of foremost importance in IT delivery. Microservice boundaries should be identified in such a way that each microservice is easily detachable from the overall system, with minimal cost of rewriting. If part of the system is just an experiment, it should, ideally, be isolated as a microservice.

An organization may develop a **recommendation engine** or a **customer ranking engine** as an experiment. If the business value is not realized, then that service should be thrown away, or replaced with another one.

Many organizations follow the startup model, where importance is given to meeting functions and quick delivery. These organizations may not worry too much about the architecture and technologies, and instead, focus on the tools or technologies that can deliver solutions faster. Organizations are increasingly choosing the approach of developing **Minimum Viable Products** (**MVPs**) by putting together a few services and allowing the system to evolve. Microservices play a vital role in such cases where the system evolves, and the services get gradually rewritten or replaced.

Coupling and cohesion

Coupling and cohesion are two of the most important parameters for deciding service boundaries. Dependencies between microservices have to be evaluated carefully to avoid highly coupled interfaces. A functional decomposition, together with a modeled dependency tree, could help in establishing microservice boundaries. Avoiding too chatty services, many synchronous request-response calls, and cyclic synchronous dependencies are three key points, as these could easily break the system. A successful equation is to keep high cohesion within a microservice and loose coupling between microservices. In addition to this, ensure that transaction boundaries are not stretched across microservices. A first-class microservice will react upon receiving an event as input, execute a number of internal functions, and finally, send out another event. As part of the compute function, it may read and write data to its own local store.

Think of the microservice as a product

DDD also recommends mapping a bounded context to a product. As per DDD, each bounded context is an ideal candidate for a product. Think about a microservice as a product in itself. When microservice boundaries are established, assess them from a product's point of view to see whether it really stacks up as product. It is much easier for business users to think of boundaries from a product point of view. A product boundary may have many parameters, such as targeted community, flexibility in deployment, sell-ability, reusability, and more.

Designing communication styles

Communication between microservices can be designed either in synchronous (request-response) or asynchronous (fire and forget) styles.

Synchronous style communication

The following diagram shows an example request-response style service:

In synchronous communication, there is no shared state or object. When the caller requests a service, it passes the required information and waits for a response. This approach has a number of advantages--an application is stateless, and from a high availability standpoint, many active instances can be up and running, accepting traffic. Since there are no other infrastructure dependencies, such as a shared messaging server, the management overhead is less. In case of an error at any stage, the error will be propagated back to the caller immediately, leaving the system in a consistent state without compromising data integrity.

The downside in a synchronous request-response communication is that the user or the caller has to wait until the requested process is completed. As a result, the calling thread will have to wait for a response, and hence, this style could limit the scalability of the system.

The synchronous style adds hard dependencies between microservices. If one service in the service chain fails, then the entire service chain will fail. In order to make a service succeed, all dependent services have to be up and running. Many of the failure scenarios have to be handled using timeouts and fallbacks.

Asynchronous style communication

The following diagram is a service designed to accept an asynchronous message as input, and to send the response asynchronously for others to consume:

The asynchronous style is based on reactive event loop semantics, which decouple microservices. This approach provides higher levels of scalability, because services are independent, and can internally spawn threads to handle an increase in load. When overloaded, messages will be queued in a messaging server for later processing. That means that if there is a slowdown in one of the services, it will not impact the entire chain. This provides higher levels of decoupling between services, and therefore, maintenance and testing will be more simple.

The downside is that it has a dependency to an external messaging server. It is complex to handle the fault tolerance of a messaging server. Messaging typically works with an active-passive semantic. Hence, handling continuous availability of messaging systems is harder to achieve. Since messaging typically uses persistence, a higher level of I/O handling and tuning is required.

How to decide which style to choose?

Both approaches have their own merits and constraints. It is not possible to develop a system with just one approach. A combination of both approaches is required based on the use cases. In principle, the asynchronous approach is great for building true, scalable microservice systems. However, attempting to model everything as asynchronous leads to complex system designs.

This is what the the aforementioned example looks like in the context where an end user clicks on a UI to get profile details:

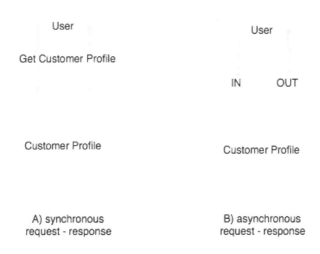

This is perhaps a simple query to the backend system to get a result in a request-response model. This can also be modeled in an asynchronous style--by pushing a message to an input queue and waiting for a response in an output queue till a response is received for the given correlation ID. However, though we use asynchronous messaging, the user is still blocked for the entire duration of the query.

Another use case is that of a user clicking a UI to search hotels, which is depicted in the following diagram:

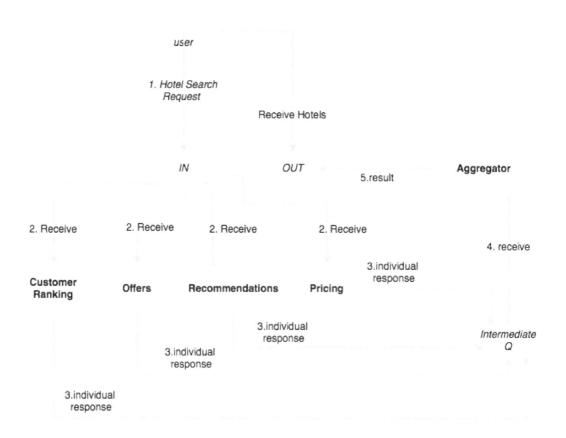

This is very similar to the previous scenario. However, in this case, we assume that this business function triggers a number of activities internally before returning the list of hotels back to the user. For example, when the system receives this request, it calculates the customer ranking, gets offers based on the destination, gets recommendations based on customer preferences, optimizes the prices based on customer values and revenue factors, and so on. In this case, we have an opportunity to do many of these activities in parallel so that we can aggregate all these results before them presenting back to the customer. As shown in the diagram, virtually any computational logic could be plugged into the search pipeline listening to the `IN` queue.

An effective approach in this case is to start with synchronous request-response, and refactor later to introduce an asynchronous style when there is value in doing that.

The following example shows a full asynchronous style of service interactions:

The service is triggered when the user clicks on the booking function. It is, again, by nature a synchronous style communication. When booking is successful, it sends a message to the customer's email address, sends a message to the hotel's booking system, updates the cached inventory, updates the loyalty points system, prepares invoices, and, perhaps, more. Instead of pushing the user into a long wait state, a better approach is to break the service into pieces. Let the user wait till a booking record is created by the Booking service. On successful completion, a Booking event will be published, and a confirmation message will be returned to the user. Subsequently, all other activities will happen in parallel and asynchronously.

In all three examples, the user has to wait for a response. With the new web application frameworks, it is possible to send requests asynchronously, and define a callback method, or set an observer for getting the response. Therefore, the users won't be fully blocked from executing other activities.

In general, the asynchronous style is always better in the microservices world, but identifying the right pattern should be purely based on merits. If there are no merits in modeling a transaction in an asynchronous style, then use a synchronous style till we find an appealing case. Use reactive programming frameworks, such as Spring Framework reactive, to avoid complexity when modeling user-driven requests modeled in asynchronous style.

Orchestration of microservices

Composability is one of the service design principles. This leads to confusion about who is responsible for the composing services. In the SOA world, ESBs are responsible for composing a set of fine-grained services. In some organizations, ESBs play the role of a proxy, and service providers themselves compose and expose coarse-grained services. In the SOA world, there were two approaches for handling such situations.

The first approach is orchestration, which is depicted in the following diagram:

In the orchestration approach, multiple services are stitched together to get a complete function. A central brain acts as the orchestrator. As shown in the diagram, the order service is a composite service that orchestrates the other services. There can be sequential as well as parallel branches from the master process. Each task is fulfilled by an atomic task service, typically, a web service. In the SOA world, ESB played the role of orchestration. The orchestrated service is exposed by ESB as a composite service.

The second approach is choreography, which is shown in the following diagram:

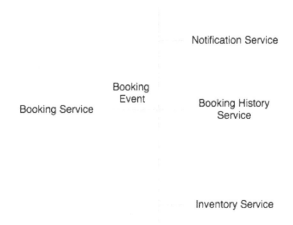

In the choreography approach, there is no central brain. An event, **Booking Event** in this case, is published by a producer, a number of consumers wait for the event and then independently apply different logic on the incoming event. Sometimes, events could even be nested where the consumers can send another event, which would be consumed by another service. In the SOA world, the caller pushes a message to the ESB, and the downstream flow is automatically determined by the consuming services.

Microservices are autonomous. This essentially means that in an ideal situation, all components that are required to complete a microservice's function should be within the service. This includes the database, orchestration of its internal services, intrinsic state management, and more. The service endpoints provide coarse-grained APIs. This is perfectly fine as long as there are no external touch points required. But in reality, a microservice may need to talk to other microservices to fulfill its function.

In such cases, **choreography** is the preferred approach for connecting multiple microservices together. Following the autonomy principle, a component sitting outside a microservice and controlling the flow is not the desired option. If the use case can be modeled in choreographic style, that would be the best possible way to handle the situation.

While choreography is the preferred approach for microservices, it may get complicated when dealing with large processes, interactions, and workflows. Netflix introduced **Conductor**, an open source microservices orchestration tool for managing large-scale microservices orchestrations.

But it may not be possible to model choreography in all cases. This is depicted in the following diagram:

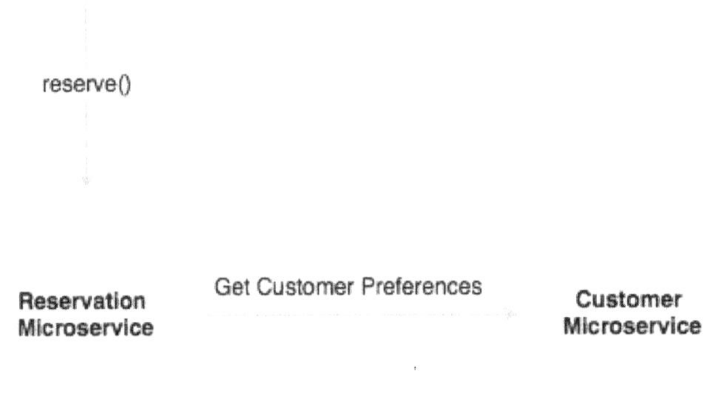

reserve()

Reservation
Microservice

Get Customer Preferences

Customer
Microservice

For example, **reservation** and **customer** are two microservices with clearly segregated functional responsibilities. A case could arise where reservation wants to get customer preferences while creating a reservation. Such scenarios are quite normal when developing complex systems.

Can we move customer to reservation so that reservation will be complete by itself? If customer and reservation are identified as two microservices based on various factors, it may not be a good idea to move customer to reservation. In such a case, we will meet another monolithic application sooner or later.

Can we make the reservation to customer call asynchronous? This example diagram shows a scenario that needs synchronous calls:

reserve()

Reservation
Microservice

Customer
Microservice

Now let us take just the orchestration bit outside and create another composite microservice, which then composes reservation and customer, as shown in the following diagram:

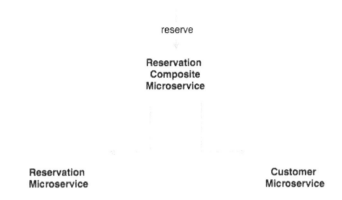

This is acceptable in an approach that composes multiple components within a microservice. But creating a composite microservice may not be a good thought. We will end up creating many fine-grained, non-autonomous microservices with no business alignment.

Let us try and duplicate customer preference by keeping a slave copy of preference data in reservation, as depicted in this diagram:

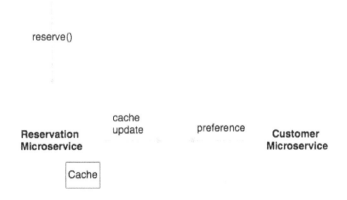

Changes will be propagated whenever there is a change in the master. In this case, reservation can use customer preference without fanning out a call. It is a valid thought, but we need to carefully analyze this. Today we replicate customer preference, but maybe, in another scenario, we would want to reach out to customer service to see whether the customer is blacklisted for reserving. You have to be extremely careful in deciding what data to duplicate. This could increase the complexity.

How many endpoints - one or many?

In many situations, developers are confused about the number of endpoints per microservice. The question really is whether to limit each microservice with one endpoint or multiple endpoints:

The number of endpoints is not really a decision point. In some cases, there may be only one endpoint, whereas in some other cases, there could be more than one endpoint in a microservice. For instance, consider a sensor data service, which collects sensor information, and has two logical endpoints--create and read. But in order to handle CQRS, we may create two separate physical microservices, as shown in the case of booking (refer to the preceding diagram). Polyglot architecture could be another scenario where we may split endpoints into different microservices.

Considering a notification engine, notifications will be sent out in response to an event. The process of notification such as the preparation of data, the identification of the person, and delivery mechanisms are different for different events. Moreover, we want to scale each of these processes differently at different time windows. In such situations, we may decide to break each notification endpoint into separate microservices.

In yet another example, a Loyalty Points microservice may have multiple services, such as accrue, redeem, transfer, and balance. We may not want to treat each of these services differently. All of these services are connected, and use the points table for data. If we go with one endpoint per service, we will end up in a situation where many fine-grained services access data from the same data store or from replicated copies of the same data store.

In short, the number of endpoints is not a design decision. One microservice may host one or more endpoints. Designing an appropriate bounded context for a microservice is more important.

How many microservices per VM - one or multiple?

One microservice could be deployed in multiple **virtual machines** (**VM**) by replicating the deployment for scalability and availability. This is a no brainer. The question is whether multiple microservices could be deployed in one virtual machine? There are pros and cons to this approach. This question typically arises when the services are simple, and have less traffic volumes.

Consider an example where we have a couple of microservices, and the overall transactions per minute is less than 10. Also assume that the smallest possible VM size available is 2 core 8 GB RAM. A further assumption is that in such cases, a 2 core 8 GB VM can handle 10-15 transactions per minute without any performance concerns. If we use different VMs for each microservice, it may not be cost effective, and we will end up paying more infrastructure and license cost, since many vendors charge on the basis of the number of cores.

The simplest way to approach this problem is to ask a few questions like these:

- Does the VM have enough capacity to run both the services under peak usage?
- Do we want to treat these services differently to achieve SLAs (selective scaling)? For example, for scalability, if we have an all-in-one VM, we will have to replicate the VMs that replicate all services
- Are there any conflicting resource requirements? For example, different OS versions, JDK versions, and more

If the answers to all the preceding questions are No, then perhaps we will start with collocated deployment until we encounter a scenario to change the deployment topology. However, we will have to ensure that these services do not share anything, and run as independent OS processes.

Having said that, in an organization with matured virtualized infrastructure or cloud infrastructure, this may not be a huge concern. In such environments, the developers need not worry about where the services are running. Developers may not even think about capacity planning. Services will be deployed in a compute cloud. Based on the infrastructure availability, SLAs, and the nature of service, the infrastructure self-manages deployments. AWS Lambda is a good example of such a service.

Rules engine - shared or embedded?

Rules are an essential part of any system. For example, an offer eligibility service may execute a number of rules before making a yes or no decision. We either hand code rules, or we may use a rules engine. Many enterprises manage rules centrally in a rules repository and execute them centrally as well. These enterprise rules engines are primarily used for providing the business an opportunity to author and manage rules, as well as to reuse rules from the central repository. Drools is one of the popular open source rules engines. IBM, FICO, and BOSCH are some of the pioneers in the commercial space. These rule engines improve productivity, reuse of rules, facts, vocabularies, and also have faster rule execution using the Rete algorithm.

In the context of microservices, a central rules engine means fanning out calls from microservices to the central rules engine. This also means that the service logic is now in two places--some within the service, and some external to the service. Nevertheless, the objective in the context of microservices is to reduce external dependencies:

Eligibility
Microservice

custom
rule engine

If the rules are simple enough, few in number, only used within the boundaries of a service, and not exposed to business users for authoring, then it may be better to hand code business rules rather than rely on an enterprise rule engine:

Eligibility
Microservice

Embedded
Rules Engine

If the rules are complex, limited to a service context, and not given to business users, then it is better to use an embedded rules engine within the service:

Eligibility
Microservice

Rule
Repository

Embedded
Rules Engine

If the rules are managed and authored by the business, or if the rules are complex, or if we are reusing rules from other service domains, then a central authoring repository with a locally embedded execution engine would be a better choice.

Note that this has to be carefully evaluated, since all vendors may not support the local rule execution approach, and there could be technology dependencies, such as running rules only within a specific application server, and so on.

Role of BPM and workflows

Business Process Management (BPM) and **Intelligent Business Process Management (iBPM)** are tool suites for designing, executing, and monitoring business processes.

Typical use cases for BPM are as follows:

- When coordinating a long running business process where some processes are realized by existing assets, whereas some other areas may be niche, and no concrete implementation of the processes are in place. BPM allows you to compose both types, and provides an end-to-end automated process. This often involves systems and human interactions.

- When process-centric organizations, such as organizations that have implemented Six Sigma, want to monitor their processes for continuous improvement in efficiency.
- In the case of process re-engineering with a top-down approach by redefining the business process of an organization.

There could be two scenarios where BPM fits in the microservices world.

The following diagram shows a loan approval process implemented as a business process:

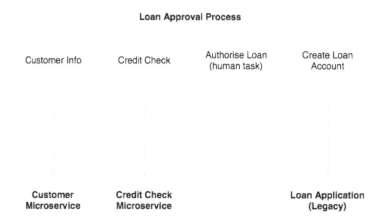

The first scenario is business process re-engineering, or threading an end-to-end, long-running business process, as stated earlier. In this case, BPM operates at a higher level, where it may automate a cross-functional, long-running business process by stitching a number of coarse-grained microservices, existing legacy connectors, and human interactions. As shown in the preceding diagram, the loan approval BPM invokes microservices as well as legacy application services. It also integrates human tasks.

In this case, microservices are headless services that implement a sub-process. From the microservices' perspective, BPM is just another consumer. Care needs to be taken in this approach to avoid accepting a shared state from the BPM process, as well as moving business logic to BPM.

The following diagram shows the order delivery process visualized through a series of bottom-up events:

The second scenario is monitoring processes and optimizing them for efficiency. This goes hand in hand with a completely automated, asynchronously choreographed microservices ecosystem. In this case, the microservices and BPM work as independent ecosystems. Microservices send events at various time intervals, such as the start of a process, state changes, end of a process, and more. These events are used by the BPM engine to plot and monitor the process states. We may not require a full-fledged BPM solution for this as we are only mocking a business process to monitor its efficiency. In this case, the Order delivery process is not a BPM implementation, but it is more of a monitoring dashboard that captures and displays the progress of the process.

In short, BPM could still be used at a higher level for composing multiple microservices in situations where end-to-end, cross-functional business processes are modeled by automated systems and human interactions. A better and simpler approach is to have a business process dashboard to which microservices feed state change events, as mentioned in the second scenario.

Can microservices share a data store?

In principle, microservices should abstract presentation, business logic, and data store. If the services are broken as per the guidelines, each microservice logically could use an independent database.

The following diagram shows order and product microservices sharing a single database:

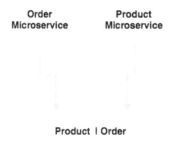

In the preceding diagram, both **Product** and **Order** microservices share one database and a shared data model. Shared data models, shared schemas, and shared tables are recipes for disasters when developing microservices. These may be good at the beginning, but when developing complex microservices, we tend to add relationships between data models, and add join queries, and so on. This can result in tightly coupled physical data models.

If the services have only a few tables, it may not be worth investing a full instance of a database, such as an Oracle database instance. In such cases, a schema-level segregation is good enough to start with.

The following diagram shows **Customer Registration** and **Customer Segmentation** reuse the same **Customer Repository**:

There could be scenarios where we tend to think of using shared database for multiple services. Take the example of a customer data repository or master data managed at the enterprise level--the customer registration and customer segmentation microservices logically share the same customer data repository.

As shown in the following diagram, an alternate approach to the given scenario is to separate the transactional data store for microservices from the enterprise data repository by adding a local transactional data store for these services:

This will help the services to have the flexibility to remodel the local data store optimized for its purpose. The enterprise customer repository sends change events when there is any change in the customer data repository. Similarly, if there is any change in any of the transactional data store, the changes have to be sent to the central customer repository.

There could be scenarios where microservices are written on top of some shared enterprise data stores, such as a Data Lake, Common Data Repositories, such as Master Data Management, and more. In such cases, you may be forced to use a shared data store. It is important to decouple such repositories from the microservices using service interfaces instead of adding native connections.

Can microservices be headless?

In many cases, microservices may be used without UIs. Such microservices are generally called **headless**. In some other cases, UIs aggregate data from multiple microservices.

Even though, in an ideal world, microservices will package UI, business logic, and the database together, this shouldn't be treated as the one and only pattern for microservices. The emerging pattern of headless microservices cannot be ignored. This is especially useful in scenarios where the same services are exposed across multiple channels, such as **Audio User Interfaces** (AUI), chatbots, gesture-based UIs, wearable user interfaces, and so on. These channel implementations, at times, need more sophisticated or specialized treatments, and may also undergo frequent changes.

In fact, headless is one of the most popular forms of microservice implementations.

Deciding transaction boundaries

Transactions in operational systems are used to maintain consistency of data stored in an RDBMS by grouping a number of operations together into one atomic block. They either commit or roll back the entire operation. Distributed systems have the concept of distributed transactions with a two-phase commit. This is particularly required if heterogeneous components such as an RPC service, JMS, and more participate in a transaction.

Is there a place for transactions in microservices? Transactions are not bad, but make use of transactions carefully by analyzing what you are trying do.

For a given microservice, if an RDBMS such as MySQL is selected as a backing store to ensure 100% data integrity (for example, a stock or inventory management service where data integrity is key), you should define transaction boundaries within the microsystem using local transactions. However, distributed global transactions should be avoided in the microservices context. Proper dependency analysis is required to ensure that transaction boundaries do not span across two different microservices as much as possible.

Altering use cases to simplify transactional requirements

Eventual consistency is a better option than distributed transactions that span across multiple microservices. Eventual consistency reduces a lot of overheads, but application developers may need to rethink the way they write application code. This could include remodeling functions, sequencing operations to minimize failures, batching insert and modify operations, remodeling data structure, and finally, compensating operations that negate the effect.

A classical problem is that of the last room selling scenario in a hotel booking use case. What if there is only one room left, and there are multiple customers booking this single available room? A business model change sometimes makes this scenario less impactful. We could set an **under booking profile**, where the actual number of bookable rooms can go below the actual number of rooms (*bookable = available - 3*) in anticipation of some cancellations. Anything in this range will be accepted as **subject to confirmation**, and customers will be charged only if payment is confirmed. Bookings will be confirmed in a set time window.

Now consider the scenario where we are creating customer profiles in a NoSQL database, such as CouchDB. In more traditional approaches with RDBMS, we insert a customer first, and then insert the customer's address, profile details, and then preferences, all in one transaction. When using NoSQL, we may not do the same steps. Instead, we may prepare a JSON object with all the details and insert this into the CouchDB in one go. In this second case, no explicit transaction boundaries are required.

Distributed transaction scenarios

The ideal scenario is to use local transactions within a microservice, if required, and to completely avoid distributed transactions. There could be scenarios where, at the end of the execution of one service, we may want to send a message to another microservice. For example, say a tour reservation has a wheelchair request. Once the reservation is successful, we will have to send a message for wheelchair booking to another microservice that handles ancillary bookings. The reservation request itself will run on a local transaction. If sending this message fails, we are still in the transaction boundary, and we can roll back the entire transaction. What if we create the reservation and send the message, but after sending, we encounter an error in the reservation, the reservation transaction failed, and subsequently, the reservation record is rolled back? Now we end up in a situation where, unnecessarily, we created an orphan wheelchair booking. This is explained in the following diagram:

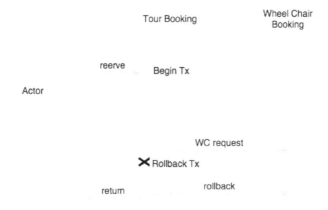

There are a couple of ways in which we can address this scenario. The first approach is to delay sending the message till the end. This will ensure that there are less chances for any failure after sending the message. Still, if failure occurs after sending the message, then using the exception handling routine, we send a compensating message to reverse the wheelchair booking.

Service endpoint design consideration

One of the important aspects of microservices is the service design. Service design has two key elements--contract design and protocol selection.

Contract design

The first and foremost principle of service design is simplicity. Often, service designers spend a considerable amount of time in future-proofing the services to make sure that they are designed for reusability. However, this may result in complex services, which are hard to consume. In reality, these future-proofed services still undergo changes.

The services should be designed for consumers to consume. A complex service contract reduces the usability of the service. The **KISS** (**Keep It Simple Stupid**) principle helps us to build services faster that are of better quality, and reduces the cost of maintenance and replacement. **YAGNI** (**You Ain't Gonna Need It**) is another principle supporting this idea. Predicting future requirements and building systems are, in reality, not future-proofed. This results in large upfront investment, as well as a higher cost of maintenance.

Evolutionary design is a great concept. Evolutionary design advocates doing just enough design to satisfy today's tasks, and keep changing and refactoring the design to accommodate new features as and when they are required. Having said that, this may not be simple, unless there is a strong governance in place.

Consumer Driven Contracts (**CDC**) is a great idea that supports evolutionary design. In many cases, when the service contract gets changed, all consuming applications have to undergo thorough testing. This makes changes difficult. CDC helps build confidence in the consumer applications. CDC advocates the each consumer provides their expectation in the form of test cases to the provider so that the provider uses them as integration tests whenever the service contract is changed.

Postel's law is also relevant in this scenario. Postel's law primarily addresses TCP communications. However, this is also equally applicable to service design. When it comes to service design, service providers should be as flexible as possible when accepting consumer requests, whereas service consumers should stick to the contract as agreed with the provider.

Protocol selection

In the SOA world, HTTP/SOAP and messaging were kind of default service protocols for service interactions. Microservices follow the same design principles for service interaction. Loose coupling is one of the core principles in the microservice world too.

Microservices fragment applications into many physically independent deployable services. This not only increases the communication cost, but also become sensitives to network failures. This could also result in poor performance of services.

Message oriented services

If we choose an asynchronous style of communication, then the user is disconnected, and therefore, response times are not directly impacted. In such cases, we may use standard JMS or AMQP protocols for communication with JSON as the payload. Messaging over HTTP is also popular, as it reduces complexity. Many new entrants in messaging services support HTTP-based communication. Asynchronous REST is also possible, and is handy when calling long-running services.

HTTP and REST endpoints

Communication over HTTP is always better for interoperability, protocol handling, traffic routing, load balancing, security systems, and so on. Since HTTP is stateless, it is more compatible for handling stateless services with no affinity. Most of the development frameworks, testing tools, runtime containers, security systems, and more friendly towards HTTP.

With the popularity and acceptance of REST and JSON, it is the default choice for microservice developers. The HTTP/REST/JSON protocol stack makes it so easy and friendly for building interoperable systems. HATEOAS is one of the design patterns emerging for designing progressive rendering and self-service navigations. As discussed in the previous chapter, HATEOAS provides a mechanism to link resources together so that the consumer can navigate between resources. RFC 5988 - Web Linking is another upcoming standard.

Optimized Communication Protocols

If the service response times are stringent, then we need to pay special attention to the communication aspects. In such cases, we may choose alternate protocols, such as Avro, Protocol Buffers, or Thrift, for communicating between services. But this limits the interoperability of services. The trade off is between performance and interoperability requirements. Custom binary protocols need careful evaluation, as they bind native objects on both sides--consumer and producer. This could run into release management issues, such as class version mismatch in Java-based, RPC style communications.

API documentations

Lastly, a good API is not only simple, but also has enough documentation for the consumers. There are many tools available today for documenting REST-based services. Swagger, RAML, and API Blueprint are good for documenting REST services.

Handling shared libraries

The underlying principle of a microservice is that it is autonomous and self-contained. In order to adhere to this principle, there may be situations where we will have to duplicate code and libraries. These could be either technical libraries or functional components:

Eligibility Rules   Eligibility Rules

Check In   **Boarding**
Microservice   **Microservice**

For example, eligibility for flight upgrade will be checked at the time of check-in, as well as when boarding. If check-in and boarding are two different microservices, we may have to duplicate the eligibility rules in both the services. This was the trade-off between adding dependency versus code duplication.

It may be easy to embed code compared to adding an additional dependency, as it enables better release management and performance. But this is against the DRY principle.

The DRY principle states that every piece of knowledge must have a single, unambiguous, and authoritative representation within a system.

The downside of this approach is that, in the case of a bug or an enhancement on the shared library, it has to be upgraded in more than one place. This may not be a severe setback, as each service can contain different versions of the shared library:

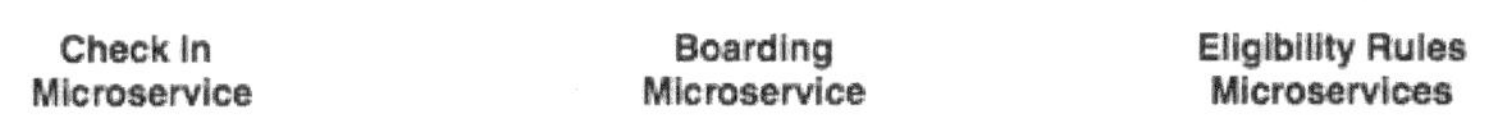

Check In Microservice	Boarding Microservice	Eligibility Rules Microservices

The alternate option for developing the shared library as another microservice itself needs careful analysis. If it does not qualify as a microservice from the business capability point of view, then it may add more complexity than usefulness. The trade-off analysis is between overhead in communication versus duplicating the libraries in multiple services.

User interfaces in microservices

The microservice principle advocates microservices as a vertical slice from database to presentation.

The following diagram shows microservices that encompasses the UI, business logic, and database:

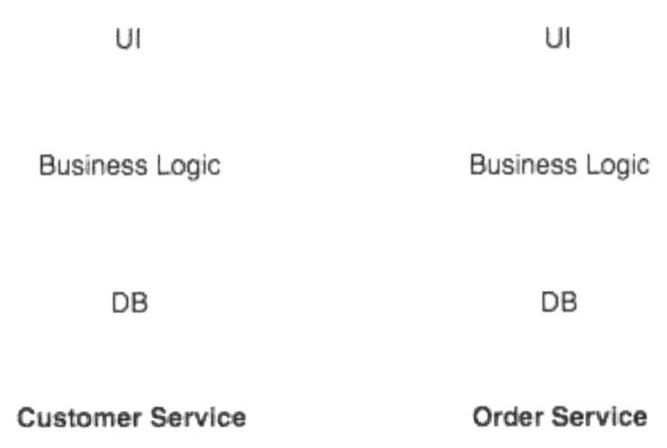

UI	UI
Business Logic	Business Logic
DB	DB
Customer Service	**Order Service**

In reality, we get the requirements to build a quick UI, and mobile applications mash up the existing APIs. This is not uncommon in the modern scenario, where business wants a quick turnaround time from IT:

The penetration of a mobile application is one of the causes of this approach. In many organizations, mobile development teams sit close to the business and develop rapid mobile applications by combining and mashing up APIs from multiple sources, both internal and external. In such situations, we may just expose services and leave it for the mobile teams to realize them in the way the business wants. In this case, we can build headless microservices and leave it to the mobile teams to build the presentation layer.

Another category of problem is that the business may want to build consolidated web applications targeted at communities, as seen in this diagram:

For example, a business may want to develop a departure control application targeting airport users. A departure control web application may have functions such as check-in, lounge management, boarding, and so on. These may be designed as independent microservices. But from the business standpoint, it all needs to be clubbed into a single web application. In such cases, we will have to build web applications by mashing up services from the backend.

One approach is to build a container web application or a placeholder web application that links to multiple microservices from behind. In this case, we will develop full stack microservices, but the screens coming out of this could be embedded into another placeholder web application. One of the advantages of this approach is that you can have multiple placeholder web applications targeting different user communities, as shown in the preceding diagram. We may use an API gateway to avoid those criss-cross connections. We will explore API gateways in the next section.

Use of API gateways in microservices

With the advancement of client-side JavaScript frameworks, such as Angular JS, the server is expected to expose RESTful services. This could lead to two issues. The first issue is the mismatch in contract expectations. The second issue is the multiple calls to the server to render a page.

We start with the contract mismatch case. For example, `GetCustomer` may return a JSON with many fields, as follows:

```
Customer {
  Name:
  Address:
  Contact :
}
```

In the preceding example, `Name`, `Address`, and `Contact` are nested JSON objects. But a mobile client may expect only basic information, such as the first name and last name. In the SOA world, an ESB or mobile middleware did this job of transformation of data for the client. The default approach in microservices is to get all the elements of `Customer`, and then the client takes up the responsibility to filter the elements. In this case, the overhead is on the network.

There are a few approaches we can think of to solve this case. Consider the following code:

```
Customer {
  id :1
  Name: /customer/name/1
  Address: /customer/address/1
  Contact : /customer/contact/1
}
```

The first is to send minimal information with links, as explained in the section on HATEOAS in the last chapter. In the preceding case, there are three links for customer ID 1, which will help the client to access specific data elements. The example is a simple logical representation, not the actual JSON. The mobile client, in this case, will get basic customer information. The client further uses the links to get the additional required information.

The second approach is that when the client makes the REST call, it also sends the required fields as part of the query string. In this scenario, the client sends a request with the first name and last name as the query string to indicate that the client only requires these two fields. The downside is that it ends up in complex server-side logic, as it has to filter based on fields. The server has to send different elements based on the incoming query.

A third approach is to introduce a level of indirection. In this, a gateway component sits between the client and the server, and transforms data as per the consumer's specification. This is a better approach, as we do not compromise on the backend service contract. This leads to what is called UI services. In many cases, the API gateway acts as a proxy to the backend, exposing a set of consumer-specific APIs.

The following diagram shows two approaches for positioning API gateways:

API Gateway	API Gateway		API Gateway
Business logic	Business logic	Business logic	Business logic
DB	DB	DB	DB
A) API gateway is part of the micro service		B) Common API gateway	

There are two ways we can deploy an API gateway. The first is to have one API gateway per microservice, as shown in diagram **A**. The second approach is to have a common API gateway for multiple services. The choice really depends on what we are looking for. If we are using the API gateway as a reverse proxy, then off-the-shelf gateways, such as Apigee, Mashery, and others, could be used as a shared platform. If we need fine-grained control over traffic shaping and complex transformations, then per-service custom API gateways may be more useful.

A related problem is that we will have to make many calls to the server from the client. If we refer to our holiday example in `Chapter 1`, *Demystifying Microservices*, we had to make a call to the server to render each widget. Though we transfer only data, it can still add a significant overhead on the network. This approach is not fully wrong, as in many cases, we use responsive design and progressive design. The data will be loaded on the demand based on user navigations. In order to do this, each widget in the client should make independent calls to the server in a lazy manner. If bandwidth is an issue, then an API gateway is the solution. The API gateway acts as a middleman to compose and transform APIs from multiple microservices.

Use of ESB and iPaaS with microservices

In theory, SOA is not all about ESBs, but the reality is that ESBs have always been at the center of many SOA implementations. What would be the role of an ESB in the microservices world?

In general, microservices are fully cloud-native systems with smaller footprints. The lightweight characteristics of microservices enable the automation of deployments, scaling, and more. In contrast, enterprise ESBs are heavyweight in nature, and most of the commercial ESBs are not cloud friendly. The key features of an ESB are protocol mediation, transformation, orchestration, and application adaptors. In a typical microservices ecosystem, we may not need any of these features.

The limited ESB capabilities that are relevant for microservices are already available with more lightweight tools, such as API gateways. Orchestration is moved from the central bus to the microservices themselves. Therefore, there is no centralized orchestration capability expected in the case of microservices. Since the services are set up to accept more universal message exchange styles using REST/JSON calls, there is no protocol mediation required. The last piece of capability we get from ESBs are adaptors to connect back to the legacy systems. In the case of microservices, the service itself provides a concrete implementation, and hence, there are no legacy connectors required. For these reasons, there is no natural space for ESBs in the microservices world.

Many organizations established ESBs as the backbone for their **Enterprise Application Integrations** (**EAI**). Enterprise architecture policies in such organizations are around ESBs. There could be a number of enterprise-level policies, such as auditing, logging, security, validation, and more, that would have been in place when integrated using ESB. Microservices, however, advocate a more decentralized governance. ESBs will be an overkill if integrated with microservices.

Not all services are going to be microservices. Enterprises will have legacy applications, vendor applications, and so on. Legacy services will still use ESBs to connect with microservices. ESBs still hold their place for legacy integration and vendor applications to integrate at the enterprise level.

With the advancement of cloud, ESB capabilities are not sufficient to manage integration between clouds, cloud to on-premise, and so on. **Integration Platform as Service** (**iPaaS**) is evolving as the next generation application integration platform, which further reduces the role of ESBs. In typical deployments, iPaaS invokes API gateways to access microservices.

Service versioning considerations

When we allow services to evolve, one of the important aspects to consider is service versioning. Service versioning should be considered upfront, not as an afterthought. Versioning will help us to release new services without breaking existing consumers. Both the old and the new versions will be deployed side by side.

Semantic versions are widely used for service versioning. A semantic version has three components, `MAJOR.MINOR.PATCH`, where `MAJOR` is used when there is a breaking change, `MINOR` is used when there is a backward compatible change, and `PATCH` is used when there is a backward compatible bug fix.

Versioning could get complicated when there is more than one service in a microservice. It is always easy to version services at the service level compared to the operations level.

Let us say that there is a service named `GreetingService` with two methods, `sayHello()` and `sayGoodBy()`, where `sayHello` and `sayGoodBy` are exposed as REST endpoints `/greetings/hello` and `/greetings/goodby` respectively. In this case, `sayHello` and `sayGoodBy` are operations of `GreetingService`.

If there is a change in one of the operations, the service will be upgraded and deployed to V2 as follows:

```
/api/v3/greetings   // service level
/api/v3/greetings/v3.1/sayhello   // service + operation level
/api/greetings/v3/sayhello   // operation level
```

The version change is applicable to all operations in the service. This is the notion of immutable services.

There are three different ways we can version REST services:

- URI versioning
- Media type versioning
- Custom header

In URI versioning, the version number will be included in the URL itself. In the URI, we just need to be worried about the major versions only. Hence, if there is a minor version change or a patch, the consumers do not need to worry about the changes. It is a good practice to alias the latest version to a non-versioned URI as follows:

```
/api/v3/customer/1234
/api/customer/1234  – aliased to v3.
@RestController("CustomerControllerV3")
@RequestMapping("api/v3/customer")
public class CustomerController {

}
```

A slightly different approach is to use the version number as part of the URL parameter, like this:

```
api/customer/100?v=1.5
```

In the case of media type versioning, the version is set by the client on the HTTP accept header as follows:

```
Accept: application/vnd.company.customer-v3+json
```

A less effective approach for versioning is to set the version in the custom header like this:

```
@RequestMapping(value = "/{id}", method =
  RequestMethod.GET, headers = {"version=3"})
public Customer getCustomer(@PathVariable("id") long id) {
  //other code goes here.
}
```

In the URI approach, it is simple for the clients to consume services. But this has some inherent issues, such as the fact that versioning nested URI resources could be complex. Indeed, migrating clients is slightly complex compared to media type approaches, with caching issues for multiple versions of the services, and so on. However, these issues are not significant enough for us to not go with the URI approach. Most of the big internet players, such as Google, Twitter, LinkedIn, and Salesforce, follow the URI approach.

Design for cross origin

With microservices, there is no guarantee that the services will run from the same host or the same domain. Composite UI web applications may call multiple microservices for accomplishing a task, and these could come from different domains and hosts.

CORS allows browser clients to send requests to services hosted on different domains. This is essential in microservices-based architecture.

One approach is to enable all microservices to allow cross-origin requests from other trusted domains. The second approach is to use an API gateway as a single trusted domain for the clients.

Handling shared reference data

When breaking large applications, one of the common issues that we see is the management of master data or reference data. Reference data is more like shared data required between different microservices. City master, country master, and more will be used in many services, such as flight schedules, reservations, and so on.

There are a few ways we can solve this. For instance, in the case of relatively static, never changing data, every service can hard code this data within all the microservices themselves.

Another approach, as shown in the following diagram, is to build it as another microservice:

This is good, clean, and neat, but the downside is that every service may need to call the master data multiple times. As shown in the following diagram, in the Search and Booking example, there are transactional microservices that use the geography microservice to access shared data:

Search
Microservice

Booking
Microservice

Geography

Geography

Another option is to replicate the data with every microservice. There is no single owner, but each service has its required master data. When there is an update, update all the services. This is extremely performance-friendly, but one has to duplicate code in all the services. It is also complex to keep data in sync across all microservices. If the code base and data is simple, or the data is more static, then this approach makes sense.

The following diagram shows that the geography local cache is replicated in both the Search and Booking service:

Yet another approach is similar to the first approach, but each service will have a local near cache of the required data, which will be incrementally loaded. A local embedded cache such as Ehcache, or data grids such as Hazelcast or Infinispan could also be used, based on the data volumes. This is the most preferred approach for a large number of microservices that have dependency on master data.

Microservices and bulk operations

Since we have broken monolithic applications into smaller, focused services, it is no more possible to use join queries across microservice data stores. This could lead to situations where one service may need many records from other services to perform its function, as seen in this diagram:

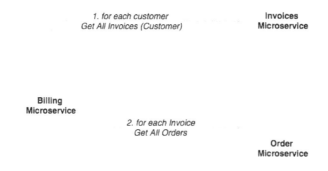

In the preceding diagram, a monthly billing function needs the invoices of many customers to process billing. To make it a bit more complicated, Invoices may have many orders. When we break billing, invoices, and orders into three different microservices, the challenge now is that the Billing service has to query the Invoice services for each customer to get all invoices, and then for each invoice, call the Order services for getting the orders. This is not a good solution, as the number of calls that go to other microservices is high.

The following diagram shows that copies of invoices and orders are replicated in the billing services:

There are two ways we can think about solving this. The first approach is to pre-aggregate data as and when it is created. When an order is created, an event will be sent out. Upon receiving the event, the Billing microservice keeps aggregating data internally for monthly processing. In this case, there is no need for the Billing microservice to go out for processing. The downside of this approach is that there is duplication of data.

The second approach, when pre-aggregation is not possible, is to use batch APIs. In such cases, we call GetAllInvoices, then we use multiple batches, and each batch further uses parallel threads to get orders. Spring Batch is useful for using in these situations.

Summary

In this chapter, we learned about handling practical scenarios that arise in microservice development.

We learned various solution options and patterns that could be applied to solve common microservice problems. We reviewed a number of challenges when developing large-scale microservices, and how to address those challenges effectively.

In the next chapter, we will establish a capability reference model for microservices.

5
Microservices Capability Model

In the previous chapter, Chapter 4, *Applying Microservices Concepts*, you learned some of the practical design aspects of the microservices development. In this chapter, we will take a step back and put together our learnings into a capability model.

What is the importance of a microservices capability model? Microservices are not as simple as developing web applications with UI, business logic, and databases. This is good enough for simple services, or when dealing with fewer microservices. Developers need to think beyond service implementation when working with large-scale microservices. There are a number of ecosystem capabilities required for the successful delivery of microservices. It is important to ensure that those required capabilities are in place as a precondition. Unfortunately, there is no standard reference model available for microservice implementations.

Even though the capabilities required for microservice implementation may vary based on the solution context, this book attempts to build a generic microservice capability model instead of building a low-level reference architecture. At the end of this chapter, we will also examine a maturity model for microservice adoption.

In the chapter, you will learn about the following:

- A capability model for the microservices ecosystem
- An overview of each capability and its importance in a microservice ecosystem
- An overview of some tools and technologies available supporting these capabilities
- A maturity model for microservices

Microservices capability model

In the service-oriented world, there are reference architectures available, which can be used as a basis for SOA implementations. For example, a comprehensive SOA Reference Architecture is defined by The Open Group, which is available for public reference.

 The Open Group SOA Reference Architecture is available at `http://www.o` `pengroup.org/soa/source-book/soa_refarch/index.htm`.

However, there is no standard or reference architecture for microservices. It is still an evolving space. Many of the architectures available publicly today are from tool vendors, and they seem to be inclined towards their own tools stack.

The microservices capability model defined in this chapter is based on design guidelines, common patterns, and best practice solutions for designing and developing microservices.

The following diagram depicts the microservices capability model, which will be used as a reference model for the rest of the chapters in this book:

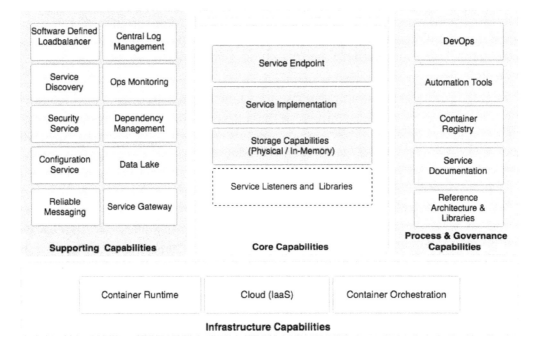

The capability model is broadly classified into four areas:

- Core capabilities, which are embedded in each microservices
- Supporting capabilities
- Infrastructure capabilities
- Process and governance capabilities

Core capabilities

Core capabilities are those components generally packaged inside a single microservice. For example, let's take an Order microservice. The Order microservice will have two key deployable parts, order.jar developed using Spring Boot and its own database--**Order DB**. The order.jar will encapsulate service listeners, libraries required for execution, service implementation code, and service APIs or endpoints, and Order DB stores all data required for Order service. Smaller microservices only require these core capabilities.

Gartner named this as **inner architecture** and the capabilities outside of this core as **outer architecture**.

In Chapter 3, *Building Microservices with Spring Boot*, we discussed the implementation of core capabilities using Spring Boot.

The core capabilities depicted in the capability model are explained in the following section.

Service listeners and libraries

Service listeners are endpoint listeners for accepting service requests coming to the microservice. HTTP and message listeners, such as AMQP, JMS, and more are used as service listeners in most of the cases. If microservices are enabled for HTTP endpoint, then the HTTP listener will be embedded within the microservices, thereby eliminating the need to have any external application server. This HTTP listener will be started at the time of the application startup. An example of embedded HTTP-based service implementations are Spring Boot services.

If the microservice is based on asynchronous communication, then, instead of an HTTP listener, a message listener will be started. This needs a reliable messaging system capable of handling large-scale messages, such as Kafka, Rabbit MQ, and more. Messaging endpoints can also be used for request-response scenarios using one of the reactive client libraries, such as RxJava.

Optionally, other protocols can also be considered for specific scenarios. There may not be any listeners if the microservice is a scheduled service.

Storage capability

The microservices will have some kind of storage mechanism to store state or transactional data pertaining to the business capability. If there is a storage required, then it will be dedicated to a microservice. However, storage is optional for microservices. There may be scenarios in which microservice is just a stateless compute service.

Depending on the capabilities that are implemented, the storage could be either a physical storage RDBMS such as MySQL, NoSQL such as Hadoop, Cassandra, Neo4J, Elasticsearch, and more; an in-memory store cache or in-memory data grid such as Ehcache, Hazelcast, Infinispan, and more; or even in-memory databases such as solidDB, TimesTen, and more.

Service implementation

This is the core of microservices, where the business logic is implemented. This could be implemented in any applicable language, such as Java, Scala, Conjure, Erlang, and so on. All required business logic to fulfill the function will be embedded within the microservice itself. Just like with normal application designs, a general modular, layered architecture is recommended for service implementations. This service implementation will provide concrete service endpoint interfaces.

As a best practice, microservice implementations may send out state changes to the external world without really worrying about the targeted consumers of these events. They could be consumed by other microservices, supporting services such as audit by replication or external applications. This will allow other microservices and applications to respond to state changes.

Service endpoint

Service endpoint refers to the APIs exposed by microservices for external consumption. These could be synchronous or asynchronous endpoints.

Synchronous endpoints are generally REST/JSON, but any other protocols, such as Avro, Thrift, or protocol buffers can also be used. Asynchronous endpoints will be through message listeners, such as Spring AMQP, Spring Cloud Streams, and more; backed by a reliable messaging solution, such as Rabbit MQ; or any other messaging servers or other messaging style implementations, such as Zero MQ.

Infrastructure capabilities

Certain infrastructure capabilities are required for a successful deployment and managing large-scale microservices. When deploying microservices at scale, not having proper infrastructure capabilities can be challenging and lead to failures.

In some cases, **Platform as a Service** (**PaaS**) vendors such as Red Hat OpenShift offer all these capabilities out of the box.

We will discuss infrastructure capabilities in `Chapter 9`, *Containerizing Microservices with Docker*.

Cloud

Microservices implementation will be difficult in a traditional data center environment with long lead time to provision infrastructures. Even a large number of infrastructure dedicated per microservice may not be very cost effective. Managing them internally in a data center may increase the cost of ownership and operations. An **Infrastructure as a Service** (**IaaS**) cloud-like infrastructure will be better for microservice deployment.

Microservices require a supporting elastic cloud-like infrastructure that can automatically provision VMs or containers. The automation will also take care of elastically scaling up by adding containers or VMs on demand and scale down when the load falls below threshold.

AWS, Azure, IBM Bluemix, or private cloud (off-premise or on-premise) are candidates for microservice deployments.

Container runtime

When there are many microservices, deploying them on large physical machines is not cost effective, and is also hard to manage. With physical machines, it is also hard to handle automatic fault tolerance of microservices.

Virtualization is adopted by many organizations because of its ability to provide optimal use of physical resources, and it provides resource isolation. It also reduces the overheads in managing large physical infrastructure components. VMWare, Citrix, and more provide virtual machine technologies.

Virtual machines are still heavy and resource intensive, and consume start-up time. Containers are a next wave of virtual machines that provide further cost saving and isolation that is required for smaller footprint microservices. Docker, Rocket, and LXD are some of the containerized technologies.

Above the host operating system, we need a software that can manage containers such as the starting and stopping containers. In this book, this is referred to as container runtime. An example of this is Docker installed on a Linux environment.

Container orchestration

Once we have a large number of containers or virtual machines, it is hard to manage and maintain them automatically. Container orchestration tools provide a uniform operating environment on top of the container runtime, and share available capacity across multiple containers. Apache Mesos, Rancher, CoreOS, and Kubernetes are examples of popular container orchestration tools. These tools are also called **container scheduler** and, sometimes, **container as service**.

One of the other challenges is manual provisioning and deployments. If a deployment has manual elements, the deployer or operational administrators should know the running topology, manually reroute traffic, and then deploy the application one by one until all services are upgraded. With many server instances running, this could lead to significant operational overheads. Moreover, chances of errors will be high in this manual approach.

Container orchestration tools generally helps us to automatically deploy applications, adjust traffic flows, replicate a new version to all instances, and gracefully fade out older versions. In a large deployment environment with many microservices, we need container orchestration tools to avoid overheads.

Container orchestration tools also helps us manage application life cycle activities, including application availability and constraints-based deployment, such as deploying across data centers, ensuring minimum number of instances to be up and running, and so on. Kubernetes supports this capability out of the box, while Mesos requires frameworks such as Marathon to address this capability. **Data Centre Operating System** (**DCOS**) from Mesosphere combines both Mesos and Marathon out of the box.

Supporting capabilities

Supporting capabilities are not directly linked to microservices, but these are essential for large-scale microservices development. These services will have a dependency on the production runtime of microservices.

Service gateway

The Service gateway or API gateway provides a level of indirection by either proxying service endpoints or composing multiple service endpoints. The API gateway is also useful for policy enforcements and routing. The API gateway can also be used for real-time load balancing in some cases.

There are many API gateways available in the market. Spring Cloud Zuul, Mashery, Apigee, Kong, WSO2, and 3scale are some examples of the API gateway providers.

We will discuss the API gateway using Spring Cloud in Chapter 7, *Scale Microservices with Spring Cloud Components*.

Software-defined load balancer

The load balancer should be smart enough to understand the changes in the deployment topology and respond accordingly. This moves away from the traditional approach of configuring static IP addresses, domain aliases, or cluster addresses in the load balancer. When new servers are added to the environment, it should automatically detect this and include them in the logical cluster by avoiding any manual interactions. Similarly, if the service instance is unavailable, it should take it out from the load balancer.

A combination of Ribbon, Eureka, and Zuul provide this capability in Spring Cloud Netflix. Alternately, container orchestration tools have an out-of-the-box capability to do load balancers. DCOS has **Marathon Load Balancer** (**marathon-lb**) for this purpose.

We will discuss Software-Defined Load balancer using Spring Cloud in Chapter 7, *Scale Microservices with Spring Cloud Components*.

Central log management

Log files are a good piece of information for analysis and debugging. Since each microservice is deployed independently, they emit separate logs, may be to a local disk. This will result in fragmented logs. When we scale services across multiple machines, each service instance could produce separate log files. This makes it extremely difficult to debug and understand the behavior of the services through log mining.

If we consider Order, Delivery, and Notification as three different microservices, we will find no way to correlate a customer transaction that runs across order processing, delivery, and notification.

When implementing microservices, we need a capability to ship logs from each services to a centrally-managed log repository. With this approach, services are not relaying on local disks or local I/Os. A second advantage is that the log files are centrally managed and are available for all sorts of analysis, such as historical, real time, and trending. By introducing a correlation ID, end-to-end transactions can be easily tracked.

We also need a capability to centralize all logs emitted by service instances with correlation IDs so that we can stitch and track end-to-end transitions based on this correlation ID.

We will discuss logging solutions in `Chapter 8`, *Logging and Monitoring Microservices*.

Service discovery

With many services running on a cloud-like environment, static service resolution is almost impossible. Therefore, large-scale microservices need an auto discovery mechanism to identify where the services are running.

A service registry provides a runtime environment for services to automatically publish their availability at runtime. A registry will be a good source of information to understand the services topology at any point so that consumers can look up for service discovery.

Eureka from Spring Cloud, Zookeeper, and Etcd are some of the service registry tools available. Alternately, container discovery services are available out of the box from container orchestration tools. For example, Mesos-DNS comes out of the box as part of the DCOS distribution.

We will discuss service discovery using Spring Cloud in `Chapter 7`, *Scale Microservices with Spring Cloud Components*.

Security service

In monolithic applications, application security was part of the application itself. Hence, it was easy to mange. With microservices, security became a more predominant issue, as there are many services, and just one service cannot hold the security master data. Distributed microservices ecosystem require a central server to manage service security. This includes service authentication and token services.

Spring Security and Spring Security OAuth are good candidates to build this capability. Single sign-on solutions provided by Microsoft, Ping, and Okta are other enterprise-grade security solutions that can be integrated well with microservices.

In Chapter 3, *Building Microservices with Spring Boot*, we discussed this capability using Spring Boot.

Service configuration

When many services, especially those running on different servers, are deployed using automated tools, it is hard to keep the application configuration static, as we practiced in the monolithic application development.

With microservices, all service configurations should be externalized, as proposed in the Twelve-Factor App. A central service for all configurations could be a good choice. Spring Cloud Config server and Archaius are out-of-the-box configuration servers. Alternately, Spring Boot profiles can be used to manage configurations for small-scale microservices if the configuration changes are not dynamic in nature.

We will discuss service configuration using Spring Cloud in Chapter 7, *Scale Microservices with Spring Cloud Components*.

Ops monitoring

With a large number of microservices, and with multiple versions and service instances, it would be difficult to find out which service is running on which server, what the health of these services is, the service dependencies, and so on. This was much easier with the monolithic applications that are tagged against a specific or a fixed set of servers.

Apart from understanding the deployment topology and health, it also poses a challenge in identifying service behaviors, debugging, and identifying hotspots. Strong monitoring capabilities are required to manage such an infrastructure.

Spring Cloud Netflix Turbine, Hysterix dashboard, and more provide service-level information. End-to-end monitoring tools, such as AppDynamic, NewRelic, and Dynatrace, and other tools, such as Statd, Sensu, and Simian Viz, could add value in microservices monitoring. Tools such as Datadog help us manage infrastructure efficiently.

We will discuss monitoring solutions in `Chapter 8`, *Logging and Monitoring Microservices*.

Dependency management

Dependency management is one of the key issues in large microservices deployments. How do we identify and reduce the impact of a change? How do we know whether all dependent services are up and running? How will the service behave if one of the dependent services is not available?

Too many dependencies could raise challenges in microservices. Four important design aspects are stated as follows:

- Reduce the dependencies by properly designing service boundaries.
- Reduce impacts by designing dependencies that are as loosely coupled as possible. Also, design service interactions through asynchronous communication styles.
- Dependency issues need to be tackled using patterns such as circuit breakers.
- Monitor dependencies using visual dependency graphs.

With many microservices, the number of **Configurable Items** (**CIs**) will be too high, and the number of servers in which these CIs are deployed might also be unpredictable. This will make it extremely difficult to manage data in a traditional **Configuration Management Database** (**CMDB**). In many cases, it is more useful to dynamically discover the current running topology than a statically configured CMDB style deployment topology. A graph-based CMDB is more obvious to manage these scenarios.

There are many tools available in the market, but a combination of tools can address the dependency issue. Some of the Ops monitoring or APM tools such as AppDynamic are useful. Cloud Craft, Light Mesh, and Simian Viz are some of the other tools.

We will discuss dependency management solutions in `Chapter 8`, *Logging and Monitoring Microservices*.

Data lake

Microservices abstract their own local transactional store, which is used for their own transactional purposes. The type of store and the data structure will be optimized for the services offered by the microservice.

For example, if we want to develop a customer relationship graph, we may use a graph database such as Neo4J, OrientDB, and more. A predictive text search to find out customers based on any related information, such as passport number, address, email, phone number, and more, could be best realized using an indexed search database, such as Elasticsearch or Solr.

This will place us into a unique situation of fragmenting data into heterogeneous data islands. For example, Customer, Loyalty Points, Reservations, and more are different microservices, and, hence, use different databases. What if we want to do a near real-time analysis of all high-value customers by combining data from all three data stores? With a monolithic application, this was easy because all the data was present in a single database.

In order to satisfy this requirement, a data warehouse or a data lake is required. Traditional data warehouses, such as Oracle, Teradata, and more, are used primarily for batch reporting. However, with NoSQL databases, such as Hadoop, and micro-batching techniques, near real-time analytics is possible with the concept of data lakes. Unlike the traditional warehouses that are purposely built for batch reporting, data lakes store raw data without assuming how the data will be used. Now, the question really is how to port data from microservices into data lakes.

Data porting from microservices to a data lake or a data warehouse can be done in many ways. Traditional ETL could be one of the options. Since we are allowing backdoor entry with ETL and breaking the abstraction, this is not considered as an effective way for data movement. A better approach is to send events from microservices as and when they occur. For example, customer registration, customer update event, and so on. Data ingestion tools will consume these events and propagate the state change to the data lake appropriately. The data ingestion tools are highly-scalable platforms, such as Spring Cloud Data Flow, Kafka, Flink, Flume, and so on.

We will discuss monitoring solutions in `Chapter 8`, *Logging and Monitoring Microservices.*

Reliable messaging

It is recommended to use a reactive style for microservices development. This will help in decoupling microservices, and, therefore, create better scalability. In a reactive system, we need a reliable, high-available messaging infrastructure service.

Messaging servers such as RabbitMQ, ActiveMQ, and Kafka are popular choices. IBM MQ and TIBCO EMS are other commercially viable enterprise-scale messaging platforms. Cloud messaging or messaging as a service such as `Iron.io` is a popular choice for internet-scale messaging.

Process and governance capabilities

The last piece in the puzzle is the process and governance capabilities that are required for microservices. These are processes, tools, and guidelines around microservices implementations.

DevOps

One of the biggest challenges in microservices implementation is the organization culture. To harness the speed of delivery of microservices, the organization should adopt agile development processes, continuous integration, automated QA checks, automated delivery pipelines, automated deployments, and automatic infrastructure provisioning.

Organizations following a waterfall development or heavyweight release management processes with infrequent release cycles are a challenge for microservices development.

DevOps is a key in successful implementations. It compliments microservices development by supporting agile development, high-velocity delivery, automation, and better change management.

We will discuss these capabilities in `Chapter 11`, *Microservice Development Life Cycle*.

Automation tools

Automation tools used in agile development, continuous integration, continuous delivery, and continuous deployment are essential for the successful delivery of microservices. Without automation, managing delivery of many smaller microservices will be a nightmare for any enterprise. Since the velocity of changes in each microservices is different, it may be worth considering different pipelines for each microservices.

Test automation is extremely important in the microservices delivery. In general, microservices also poses a challenge for the testability of services. In order to achieve a full-service functionality, one service may rely on another service, and that in turn, may rely on another service--either synchronously or asynchronously. The issue is how do we test an end-to-end service to evaluate its behavior. The dependent services may or may not be available at the time of testing.

Service virtualization and **service mocking** is one of the techniques used to test services without actual dependencies. In testing environments, when the services are not available, mock services can simulate behavior of the actual service. The microservices ecosystem needs service virtualization capabilities. However, this may not give us full confidence, as there may be many corner cases that mock services do not simulate, especially when there are deep dependencies.

Another approach is to use a consumer-driven contract. The translated integration test cases can cover more or less all corner cases of the service invocation.

A lot of emphasis is required in automated functional, real-user testing, synthetic testing, integration, release, and performance testing. Test automation and continuous delivery approaches such as AB Testing, Future Flags, Canary Testing, Blue-Green deployments, and Red-Black deployments, all reduce the risks of production releases.

In-production destructive testing is also a useful technique in microservice development. Netflix uses Simian Army for anti-fragile testing. Matured services need consistent challenges to see the reliability of the services and how good fallback mechanisms are. Simian Army components create various error scenarios to explore the behavior of the system under the failure scenarios.

We will discuss these capabilities in `Chapter 11`, *Microservice Development Life Cycle*.

Container registry

A microservices registry is where the versioned binaries of microservices are placed. These could be a simple artifactory repository or truly container repository, such as a Docker registry. Generally, a Docker registry stores base images as well as application images built using those base images. Automation tools will be integrated with the Docker registry as part of the development and delivery pipeline to upload and download images.

It is arguable that container registry is part of the supporting capability or process and governance capability. In this reference model, it is added as a part of the process and governance mainly because it is more of a part of automation tools and doesn't play any role beyond deployments. Registry is also fundamental for the governance. Many organizations set polices around base container images to avoid security-related issues.

Docker Hub, Google Container Repository, Core OS Quay, and Amazon EC2 container registry are some of the examples. Registry can be either private or public, based on the organizations the cyber security policies.

We will discuss Docker registry in `Chapter 9`, *Containerizing Microservices with Docker*.

Microservice documentation

Microservices impose decentralized governance, and this is quite in contrast with the traditional SOA governance. Organizations may find it hard to come up with this change, and that could negatively impact the microservices development.

There are a number of challenges that come with a decentralized governance model. How do we understand who is consuming a service? How do we ensure service reuse? How do we define which services are available in the organization? How do we ensure enforcement of enterprise polices?

One of the most important considerations is to have a place where all stakeholders can see all the services, their documentations, contracts, and service-level agreements. Especially in a distributed agile development environment where scrum teams are empowered to do their designs, it is important to understand what endpoints are available, what they offer, and how to access them, hosted in a central repository.

A good API repository should do the following:

- Expose repository via a web browser
- Provide easy ways to navigate APIs
- Be nicely organized
- Have the ability to invoke and test those endpoints with samples

Swagger, RAML, or API blueprint are helpful in achieving good microservices documentation. Swagger is popular and commonly used by many enterprises.

Spotify's service documentation in their public developer portal is a good example of microservices documentation:
`https://developer.spotify.com/web-api/endpoint-reference/`

We discussed the microservice documentation using Swagger in Chapter 3, *Building Microservice with Spring Boot*.

Reference architecture and libraries

Decentralized governance also poses challenges in developing microservices in silos with different patterns, tools, and technologies. This will limit organizations that are extended to deploy cost-effective solutions and also reusing services.

The first and foremost factor to consider in a decentralized governance model is to have a set of standards, reference models, best practices, and guidelines on how to implement better services. These should be available to the organization in the form of standard libraries, tools, and techniques. This ensures that the services developed are top quality, and that they are developed in a consistent manner.

The reference architecture provides a blueprint at the organization level to ensure that services are developed according to certain standards and guidelines in a consistent manner. Many of these could then be translated to a number of reusable libraries that enforce service development philosophies.

Standardization on tools helps enterprises to avoid different flavors of microservices implementations which are not interoperable, for example, different teams using different tools for microservice documentation, different image registries, or different container orchestration tools.

This reference architecture and libraries, together with a strong commitment to documentation, is essential when dealing with decentralized microservices governance.

We will discuss these capabilities in Chapter 11, *Microservice Development Life Cycle*.

Microservices maturity model

Microservice adoption needs some careful thoughts. A quick maturity assessment will be helpful to understand the maturity of the organization and some of the challenges the organization can expect.

The maturity model in the following diagram is derived from the capability model discussed earlier in this chapter:

	Level 0 Traditional	Level 1 Basic	Level 2 Intermediate	Level 3 Advanced
Application	Monolithic	Service Oriented Integrations	Service Oriented Applications	API Centric
Database	One Size Fit All Enterprise DB	Enterprise DB + No SQLs and Light databases	Polyglot, DBaaS	Matured Data Lake / Near Realtime Analytics
Infrastructure	Physical Machines	Virtualization	Cloud	Containers
Monitoring	Infrastrucure	App & Infra Monitoring	APMs	APM & Central Log Management
Process	Waterfall	Agile and CI	CI & CD	DevOps

The 4*5 maturity model is simple enough for a quick self-evaluation. Four levels of maturities are mapped against five characteristics of application development--**Application**, **Database**, **Infrastructure**, **Monitoring**, and **Processes**.

Level 0 - Traditional

Characteristics of the Traditional maturity level are explained as follows:

- Organizations still develop applications in a monolithic approach. There may be internal modularizations using subsystem designs, but packaged as a monolithic WAR. Use of proprietary service interfaces instead of RESTful service.
- Organizations use the *one size fits all* database model based on an enterprise standard and license model, irrespective of application types or application size.
- The infrastructure will be primarily based on physical machines with no virtualization implemented.
- The infrastructure monitoring may exist, but only as a limited application-level monitoring, for example, the application's URL monitoring.
- These organizations will be primarily based on waterfall development methods with long and fat release cycles.

These characteristics are not fully suitable for microservice development. Such organizations may struggle when attempting large-scale microservice developments. The recommended approach is to start small and adopt in small scale. A big stride needs careful planning and adoption of all related capabilities.

Level 1 - Basic

The characteristics of the Basic maturity level are explained as follows:

- Organizations still develop applications in a monolithic model, but uses Service-Oriented Integration for application-to-application communications
- While predominantly these organizations use one size fit for all database models, there may be some footprints of NoSQL and other lightweight databases
- The infrastructure will be primarily based on virtual machines, with no cloud adoption yet
- The infrastructure monitoring may be sophisticated, which includes somewhat matured application layer monitoring
- These organizations use agile development methods with automated tools for continuous integration

These characteristics are still not fully suitable for microservice development. Such organizations will face issues around optimal infrastructure usage and faster application delivery. The recommended approach for organizations at this level is to identify candidates for microservices and carefully approach them with some tactical decisions on infrastructure to start with, such as sharing a single instance of database. The risk level is less compared to Level 0, Traditional.

Level 2 - Intermediate

The characteristics of the Intermediate maturity level are explained as follows:

- Organizations develop SOA-based applications with a strong focus on service-based developments. For optimization purposes, they may still use proprietary protocols at application level.
- These organizations use polyglot persistence as a first class citizen. These organizations will have the culture of choosing the right databases for the right purpose without much worry about the economies of the scale.

- The infrastructure will be primarily based on cloud--either public or private.
- Organizations use both infrastructure monitoring as well as APM tools for end-to-end application monitoring.
- These organizations use agile development methods with automated tools for continuous integration and delivery.

Such organizations are more or less just one step away from full-scale microservices developments. Microservices is their natural progression as their next phase of architecture adoption. The risk is very minimal at this level.

Level 3 - Advanced

The characteristics of the Advanced maturity level are explained as follows:

- Organizations use APIs as first-class citizens for development. They use an API-first design philosophy.
- These organizations use polyglot persistence as first class citizen. Also, these organizations are matured in terms of data lake and near real-time analytics.
- The infrastructure will be primarily based on cloud, but also use containers and container-orchestration tools.
- Organizations use both infrastructure monitoring as well as APM tools for end-to-end application monitoring, including synthetic and real-user monitoring. They also use the centralized log management solutions.
- These organizations use full DevOps philosophies for application/product developments.

Such organizations may already be using some form of microservices, and they are ready to quickly move to large-scale microservice developments.

Entry points for adoption

When adopting microservices, organizations generally use one of the two entry points mentioned in the following diagram:

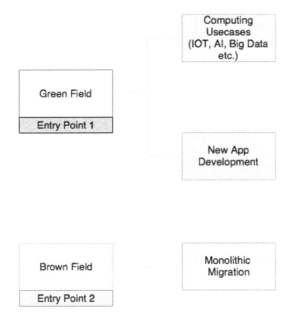

The first entry point is termed as the **Green Field** approach. In this approach, organizations will use microservice for developing new capabilities. There are a couple of use cases for Green Field development:

- Development of computing services, such as IoTs, AI algorithms, Big Data processing, and more
- New ground-up application developments

The second entry point is termed as the **Brown Field** approach. In this case, organizations will use microservices for monolithic migrations.

Summary

In this chapter, we established a technology and tool agnostic capability model for microservice based on best practices, common patterns, and design guidelines, inspired from successful microservices implementations across the industry. This will be useful for organizations thinking about the microservices journey to understand the different areas to be considered before attempting microservice adoption.

We expanded each of these capabilities in the capability model and learned their importance in microservices implementations. Along side, we also learned various technology solutions available to support these capabilities. Finally, we explored a maturity model for microservices adoption.

Next, we will take a real-world problem and model using the microservices architecture to see how to translate our learnings into practice.

6
Microservices Evolution – A Case Study

Like SOA, a microservices architecture can be interpreted differently by different organizations, based on the problem in hand. Unless a sizable, real-world problem is examined in detail, the microservices concepts are hard to understand.

This chapter will introduce **BrownField Airline** (**BF**), a fictitious budget airline, and their journey from a monolithic **Passenger Sales and Service** (**PSS**) application to a next-generation microservices architecture. This chapter examines the PSS application in detail, and explains the challenges, approach, and transformation steps of a monolithic system to a microservices-based architecture, adhering to the principles and practices that were explained in the previous chapter.

The intention of this case study is to get us as close as possible to a live scenario so that the architecture concepts can be set in stone.

At the end of this chapter, you will have learned about the following:

- A real-world case for migrating monolithic systems to microservices-based ones with the BrownField Airline's PSS application as an example
- Various approaches and transition strategies for migrating a monolithic application to microservices
- Designing a new futuristic microservices system, replacing the PSS application using Spring Framework components
- Implementation of microservices using Spring Framework and Spring Boot

The full source code of this chapter is available under the `chapter6` folder in the code files available at `https://github.com/rajeshrv/Spring5Micr oservice`.

Understanding the PSS application

The BrownField Airline is one of the fastest growing, low-cost, regional airlines, flying directly to more than one hundred destinations from its hub. As a start-up airline, BrownField Airline has started its operations with a few destinations and a few aircrafts. The BrownField has developed its home-grown PSS application to handle their passenger sales and services.

Business process view

For discussion purposes, this use case is considerably simplified. The process view in the following diagram shows BrownField Airline's end-to-end passenger services operations covered by the current PSS solution:

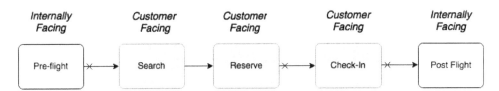

The current solution automates certain customer-facing functions, as well as certain internally-facing functions. There are two internally-facing functions, **Pre-flight** and **Post Flight**. **Pre-flight** is in the planning phase, used for preparing flight schedules, plans, aircrafts, and so on. **Post Flight** is used by the back office for revenue management, accounting, and so on. **Search** and **Reserve** are functions, which are part of the online seat reservation process, and the **Check-In** function is the process of accepting passengers at the airport. The Check-In function is also accessible to the end users over the Internet for online check-in.

The cross marks at the beginning of the arrows in the diagram indicate that they are disconnected, and occur at different timelines. For example, passengers are allowed to book 360 days in advance, whereas, check-in generally happens 24 hours before flight departure.

Functional view

The following diagram shows the functional building blocks of BrownField Airline's PSS landscape. Each business process and its related sub-functions are represented in a row:

Each sub-function shown in the preceding diagram explains its role in the overall business process. Some sub-functions participate in more than one business process. For example, the **Inventory** is used in both search as well as in booking. To avoid complication, this is not shown in the diagram. The **Data Management** and **Cross Cutting** sub-functions are used across many business functions.

Architecture view

In order to effectively manage the end-to-end passenger operations, BrownField had developed an in-house PSS application, almost ten years back. This well-architected application was developed using Java and JEE technologies combined with the best-of-the-breed open source technologies available at the time.

The overall architecture and technologies are shown in the following diagram:

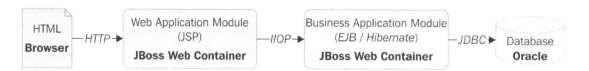

The architecture has well-defined boundaries. Also, different concerns are separated into different layers. The web application was developed as an *n*-tier, component-based modular system. The functions interact with each other through well-defined service contracts defined in the form of EJB endpoints.

Design view

The application has many logical functional groupings or subsystems. Further, each subsystem has many components organized as depicted in the following diagram:

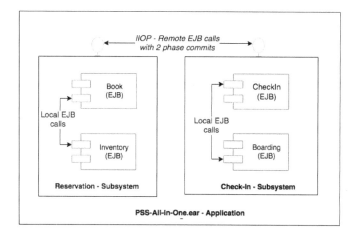

Subsystems interact with each other through remote EJB calls, using the IIOP protocol. The transactional boundaries are spanned across subsystems. Components within the subsystems communicate with each other through local EJB component interfaces. In theory, since subsystems use remote EJB endpoints, they could run on different, physically separated application servers. This was one of the design goals.

Implementation view

The implementation view in the following diagram showcases the internal organization of a subsystem and its components. The purpose of the diagram is also to show the different types of artifacts:

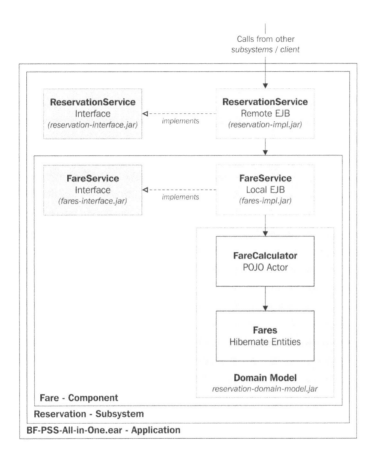

The grey-shaded boxes are treated as different Maven projects and translate into physical artifacts, as shown in the diagram. Subsystems and components are designed adhering to the **program to an interface** principle. Interfaces are packaged as separate jar files so that clients are abstracted from the implementations. The complexity of the business logic is buried in the domain model. Local EJBs are used as component interfaces. Finally, all subsystems are packaged into a single all-in-one EAR and deployed in the application server.

Deployment view

The application's initial deployment was simple and straightforward as follows:

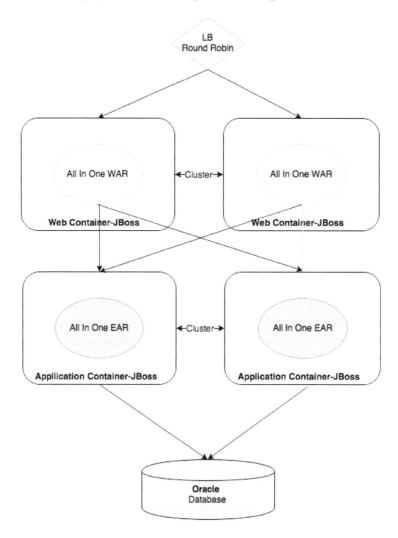

The web modules and business modules were deployed into separate application server clusters. The application was scaled horizontally by adding more and more application servers to the cluster.

Zero downtime deployments were handled by creating a standby cluster and gracefully diverting traffic to the standby cluster. The standby cluster is destroyed once the primary cluster is patched with the new version and brought back to service. Most of the database changes were designed for backward compatibility, but breaking changes are promoted with application outages.

Death of the monolith

The PSS application was performing well, successfully supporting all business requirements, as well as expected service levels. The system had no issues in scaling with the organic growth of the business in the initial years.

The business has seen tremendous growth over a period of time. The fleet size increased significantly and new destinations got added to the network. As a result of this rapid growth, the number of bookings has gone up, resulting in a steep increase in transaction volumes--up to 200 to 500 fold of what was originally estimated.

Pain points

The rapid growth of business has eventually put the application under pressure. Odd stability issues and performance issues surfaced. New application releases started breaking the working code. Moreover, the cost of change and the speed of delivery profoundly started impacting the business operations.

An end-to-end architecture review was ordered, and exposed the weaknesses of the system as well as the root causes of many failures, which are as follows:

- **Stability**: The stability issues are primarily due to stuck threads, which limit the application server's capability to accept more transactions. The stuck threads are mainly due to database table locks. Memory issues are another contributor to the stability issues. Additionally, issues in certain resource-intensive operations were impacting the whole application.
- **Outages**: The outage window increased largely because of the increase in server startup time. The root cause of this issue boiled down to the large size of the EAR. Message pile-up during any outage window causes heavy usage of the application immediately afterwards. Since everything was packaged into a single EAR, any small application code change resulted in full redeployment. The complexity of the zero-downtime deployment model described earlier, together with the server startup times, increased both the outage number and outage durations.

- **Agility**: The complexity of the code has also increased considerably over time, partially due to the lack of discipline in implementing the changes. As a result, changes became hard to implement. Also, the impact analysis became too complex to perform. As a result, inaccurate impact analysis often led to fixes that broke the working code. The application build time went up severely, from a few minutes to hours, causing unacceptable drops in the development productivity. The increase in build time also led to difficulty in build automation, and eventually, stopped **continuous integration (CI)** and unit testing.

Stopgap fix

Performance issues were partially addressed by applying the *Y*-scale method in the scale cube, as described in `Chapter 1`, *Demystifying Microservices*. The monolithic all in one EAR is deployed into multiple disjoint clusters. A software proxy was installed to selectively route traffic to designated clusters as shown here:

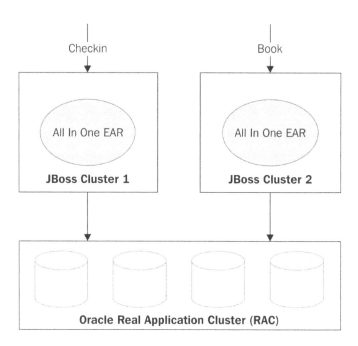

This helped BrownField's IT to scale the application servers. Therefore, the stability issues are controlled. However, soon this resulted in a bottleneck at the database level. Oracle **Real Application Cluster (RAC)** was implemented as a solution to this problem at the database layer.

This new scaling model reduced the stability issues, but at a premium of increased complexity and cost of ownership. The technology debt also increased over a period of time, leading to a state where a complete rewrite is the only option for reducing this technology debt.

Retrospection

Although the application was well-architected, there was a clear segregation between functional components. They were loosely coupled, programmed to interfaces, with access through standards-based interfaces, and had a rich domain model.

The obvious question is, how come such a well-architected application failed to live up to expectations? What else could the architects have done?

It is important to understand what went wrong over a period of time. In the context of this book, it is also important to understand how microservices can avoid a recurrence of these scenarios. We will examine some of these scenarios in the subsequent sections.

Precedence on data sharing over modularity

Almost all functional modules require reference data, such as the airline's details, airplane details, a list of airports and cities, countries, currencies, and more. For example, a fare is calculated based on the point of origin (city), a flight is between an origin and a destination (airports), check-in is at the origin airport (airport), and so on. In some functions, the reference data is a part of the information model, whereas, in some other functions, it is used for validation purposes.

Most of this reference data is neither fully static nor fully dynamic. Addition of a country, city, airport, and more could happen when the airline introduces new routes. Aircraft reference data could change when the airline purchases a new aircraft, or changes an existing airplane's seat configuration.

One of the common usage scenarios of reference data is to filter operational data based on certain reference data. For instance, when a user wishes to see all the flights to a country. In this case, the flow of events could be: find all cities in the selected country, then all airports in the cities, and then, fire a request to get all flights to the list of resulting airports identified in that country.

The architects considered multiple approaches when designing the system. Separating reference data as an independent subsystem, like other subsystems, was one of the options considered, but this could lead to performance issues. The team has taken a decision to follow an exception approach for handling reference data compared to other transactions. Considering the nature of query patterns as discussed previously, the approach was to use reference data as a shared library. In this case, the subsystems were allowed to access the reference data directly using pass-by-reference semantic data instead of going through EJB interfaces. This also meant that, irrespective of the subsystems, hibernate entities could use reference data as a part of their entity relationships.

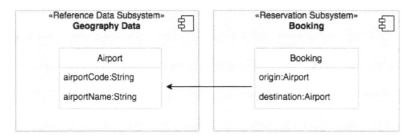

As depicted in the preceding diagram, the **Booking** entity in the reservation subsystem is allowed to use reference data entities, in this case **Airport**, as part of their relationships.

Single monolithic database

Though there was enough segregation enforced at the middle tier, all functions pointed to a single database, even to the same database schema. The single schema approach has opened a plethora of issues.

Native queries

The Hibernate framework provides a good abstraction over the underlying databases. It generates efficient SQL statements, in most of the cases targeting the database using specific dialects. However, sometimes, writing native JDBC SQLs offers better performance and resource efficiency. In some cases, using native database functions gives even better performance.

The single database approach was working good at the beginning. But over a period of time, it opened up a loophole for the developers by connecting database tables owned by different subsystems. Native JDBC SQL was a good vehicle for doing this.

The following diagram shows an example of connecting two tables owned by two subsystems using a native JDBC SQL:

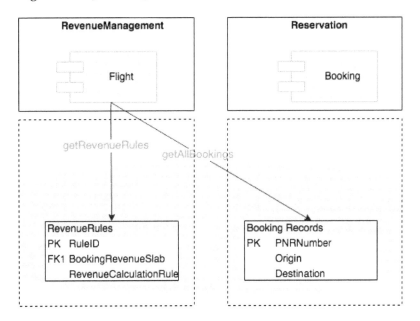

As shown in the preceding diagram, the **Accounting** component requires all booking records for a day for a given city from the **Booking** component to process the day-end billing. The subsystem-based design enforces **Accounting** to make a service call to **Booking** to get all the booking records for a given city. Assume this results in n booking records. Now, for each booking record, **Accounting** have to execute a database call to find the applicable rules based on the fare code attached to each of the booking records. This could result in $N+1$ JDBC calls, which is inefficient. Workarounds are available, such as batch queries or parallel and batch executions, but this would lead to increased coding efforts and higher complexity. The developers tackled this issue with a native JDBC query as an easy-to-implement shortcut. Essentially, this approach could reduce the number of calls from $N+1$ to a single database call, with minimal coding efforts.

This habit continued with many JDBC native queries connecting tables across multiple components and subsystems. This resulted not only in tightly coupled components, but also led to undocumented, hard-to-detect code.

Stored procedures

Another issue that surfaced as a result of the use of a single database was the use of complex stored procedures. Some of the complex data-centric logic written at the middle layer was not performing well, causing slow response, memory issues, and thread-blocking issues.

In order to address this problem, the developers had taken the decision to move some of the complex business logic from the middle tier to the database tier by implementing the logic directly within the stored procedures. This decision resulted in better performance of some of the transactions, and removed some of the stability issues. More and more procedures were added over a period of time. However, this eventually broke the application's modularity.

Compromised on domain boundaries

Though the domain boundaries are well established, all components are packaged as a single EAR file. Since all components are set to run on a single container, there was no stopping for the developers to reference objects across these boundaries. Over a period of time, the project teams changed, delivery pressure increased, and the complexity grew tremendously. The developers started looking for quick solutions rather than the right ones. Slowly, but steadily, the modular nature of the application went away.

As depicted in the following diagram, hibernate relationships are created across the subsystem boundaries:

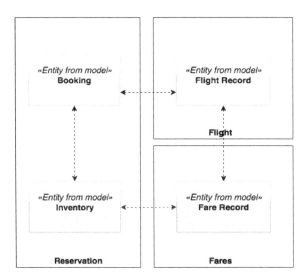

Microservices to the rescue - a planned approach for migration

There are not many improvement opportunities left to support the growing demand of BrownField Airline's business. BrownField Airline was looking to re-platform the system with an evolutionary approach rather than a revolutionary model.

Microservices is an ideal choice in such situations, for transforming a legacy monolithic application with minimal disruption to the business.

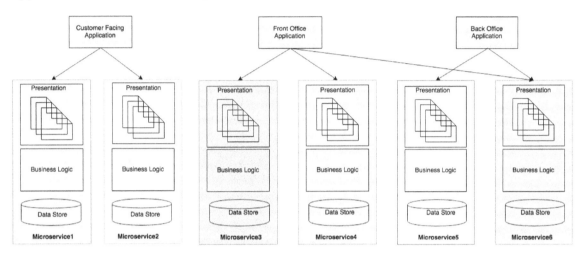

As shown in the preceding diagram, the objective is to move to a microservices-based architecture aligned to the business capabilities. Each microservice will hold the data store, the **Business Logic** and the **Presentation** layer.

The approach taken by BrownField Airline was to build a number of web portal applications targeting specific user communities such as customer facing, front office, and back office. The advantage of this approach lies in the flexibility for modelling, and also in the possibility to treat different communities differently. For example, the policies, architecture, and testing approaches for Internet facing are different from the Intranet-facing web application. Internet-facing applications may take advantage of **CDNs** (**Content Delivery Networks**) to moves pages as close to the customer as possible, whereas, intranet applications could serve pages directly from the data center.

The business case

When building business cases for migration, one of the commonly asked questions is *how do microservices architecture avoid the resurfacing of the same issues in another five years' time?*

Microservices offers a full list of benefits, which we discussed in Chapter 1, *Demystifying Microservices*, but it is important to list a few here, which are critical in this situation:

- **Service dependencies**: While migrating from monolithic to microservices, the dependencies are better known, and therefore, the architects and developers are much better placed to avoid breaking dependencies, and to future proof dependency issues. Learnings from the monolithic application help architects and developers to design a better system.
- **Physical boundaries**: Microservices enforce physical boundaries in all areas, including the data store, the business logic, and the presentation layer. Access across subsystems or microservices is truly restricted due to their physical isolation. Beyond the physical boundaries, they could even run on different technologies.
- **Selective scaling**: Selective scale out is possible in microservices architecture. This provides a much more cost-effective scaling mechanism compared to the Y scale approach used in the monolithic scenario.
- **Technology obsolesces**: Technology migrations could be applied at the microservices level rather than at the overall application level. Therefore, it does not require a humongous investment.

Migration approach

It is not simple to break an application that has millions of lines of code, especially, if the code has complex dependencies. How do we break it? More importantly, where do we start, and how do we approach this problem?

The best way to address this problem is to establish a transition plan and gradually migrate functions as microservices. At every step, a microservice will be created outside of the monolithic application, and traffic will be diverted to the new service as shown in the following diagram:

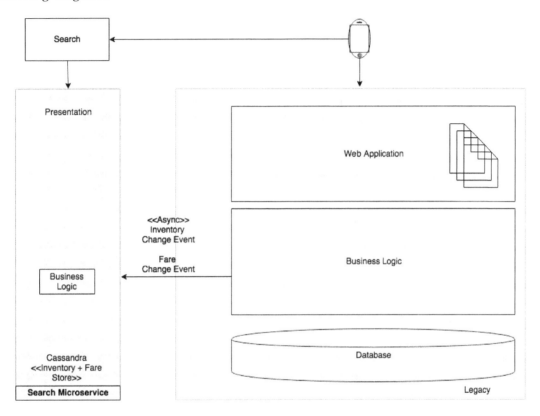

In order to run this migration successfully, a number of key questions need to be answered from the transition point of view. These are listed as follows:

- Identification of microservices' boundaries
- Prioritizing microservices for migration
- Handling data synchronization during the transition phase
- Handling user interface integration, working with old and new user interfaces
- Handling of reference data in the new system
- Testing strategy to ensure the business capabilities are intact and correctly reproduced
- Identification of any prerequisites for microservice development, such as microservices capabilities, frameworks, processes, and more

Identification of microservices' boundaries

The first and foremost activity is to identify the microservices' boundaries. This is the most interesting part of the problem, and the most difficult part as well. If identification of the boundaries is not done properly, the migration could lead to more complex manageability issues.

As in SOA, a service decomposition is the best way to identify services. However, it is important to note that decomposition stops at a business capability or bounded context. In SOA, service decomposition goes further into an atomic granular service level.

A top-down approach is typically used for domain decomposition. Bottom-up is also useful in the case of breaking an existing system, as it can utilize a lot of practical knowledge, functions, and behaviors of the existing monolithic application.

The previous decomposition step will give a potential list of microservices.

 It is important to note that this isn't the final list of microservices, but it serves as a good starting point. We will run through a number of filtering mechanisms to get to a final list. The first cut of functional decomposition will, in this case, be similar to the diagram shown under the functional view introduced earlier in this chapter.

Analyze dependencies

The next step is to analyse dependencies between the initial set of candidate microservices, which we created in the previous section. At the end of this activity, a dependency graph will be produced.

 A team of architects, business analysts, developers, release management, and support teams is required for this exercise.

One way to produce a dependency graph is to list out all the components of the legacy system, and overlay dependencies. This could be done by combining one or more of the approaches listed as follows:

- Manual code analysis and regenerating dependencies.
- Using the experience of the development team to regenerate dependencies.
- Using a Maven dependency graph. There are a number of tools we could use to regenerate a dependency graph, such as PomExplorer, PomParser, and more.

- Using performance engineering tools such as AppDynamics to identify the call stack and roll up dependencies.

Let us assume that we have reproduced the functions and their dependencies as shown in the following diagram:

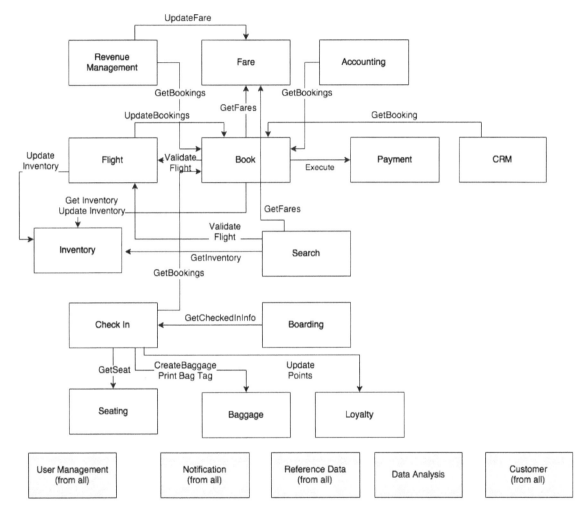

There are many dependencies going back and forth between different modules. The bottom layer shows cross-cutting capabilities, which are used across multiple modules. At this point, the modules are more like a spaghetti rather than autonomous units.

The next step is to analyze these dependencies, and come up with a better, simplified dependency map.

Events as opposed to query

Dependencies could be query-based or event-based. Event-based is better for scalable systems. Sometimes, it is possible to convert query-based communications to event-based ones. In many cases, these dependencies exist because either the business organizations are managed like that, or by virtue of the way the old system handled the business scenario.

Let us now focus on the Revenue Management and the Fare services mentioned in the previous diagram.

Revenue Management is a module used for calculating optimal fare values based on the booking demand forecast. In case of a fare change between an origin and a destination, update fare on the **Fare** modules is called by the **Revenue Management** to update the respective fares in the **Fare** module.

An alternate way of thinking is that the **Fare** module is subscribed to the **Revenue Management** for any changes in fares, and **Revenue Management** publishes whenever there is a fare change. This reactive programming approach gives an added flexibility such that the **Fares** and the **Revenue Management** modules could stay independent, but connected through a reliable messaging system. This same pattern could be applied in many other scenarios such as **Check In** to **Loyalty** and **Boarding**.

Next, examine the scenario of **CRM** and **Booking**:

This scenario is slightly different from the previously explained scenario. The **CRM** module is used to manage passenger complaints. When **CRM** receives a complaint, it retrieves the corresponding passenger **Booking**. In reality, the number of complaints are negligibly small when compared to the number of bookings. If we blindly apply the previous pattern, where **CRM** subscribes to all bookings, we will find that this is not cost effective.

Examine another scenario between **Check-in** and **Booking**. Instead of **Check-in** calling the **GetBookings** service on the **Booking**, can **Check-in** listen to booking events? This is possible, but the challenge here is that booking could happen 360 days in advance, whereas **Check-in** generally starts only 24 hours before the flight departure. Duplicating all bookings and booking changes in the **Check-in** module 360 days in advance will not be a wise decision, as **Check-in** does not require this data until 24 hours before the flight departure.

An alternate option is, when **Check-in** opens for a flight (24 hours before departure), **Check-in** calls a service on the **Booking** to get a snapshot of bookings for a given flight. Once this is done, **Check-in** could subscribe for booking events specifically for that flight. In this case, the approach is a combination of query based as well as event based. By doing so, we reduce unnecessary events and storage, as well as the number of queries between these two services.

In short, there is no single policy that rules all scenarios. Each scenario requires logical thinking, and it then applies the most appropriate pattern.

Events as opposed to synchronous updates

Apart from the query model, a dependency could be an update transaction as well. Consider this scenario between **Revenue Management** and **Booking**:

In order to do a forecast and analysis of the current demand, **Revenue Management** requires all bookings across all flights. The current approach, as depicted in the dependency graph, is that **Revenue Management** has a schedule job, which calls **GetBooking** on **Booking** to get all incremental bookings (new and changed) since the last synchronization.

An alternative approach is to send new bookings and changes of bookings, as soon as they take place in **Booking**, as an asynchronous push. The same pattern could be applied in many other scenarios such as from **Booking** to **Accounting**, from **Flight** to **Inventory**, and also from **Flight** to **Booking**. In this approach, the source service publishes all state-change events to a topic. All interested parties could subscribe to this event stream, and store locally. This approach removes many hard wirings, and keeps the systems loosely coupled.

The dependency is depicted as follows:

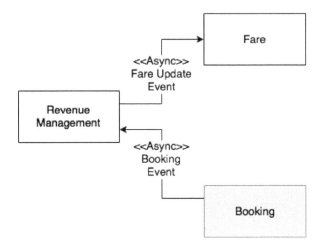

In this case, we changed both the dependencies, and converted them to asynchronous events.

A last case to analyze is the **Update Inventory** call from the **Booking** module to the **Inventory** module:

When a booking is completed, it has to update the inventory status by depleting the inventory stored in the **Inventory** service. For example, when there are 10 economy class seats available, at the end of the booking, we have to reduce it to 9. In the current system, **Booking** and **Update Inventory** are executed within the same transaction boundaries. This is to handle a scenario in which there is only one seat left, and multiple customers are trying to book. In the new design, if we apply the same event-driven pattern--sending the inventory update as an event to **Inventory**--it may leave the system in an inconsistent state. This needs further analysis, which we will address later in this chapter.

Challenge requirements

In many cases, the targeted state could be achieved by relooking at the requirements as follows:

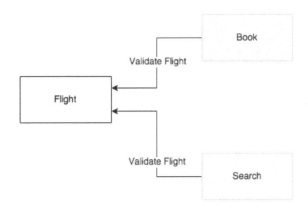

There are two validate flight calls, one from the **Booking** module, and another one from **Search**. The validate flight call is to validate the input flight data coming from different channels. The end objective is to avoid incorrect data being stored or serviced. When a customer does a flight search, say **BF100**, the system validates this flight to see the following:

- Is this is a valid flight?
- Does the flight exist on that particular date?
- Are there any booking restrictions set on this flight?

An alternate way of solving this is to adjust the inventory of the flight based on the aforementioned conditions. For example, if there is a restriction on the flight, update the inventory as zero. In this case, the intelligence will remain with **Flight**, and it keeps updating the inventory. As far as **Search** and **Booking** are concerned, both just look up the inventory instead of validating flights for every request. This approach is more efficient compared to the original approach.

Next, we will review the **Payment** use case. Payment is typically a disconnected function due to the nature of security constraints such as the **Payment Card Industry Data Security Standard** (**PCI-DSS**)-like standards. The most obvious way to capture a payment is to do a browser redirect to a payment page hosted in the Payment service. Since card handling applications come under the purview of PCI-DSS, it is wise to remove any direct dependencies from the payment service. Therefore, we can remove **Booking** to **Payment** direct dependency, and opt for a UI-level integration.

Challenge service boundaries

In this section, we will review some of the service boundaries based on the requirements and dependency graph, considering **Check In** and its dependencies to **Seating** and **Baggage**.

The seating function runs a few algorithms based on the current state of seat allocation in the airplane, and finds out the best way to position the next passenger so that the weight and balance requirements can be met. This is based on a number of pre-defined business rules. However, other than **Check In**, no other module is interested in the seating function. From a business capability perspective, seating is just a function of check-in, not a business capability by itself. Therefore, it is better to embed this logic inside check-in itself.

The same is applicable to **Baggage** as well. BrownField has a separate baggage handling system. The baggage function, in the PSS context, is to print the baggage tag as well as store baggage data against the **Check In** records. There is no business capability associated with this particular functionality. Therefore, it is ideal to move this function to **Check In** itself.

The **Book**, **Search**, and **Inventory** functions after the redesign are shown as follows:

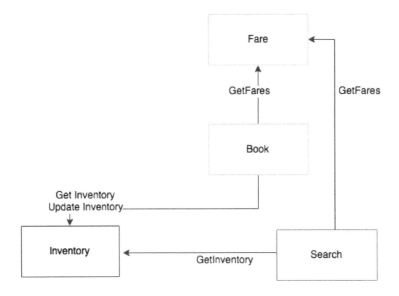

Similarly, **Inventory** and **Search** are more of supporting functions of the **Booking** module. They are, as such, not aligned with any of the business capabilities. Similar to the previous judgement, it is ideal to move both **Search** and **Inventory** to **Booking**. Assume, for the time being, that **Search**, **Inventory**, and **Booking** are moved to a single microservice named **Reservation**.

As per the statistics of BrownField, search transactions are 10 times more frequent than booking transactions. Moreover, search is not a revenue-generating transaction like booking. Due to these reasons, we need different scalability models for search and booking. Booking should not get impacted if there is a sudden surge of transactions in search. From a business point of view, dropping a search transaction in favor of saving a valid booking transaction is more acceptable.

This is an example of a polyglot requirement, which overrules the business capability alignment. In this case, it makes more sense to have **Search** as a separate service from the **Booking** service. Let us assume that we move **Search** out. Only **Inventory** and **Booking** remain under **Reservation**. Now **Search** has to hit back to the **Reservation** module to perform inventory searches. This could impact the booking transactions as follows:

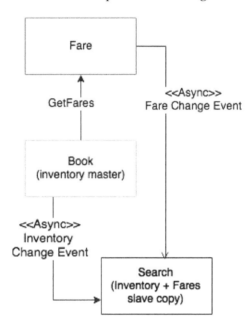

A better approach is to keep the **Inventory** module with **Booking**, and keep a read-only copy of the inventory under **Search**, continuously synchronizing the inventory data over a reliable messaging system. Since both **Inventory** and **Booking** are collocated, this will also solve the need to have two phase commits. Since both of them are local, they could work well with local transactions.

Let us now challenge the **Fare** module design. When a customer searches for a flight between **A** and **B** for a given date, we want to show the flights and fares together. That means our read-only copy of inventory can also combine both fares as well as inventory. Search will then subscribe to **Fare** for any fare-change events. The intelligence still stay with the **Fare** service, but it keeps sending fare updates to the cached fare data under the **Search**.

Final dependency graph

There are still few synchronized calls, which for the time being, we will keep as it is. By applying all these changes, the final dependency diagram will look as follows:

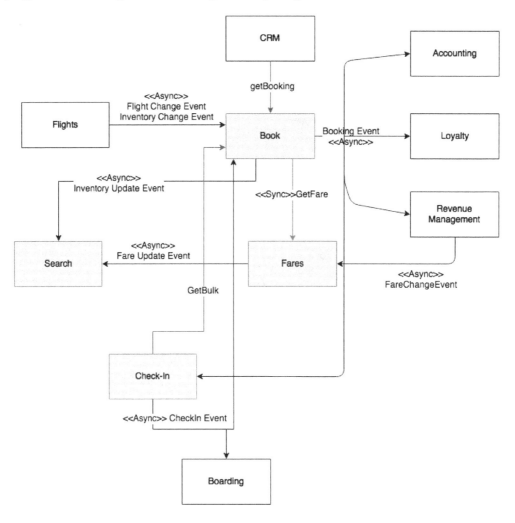

Now we can safely consider each box in the preceding diagram as a microservice. We have nailed down many dependencies, and modeled many of them as asynchronous as well. The overall system is more or less designed in the reactive style. Still, there are some synchronized calls shown in the diagram with bold lines, such as **GetBulk** from **Check-In**, **getBooking** from **CRM**, and **GetFare** from **Booking**. These synchronous calls are essentially required as per the trade-off analysis.

Prioritizing microservices for migration

We have identified a first-cut version of our microservices-based architecture. As the next step, we will analyze the priorities, and identify the order of migration. This could be done by considering multiple factors as explained next:

- **Dependency**: One of the parameters for deciding the priority is the dependency graph. From the service dependency graph, services with less dependency or no dependency at all are easy to migrate, whereas, complex dependencies are way harder. Services with complex dependencies will need dependent modules to also be migrated along with them. **Accounting**, **Loyalty**, **CRM**, and **Boarding** have less dependencies compared to **Booking** and **Check-In**. Modules with high dependencies will also have higher risks in their migration.

- **Transaction volume**: Another parameter that can be applied is analyzing the transaction volumes. Migrating services with the highest transaction volumes will relieve the load on the existing system. This will have better values from an IT support and maintenance perspective. However, the downside of this approach is the higher risk factor. As stated earlier, Search requests are ten times higher in volume compared to the **Booking** requests. **Check-In** has the third highest volume transaction after **Search** and **Booking**.

- **Resource utilization**: This is measured based on current utilizations such as CPU, memory, connection pools, thread pools, and more. Migrating resource-intensive services out of the legacy system provides relief to other services. This will help the remaining modules to function better. **Flight**, **Revenue Management**, and **Accounting** are resource-intensive services, as they involve data-intensive transactions such as forecasting, billing, flight schedule changes, and more.

- **Complexity**: The complexity is perhaps measured in terms of the business logic associated with a service such as function points, lines of code, number of tables, number of services, and more. Less complex modules are easy to migrate as compared to complex modules. Booking is extremely complex compared to **Boarding**, **Search**, and **Check-In** services.

- **Business criticality**: Business criticality could be either based on revenue or customer experience. Highly critical modules deliver higher business value. **Booking** is the most revenue generating service from the business standpoint, whereas, **Check-In** is business critical, as it could lead to flight departure delays, which could lead to revenue loss as well as customer dissatisfaction.

- **Velocity of changes**: Velocity of change indicates the number of change requests targeting a function in a short timeframe. This translates to speed and agility of delivery. Services with high velocity of change requests are better candidates for migration as compared to stable modules. Statistics show that **Search**, **Booking**, **Fares** go through frequent changes, whereas, **Check-In** is the most stable function.

- **Innovation**: Services that are part of a disruptive innovative process need to get priority over back-office functions, which are based on more established business processes. Innovations on legacy systems are harder to achieve as compared to applying innovations in the microservices world. Most of the innovations are around **Search**, **Booking**, **Fares**, **Revenue Management**, and **Check-In** compared to back-office **Accounting**.

Based on BrownField's analysis, **Search** has the highest priority, as it requires innovation, has high velocity of changes, is less business critical, and gives better relief for both business and IT. The **Search** service has minimal dependency with no requirements to synchronize data back to the legacy system.

Data synchronization during migration

During the transition phase, the legacy system and the new microservices will run in parallel. Therefore, it is important to keep the data synchronized between the two systems.

The straightforward option is to synchronize data between the two systems at the database level by using any data synchronization tool. This approach works well when both old and new systems are built on the same data store technologies. The complexity will be higher if the data store technologies are different. The second problem with this approach is that we are allowing a backdoor entry, hence, exposing the microservices' internal data store outside. This is against the microservices' principles.

Let us take this on a case-by-case basis before we can conclude with a generic solution. The following diagram shows the data migration and synchronization aspect once **Search** is taken out:

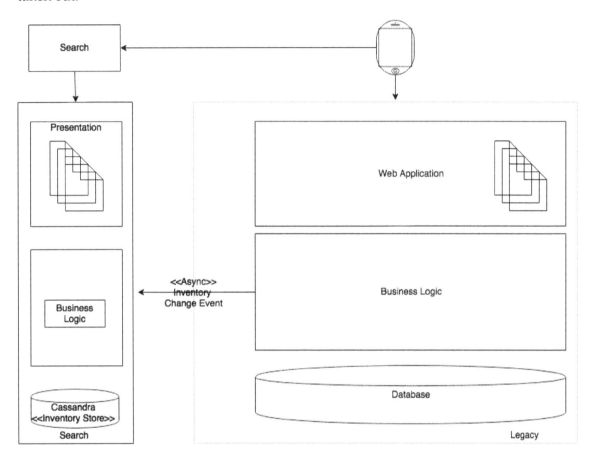

Let us assume that we use a NoSQL database for keeping inventory and fares under the **Search** service. In this particular case, all we need is the legacy system to supply data to the new service using asynchronous events. We will have to make some changes in the existing system to send fare changes or any inventory changes as events. The **Search** service then accepts these events, and stores them locally into the local NoSQL store.

This is a bit more tedious in the case of the complex **Booking** service.

In this case, the new **Booking** microservice sends inventory change events to the **Search** service. In addition to this, the legacy application has to also send the fare change events to **Search**. Booking will then store them in the new **Booking** service, in its MySQL data store as seen in the following diagram:

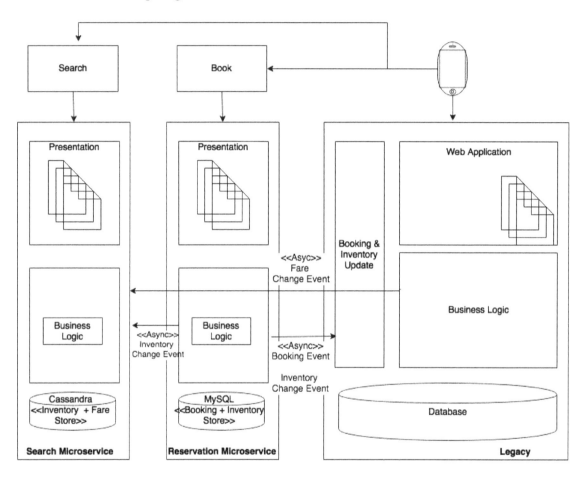

The most complex piece, the **Booking** service, has to send the booking events and inventory events back to the legacy system. This is to ensure that the functions in the legacy system continue to work as before. The simplest approach is to write an update component, which accepts the events and updates the old booking records table so that there are no changes required in the other legacy modules. We will continue this until none of the legacy components are referring booking and inventory data any longer. This will help us to minimize changes in the legacy system, and therefore, reduce the risk of failures.

In short, a single approach may not be sufficient. A multi-pronged approach based on different patterns is required.

Managing reference data

One of the biggest challenges in migrating monolithic applications to microservices is to manage reference data. A simple approach is to build the reference data as another microservice itself, as shown in the following diagram:

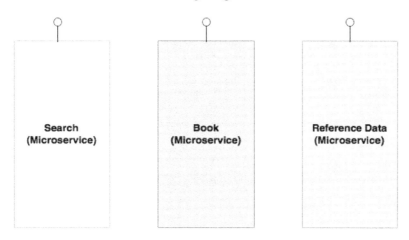

In this case, whoever needs reference data should access them through the microservice endpoints. This is a well-structured approach, but could lead to performance issues, as encountered in the original legacy system.

An alternate approach is to have reference data as a microservice service for all the admin and CRUD functions. A near cache will then be created under each service to incrementally cache data from the master services. A thin reference data access proxy library will be embedded in each of these services. The reference data access proxy abstracts whether data is coming from the cache or from a remote service.

This is depicted in the following diagram. The following **Master Node** is the actual reference data microservice:

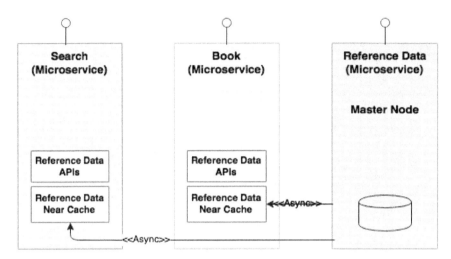

The challenge is to synchronize the data between the master and slave. A subscription mechanism is required for those data caches that change frequently.

A better approach is to replace the local cache with an in-memory data grid, as shown in the following diagram:

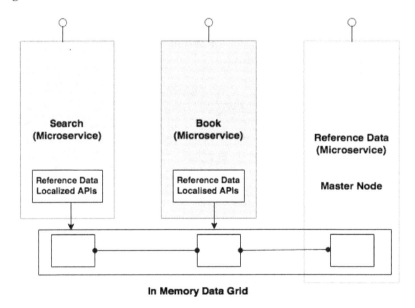

The reference data microservice will write to the data grid, whereas, the proxy libraries embedded in other services will have read-only APIs. This eliminates the requirement to have subscription of data, and is much more efficient and consistent.

User interfaces and web applications

During the transition phase, we have to keep both old and new user interfaces together. There are three general approaches usually taken in this scenario.

The first approach is to have the old and new user interfaces as separate user applications with no link between them, as shown in this diagram:

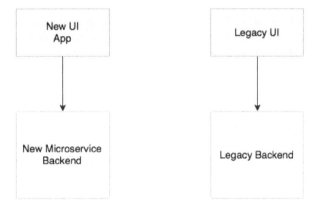

A user signs into the new application as well as into the old application, much like two different applications with no **Single Sign On** (**SSO**) between them. This approach is simple, and there is no overhead. In most of the cases, this may not be acceptable to the business, unless it is targeted at two different user communities.

The second approach is to use the legacy user interface as the primary application, and then transfer page controls to the new user interfaces when the user requests pages of the new application:

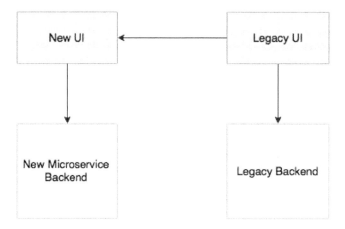

In this case, since the old and the new application are web-based applications running on a web browser window, users will get a seamless experience. SSO has to be implemented between the old and the new user interfaces.

The third approach is to integrate the existing legacy user interface directly to the new microservices backend, as seen in the following diagram:

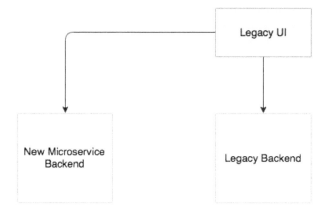

In this case, the new microservices are built as headless applications with no presentation layer. This could be challenging, as it may require many changes in the old user interface, such as introducing service calls, data model conversions, and more.

Another issue in the last two cases is how to handle the authentication of resources and services.

Session handling and security

Assume that the new services are written based on Spring Security with a token-based authorization strategy, whereas, the old application uses a custom-build authentication with its local identity store.

The following diagram shows how to integrate between the old and the new services:

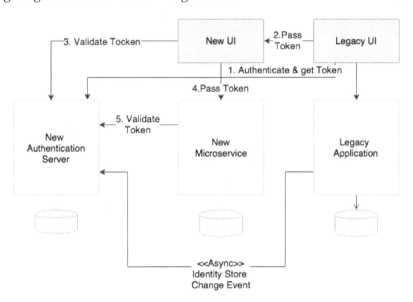

The simplest approach, as shown in the diagram, is to build a new identity store with an authentication service as a new microservice using Spring Security. This will be used for all our future resource and service protections, for all microservices.

The existing user interface application authenticates itself against the new authentication service, and secures a token. This token will be passed to the new user interface or new microservice. In both cases, the user interface or microservice will make a call to the authentication service to validate the given token. If the token is valid, then the UI or microservice accepts the call.

The catch here is that the legacy identity store has to be synchronized with the new one.

Test strategy

One important question to answer from a testing point of view is how can we ensure that all functions work in a similar way as before the migration?

Before the migration or refactoring, integration test cases should be written for the services that are getting migrated. This will ensure that, once migrated, we get the same expected result, and the behavior of the system remains the same. An automated regression test pack has to be in place, and has to be executed every time we make a change in the new or old system.

In the following diagram, for each service, we need one test against the EJB endpoint and another one against the microservices endpoint:

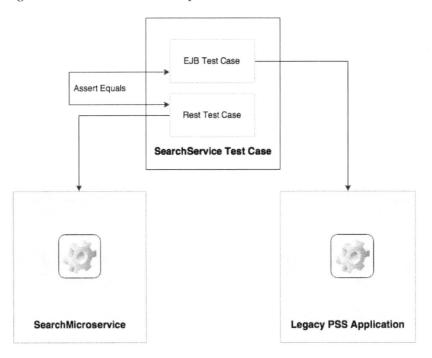

Building ecosystem capabilities

Before we embark on the actual migration, we will have to build all the microservices capabilities mentioned under the capability model, as documented in Chapter 3, *Building Microservices with Spring Boot*. These are the prerequisites for developing microservices based systems.

In addition to these capabilities, certain application functions are also required to be built upfront, such as reference data, security and SSO, Customer, and Notification. A data warehouse or a data lake is also required as a prerequisite.

 An effective approach is to build these capabilities in an incremental fashion, delaying development until it is really required.

Migrate modules only if required

In the previous chapters, we examined approaches and steps for transforming from monolithic to microservices. It is important to understand that it is not necessary to migrate all modules to the new microservices architecture unless it is really required. A major reason is that these migrations incur costs.

We will review a few such scenarios here. BrownField has already taken a decision to use an external Revenue Management system in place of the PSS revenue management function. BrownField is also in the process of centralizing their accounting functions, and therefore, need not migrate the accounting function from the legacy system. Migration of CRM does not add much value at this point to the business. Therefore, it is decided to keep the CRM in the legacy system itself. The business has plans to move to a SaaS-based CRM solution as part of their cloud strategy. Also note that stalling the migration halfway through could seriously impact the complexity of the system.

Internal layering of microservices

In this section, we will further explore the internal structure of microservices. There is no standard to be followed for the internal architecture of a microservice. The rule of thumb is to abstract realizations behind simple service endpoints.

A typical structure would look like the one shown here:

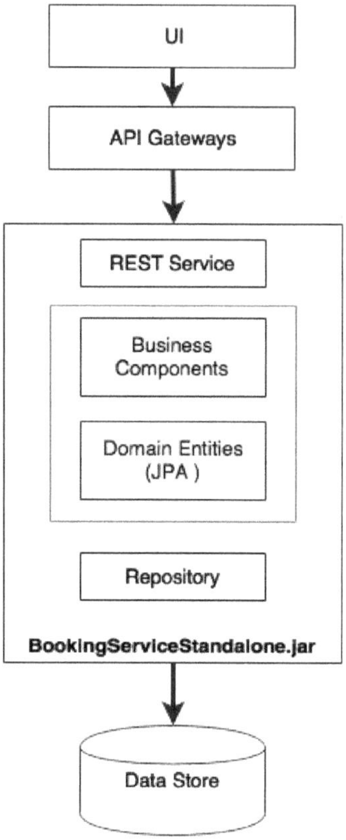

The UI accesses the REST services through a service gateway. The API Gateway may be one per microservice or one for many microservices--it depends on what we want to do with the API gateway. There could be one or more rest endpoints exposed by microservices. These endpoints, in turn, connect to one of the business components within the service. Business components then execute all business functions with the help of domain entities. A repository component is used for interacting with the backend data store.

Orchestrating microservices

The logic of the booking orchestration and the execution of rules sits within the Booking service. The brain is still inside the Booking service in the form of one or more booking business components. Internally, business components orchestrate private APIs exposed by other business components or even external services.

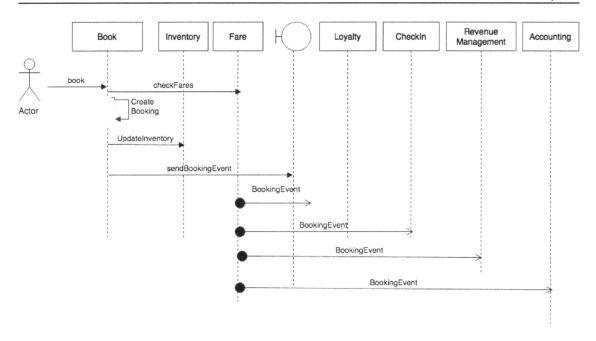

As shown in the preceding diagram, the booking service internally calls to update the inventory of its own component, as well as calls the **Fare** service.

Is there any orchestration engine required for this activity? It depends on the requirements. In complex scenarios, we may have to do a number of things in parallel. For example, create booking internally, apply a number of booking rules, validate the fare, and validate the inventory before creating a booking. We may want to execute them in parallel. In such cases, we may use Java concurrency APIs or reactive Java libraries.

 In extremely complex situations, we may opt for an integration framework such as Spring Integration or Apache Camel in embedded mode.

Integration with other systems

In the microservices world, we use an API gateway or a reliable message bus for integrating with other non-microservices.

We will assume that there is another system in BrownField that needs booking data. Unfortunately, the system is not capable of subscribing to the booking events that Booking microservice is publishing. In such cases, an **Enterprise Application integration** (**EAI**) solution could be employed, which listens to our booking events, and then uses a native adaptor to update the database.

Managing shared libraries

Certain business logic or libraries may be used in more than one microservice in which the library logic itself is not qualified as a business service. For example, Search and Reservation microservices may use a built technical library for natural language processing. In such cases, these shared libraries will be duplicated in both the microservices.

Handling exceptions

Examine the booking scenario to understand different exception-handling approaches.

In the service sequence diagram below, there are three lines marked with a cross mark. These are potential areas where exceptions could occur.

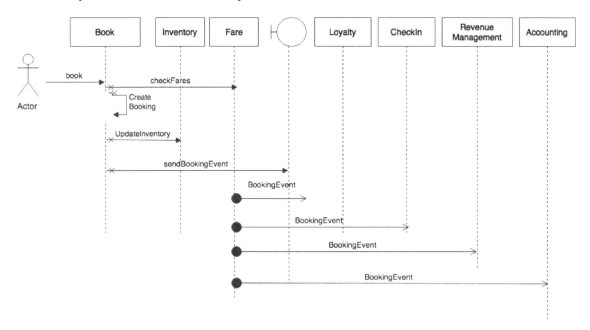

There is a synchronous communication between Booking and Fare. What if the fare service is not available? If the Fare service is not available, throwing an error back to the user may cause revenue loss. An alternate thought is to trust the fare which is coming as part of the incoming request. When we serve search, the search results will have the fare as well. When the user selects a flight and submits, the request will have the selected fare. In case the Fare service is not available, we trust the incoming request and accept the Booking. We will use a circuit breaker and a fallback service, which simply creates the booking with a special status, and queues the booking for manual action or a system retry.

What if creating the booking fails? If creating booking fails unexpectedly, a better option is to throw a message back to the user. We could try alternative options, but that would increase the overall complexity of the system. The same is applicable for inventory updates.

In the case of creating a booking and updating the inventory, we avoid a situation where a booking is created and the inventory update somehow fails. As the inventory is critical, it is better to have both create booking and update inventory to be in a local transaction. This is possible, as both components are under the same subsystem.

If we consider the **CheckIn** scenario, **CheckIn** sends an event to **Boarding** and **Booking** as shown in this diagram:

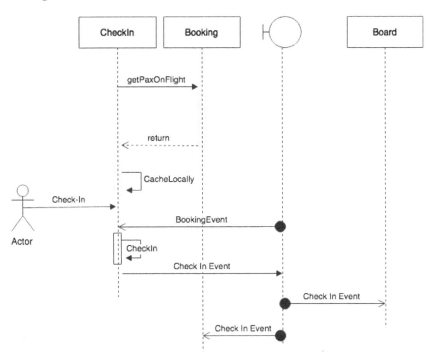

Consider a scenario where the check-in services fail immediately after the check-in complete event is sent out. The other consumers processed this event, but the actual check-in is rolled back. This is because we are not using a two-phase commit. In this case, we need a mechanism for reverting that event. This could be done by catching the exception, and sending another check-in cancelled event.

In the preceding case, note that, to minimize the use of the compensating transaction, sending the check-in event is moved towards the end of the check-in transaction. This reduces the chance of failure after sending out the event.

On the other hand, what if the check-in is successful, but sending the event failed? We could think of two approaches: invoke a fallback service to store it locally, and then use another sweep and scan program to send the event at a later time. It could even retry multiple times. This could add more complexity, and may not be efficient in all cases. An alternate approach is to throw the exception back to the user so that the user can retry. However, this might not always be good from a customer engagement standpoint. On the other hand, the earlier option is better for the system's health. A trade-off analysis is required to find out the best solution for the given situation.

Target implementation

The following diagram represents the implementation view of the BrownField PSS microservices system:

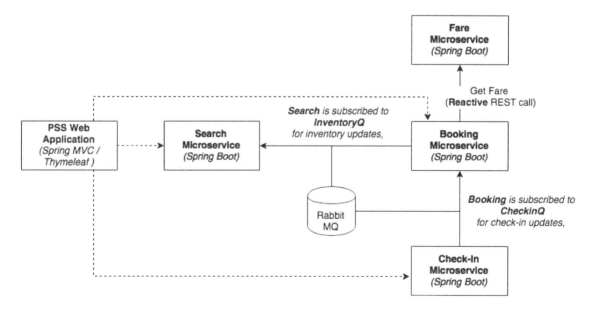

As shown in the preceding diagram, as an example, we are implementing four microservices--**Search**, **Fare**, **Booking**, and **Check-In**. In order to test the application, there is a website application developed using Spring MVC with Thymeleaf templates. The asynchronous messaging is implemented with the help of RabbitMQ. In this sample implementation, the default H2 database is used as the in-memory store for demonstration purposes.

As shown in the preceding diagram, the call from **Booking** to **Fare** uses Spring WebFlux. It uses **Mono** construct to reactively collect remote fare data, as shown in the following code snippet:

```
public void validateFareReactively(BookingRecord record){
  Mono<Fare> result = webClient.get().uri("/fares/get?
    flightNumber="+record.getFlightNumber()
    +"&flightDate="+record.getFlightDate())
    .accept(MediaType.APPLICATION_JSON)
    .exchange().flatMap(response ->
    response.bodyToMono(Fare.class));
  result.subscribe(fare ->
    checkFare(record.getFare(),fare.getFare()));
}
```

If your microservice is set to use one of the reactive database drivers, then it makes more sense to change all internal coding based on Reactive constructs. In this example, since we are using an embedded database with no reactive support, only inter-service calls are implemented in a non-blocking manner.

Implementation projects

The basic implementation of the BrownField Airline's PSS microservices system has five core projects, as summarized in the following table. The table also shows the port range used for these projects to ensure consistency throughout the book.

Microservices	Projects	Port Range
Book Microservice	chapter6.book	8060-8069
Check-in Microservice	chapter6.checkin	8070-8079
Fare Microservice	chapter6.fares	8080-8089
Search Microservice	chapter6.search	8090-8099
Website	chapter6.website	8001

The website is the UI application for testing the PSS microservices.

All microservice projects in this example follow the same pattern for package structure, as shown here:

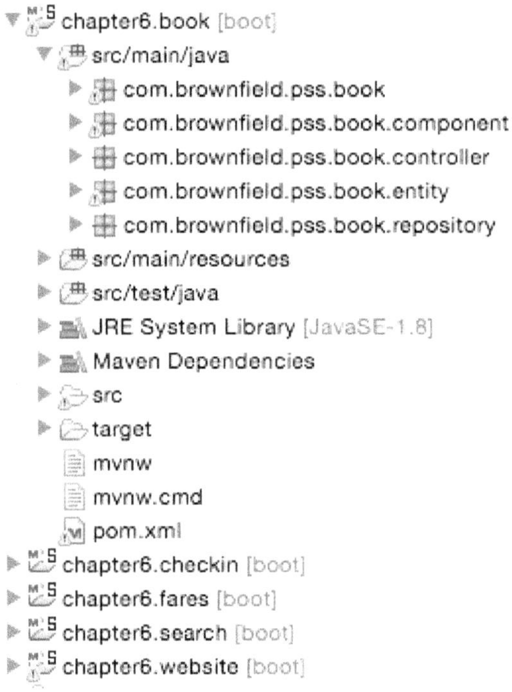

```
▼ 🗂 chapter6.book [boot]
    ▼ 📁 src/main/java
        ▶ 🗒 com.brownfield.pss.book
        ▶ 🗒 com.brownfield.pss.book.component
        ▶ 🗒 com.brownfield.pss.book.controller
        ▶ 🗒 com.brownfield.pss.book.entity
        ▶ 🗒 com.brownfield.pss.book.repository
    ▶ 📁 src/main/resources
    ▶ 📁 src/test/java
    ▶ 🗄 JRE System Library [JavaSE-1.8]
    ▶ 🗄 Maven Dependencies
    ▶ 📁 src
    ▶ 📁 target
        📄 mvnw
        📄 mvnw.cmd
        📄 pom.xml
▶ 🗂 chapter6.checkin [boot]
▶ 🗂 chapter6.fares [boot]
▶ 🗂 chapter6.search [boot]
▶ 🗂 chapter6.website [boot]
```

The different packages and their purposes are explained as follows:

- The root folder (`com.brownfield.pss.book`) contains the default Spring Boot application.
- The component package hosts all the service components where the business logic is implemented.
- The controller package hosts the REST endpoints and the messaging endpoints. Controller classes internally utilize the component classes for execution.
- The entity package contains the JPA entity classes for mapping to the database tables.
- Repository classes are packaged inside the repository package, and are based on Spring Data JPA.

Running and testing the project

Perform the following steps to build and test the microservices developed in this chapter:

1. Build each of the projects using Maven. Ensure that the test flag is switched off. The test programs assume other dependent services are up and running. It fails if the dependent services are not available:

   ```
   mvn –Dmaven.test.skip=true install
   ```

2. Run the RabbitMQ server as follows:

   ```
   rabbitmq_server-3.5.6/sbin$ ./rabbitmq-server
   ```

3. Run the following commands in separate terminal windows:

   ```
   java –jar target/fares-1.0.jar

   java –jar target/search-1.0.jar

   java –jar target/checkin-1.0.jar

   java –jar target/book-1.0.jar

   java –jar target/website-1.0.jar
   ```

4. The website project has a CommandLineRunner, which will execute all the test cases at startup. Once all the services are successfully started, open the following URL in a browser:

   ```
   http://localhost:8001
   ```

5. The browser will ask for basic security credentials (if basic authentication is enabled). Use guest/guest123 as the credentials. This example only shows the website security with basic authentication mechanism. As explained in Chapter 3, *Building Microservices with Spring Boot,* service-level security can be achieved using OAuth2.

6. This will display the following screen. This is the home screen of our BrownField PSS application:

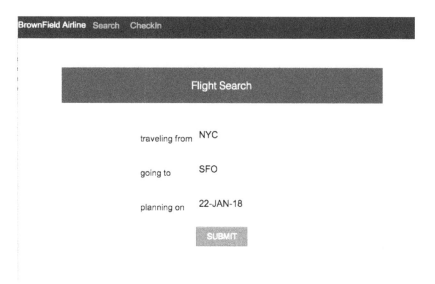

7. The **SUBMIT** button will invoke the Search microservice to fetch the available flights, which meet the conditions mentioned on the screen. There are a few flights pre-populated at startup of the Search microservice. Edit the Search microservice code to feed in additional flights if required.

8. The output screen with a list of flights is shown in the following screenshot. The **Book** link will take us to the booking screen for the selected flight:

9. The booking screen is as shown in the following screenshot. The user can enter the passenger details, and create a booking by clicking on the **CONFIRM** button. This will invoke the Booking microservice, and internally, the Fare service as well. It also sends a message back to Search microservice.

10. If the booking is successful, the following confirmation screen will be displayed with the booking reference number:

11. Let us test the Check-in microservice. This can be done by clicking on **CheckIn** from the top menu. Use the booking reference number obtained in the previous step to test check-in. This is shown in the following screenshot:

12. Clicking on the **SEARCH** button in the previous screen will invoke the Booking microservice, and retrieve the booking information. Click on the **CheckIn** link to perform the check-in. This will invoke the Check-in microservice:

13. If check-in is successful, it will display the confirmation message, as shown next, with a confirmation number. This will be done by internally calling the Check-in service. The Check-in service internally sends a message to Booking to update the check-in status.

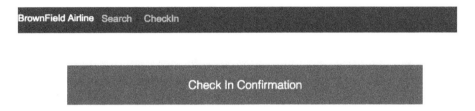

In this chapter, we implemented and tested the BrownField PSS microservices with basic Spring Boot capabilities.

Potential next steps

We are now halfway through this book. So far, we have developed a set of microservices using Spring Boot. The following goals have been met:

- Understanding the basic concepts of microservices architecture.
- Learning the design practices and trade-offs between various design choices.
- Understanding practical challenges by developing a complex use case ground up.
- Implementing five microservices using Spring Boot. We also examined a number of useful Spring boot features for developing microservices.

This implementation is good and serves as the basic building block. The next area that we will try and understand is how to scale these microservices in an enterprise environment.

 There are generally two paths we can take from here--it largely depends on whether we want to go with Containers such as Docker or with plain Spring Boot applications.

The following two options are available to choose from:

- Use Spring Boot to develop microservices, and run them as standalone services. In this approach, it is best to use Spring Cloud for scaling and managing microservices. This approach is explained in `Chapter 7`, *Scale Microservices with Spring Cloud Components* and `Chapter 8`, *Logging and Monitoring Microservices*.
- If the approach taken is to go with Containers, then Docker, together with a container services tool such as Mesos and Marathon, is the best way forward. `Chapter 9`, *Containerizing Microservices with Docker*, and `Chapter 10`, *Scaling Dockerized Microservices with Mesos and Marathon* explain this approach.

Both these approaches are mutually exclusive. Having said that, Spring Cloud components can also be used in conjunction with the Container approach. However, this can result in complex deployment environments.

Summary

In this chapter, you learned how to approach a real use case with a microservices architecture.

We examined various stages of a real-world evolution towards microservices from a monolithic application. We also evaluated the pros and cons of multiple approaches and obstacles when migrating a monolithic application. Finally, we explained the end-to-end microservices design for the use case that we examined. Design and implementation of a full-fledged microservice implementation was also validated.

In the next chapter, we will see how the Spring Cloud project helps us to transform the BrownField PSS microservices developed to Internet-scale deployments.

7
Scale Microservices with Spring Cloud Components

In order to manage Internet-scale microservices, one requires more capabilities than what is offered by the Spring Boot framework. The Spring Cloud project has a suite of purpose-built components to achieve these additional capabilities effortlessly.

This chapter will provide a deep insight into the various components of the Spring Cloud project, such as Eureka, Zuul, Ribbon, and Spring Config, by positioning them against the microservices capability model discussed in `Chapter 4`, *Applying Microservices Concepts*. This chapter will demonstrate how the Spring Cloud components help to scale the BrownField Airline's PSS microservices system, developed in the previous chapter.

At the end of this chapter, we will have learned about the following:

- The Spring **Config Server** for externalizing configuration
- The Eureka Server for service registration and discovery
- Understanding the relevance of Zuul as a service proxy and gateway
- The implementation of automatic microservice registration and service discovery
- Spring Cloud messaging for asynchronous reactive microservice composition

What is Spring Cloud?

Add a link to Netflix OSS. The Spring Cloud project is an umbrella project from the Spring team, which implements a set of common patterns required by distributed systems as a set of easy-to-use Java Spring libraries. Despite its name, Spring Cloud by itself is not a cloud solution. Rather, it provides a number of capabilities, which are essential when developing applications targeting cloud deployments that adhere to the Twelve-Factor Application principles. By using Spring Cloud, developers just need to focus on building business capabilities using Spring Boot, and leverage the distributed, fault-tolerant, and self-healing capabilities available out-of-the-box from Spring Cloud.

The Spring Cloud solutions are agnostic to the deployment environment and can be developed and deployed on a desktop PC or in an elastic cloud. The cloud-ready solutions, which are developed using Spring Cloud, are also agnostic, and portable across many cloud providers, such as Cloud Foundry, AWS, Heroku, and others. When not using Spring Cloud, developers will end up using services natively provided by the cloud vendors, resulting in deep coupling with the PaaS providers. An alternate option for developers is to write quite a lot of boilerplate code to build these services. Spring Cloud also provides simple, easy-to-use Spring-friendly APIs, which abstract the cloud provider's service APIs, such as those APIs coming with the AWS Notification service.

Built on Spring's *convention over configuration* approach, Spring Cloud defaults all configurations, and helps developers to a quick start. Spring Cloud also hides complexities, and provides simple declarative configurations to build systems. The smaller footprints of the Spring Cloud components make it developer-friendly, and also make it easy to develop cloud-native applications.

Spring Cloud offers many choices of solutions for developers based on their requirements. For example, the service registry can be implemented using popular options such as Eureka, Zookeeper, or Consul. The components of Spring Cloud are fairly decoupled, hence, developers get the flexibility to pick and choose what is required.

 What is the difference between Spring Cloud and Cloud Foundry? Spring Cloud is a developer kit for developing Internet-scale Spring Boot applications, whereas, Cloud Foundry is an open source Platform as a Service for building, deploying, and scaling applications.

Spring Cloud releases

The Spring Cloud project is an overarching Spring project, which includes a combination of different components. The versions of these components are defined in the *spring-cloud-starter-parent* BOM.

 In this book, we are relying on the **Dalston SR1** version of the Spring Cloud. Dalston does not support Spring Boot 2.0.0 and Spring Framework 5. Spring Cloud Finchley, planned for the end of this year, is expected to support Spring Boot 2.0.0. Hence, examples in the previous chapters need to downgrade to the Spring Boot 1.5.2.RELEASE version.

Add the following dependency in `pom.xml` to use Spring Cloud Dalston dependency:

```
<dependency>
  <groupId>org.springframework.cloud</groupId>
  <artifactId>spring-cloud-dependencies</artifactId>
  <version>Dalston.SR1</version>
  <type>pom</type>
  <scope>import</scope>
</dependency>
```

Setting up the environment for the BrownField PSS

In this chapter, we will amend the BrownField's PSS microservices developed in `Chapter 6`, *Microservices Evolution - A Case Study*, using the Spring Cloud capabilities. We will also examine how to make these services enterprise grade using the Spring Cloud components.

In order to prepare the environment for this chapter, import and rename (`chapter6.*` to `chapter7.*`) projects into a new STS workspace.

 The full source code of this chapter is available under the `chapter7` project in the code files under `https://github.com/rajeshrv/Spring5Microservice`.

Spring Cloud Config

Simplify this section. The Spring Cloud Config Server is an externalized configuration server in which applications and services can deposit, access, and manage all runtime configuration properties. The Spring Config Server also supports version control of the configuration properties.

In earlier examples with Spring Boot, all configuration parameters were read from a property file packaged inside the project, either `application.properties` or `application.yaml`. This approach is good, since all properties are moved out of code to a property file. However, when microservices are moved from one environment to another, these properties need to undergo changes, which require application rebuild. This is in violation of one of the Twelve-Factor Application principles, which advocates one time build and moving the binaries across environments.

A better approach is to use the concept of profiles. Profiles, as discussed in `Chapter 3`, *Building Microservices with Spring Boot*, is used to partition different properties for different environments. The profile specific configuration will be named as `application-{profile}.properties`. For example, `application-development.properties` represents a property file targeted for the development environment.

However, the disadvantage of this approach is that the configurations are statically packaged along with the application. Any changes in the configuration properties require the application to be rebuilt.

There are alternate ways to externalize configuration properties from the application deployment package. Configurable properties can also be read from an external source in a number of ways, which are as follows:

- From an external JNDI server using the JNDI namespace (`java:comp/env`)
- Using the Java system properties (`System.getProperties()`), or by using the `-D` command-line option
- Using the `PropertySource` configuration

  ```
  @PropertySource("file:${CONF_DIR}/application.properties")
  public class ApplicationConfig {
  }
  ```

- Using a command-line parameter pointing a file to an external location

  ```
  java -jar myproject.jar --spring.config.location=<file location>
  ```

JNDI operations are expensive, lack flexibility, have difficulties in replication, and are not version controlled. System.properties is not flexible enough for large-scale deployments. The last two options rely on a local or a shared filesystem mounted on the server.

For large-scale deployments, a simple, yet powerful, centralized configuration management solution is required.

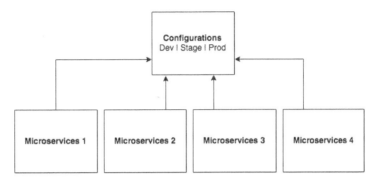

As shown in the preceding diagram, all microservices point to a central server to get the required configuration parameters. The microservices then locally cache these parameters to improve performance. The Config Server propagates the configuration state changes to all subscribed microservices so that the local cache's state can be updated with the latest changes. The Config Server also uses profiles to resolve values specific to an environment.

As shown in the next diagram, there are multiple options available under the Spring Cloud project for building the configuration server. Config Server, Zookeeper Configuration, and Consul Configuration are available as options. However, this chapter will only focus on the Spring Config Server implementation:

Cloud Config

☐ Config Client

   spring-cloud-config Client

☐ Config Server

   Central management for configuration via a git or svn backend

☐ Zookeeper Configuration

   Configuration management with Zookeeper and spring-cloud-zookeeper-config

☐ Consul Configuration

   Configuration management with Hashicorp Consul

The Spring Config Server stores properties in a version-controlled repository such as Git or SVN. The Git repository can be local or remote. A highly available remote Git server is preferred for large-scale distributed microservices deployments.

The Spring Cloud Config Server architecture is shown in the following diagram:

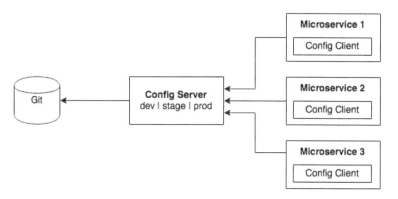

As shown in the diagram, the **Config Client** embedded in the Spring Boot microservices does a configuration lookup from a central configuration server using simple declarative mechanisms and stores properties into the Spring environment. The configuration properties can be application-level configurations such as trade limit per day, or infrastructure-related configurations such as server URLs, credential and so on.

Unlike Spring Boot, Spring Cloud uses a bootstrap context, which is a parent context of the main application. Bootstrap context is responsible for loading configuration properties from the **Config Server**. The bootstrap context looks for `bootstrap.yaml` or `bootstrap.properties` for loading the initial configuration properties. To make this work in a Spring Boot application, rename the `application.*` file as `bootstrap.*`.

Building microservices with Config Server

The next few sections demonstrate how to use the Config Server in a real-world scenario. In order to do this, we will modify our search microservice (`chapter7.search`) to use the Config Server. The following diagram depicts the scenario:

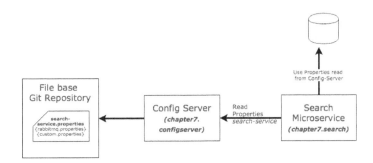

In this example, the search service will read the **Config Server** at startup by passing the service name. In this case, the service name of the search service will be **search-service**. The properties configured for the **search-service** include the RabbitMQ properties as well as a custom property.

Setting up the Config Server

The following steps need to be followed to create a new Config Server using STS:

1. Create a new Spring Starter project and select **Config Server** and **Actuator**, as shown in this screenshot:

2. Set up a Git repository. This could be done by pointing to a remote Git configuration repository, such as `https://github.com/spring-cloud-samples/config-repo`. This URL is an indicative one, a Git repository used by the Spring Cloud examples. We will have to use our own Git repository instead.

3. Alternatively, a local-file-system-based Git repository can be used. In a real production scenario, an external Git is recommended. The Config Server in this chapter will use a local-file-system-based Git repository for demonstration purposes.

4. Use the following set of commands to set up a local Git repository:

```
$ cd $HOME
$ mkdir config-repo
$ cd config-repo
$ git init .
$ echo message : helloworld > application.properties
$ git add -A .
$ git commit -m "Added sample application.properties"
```

This will create a new Git repository on the local filesystem. A property file, named `application.properties`, with a property message and value `helloworld` is also created.

 `application.properties` is created for demonstration purposes. We will change this in subsequent sections.

5. The next step is to change the configuration in the Config Server to use the Git repository created in the previous step. In order to do this, rename `application.properties` as `bootstrap.properties`:

6. Edit the contents of the new `bootstrap.properties` to match the following:

```
server.port=8888
spring.cloud.config.server.git.uri:
  file://${user.home}/config-repo
```

 Port `8888` is the default port for the Config Server. Even without configuring the `server.port`, the Config Server should bind to `8888`. In a Windows environment, an extra `/` is required in the file URL.

7. Also add `management.security.enabled=false` to disable security validation.

8. Optionally, rename the default package of the autogenerated `Application.java` from `com.example` to `com.brownfield.configserver`. Add `@EnableConfigServer` in `Application.java`.

```
@EnableConfigServer
@SpringBootApplication
public class ConfigserverApplication {
```

9. Run the Config Server by right-clicking the project, and run as Spring Boot App.

10. Check `curl http://localhost:8888/env` to see whether the server is running. If everything is fine, this will list all environment configurations. Note that `/env` is an Actuator endpoint.

11. Check `http://localhost:8888/application/default/master` to see the properties specific to `application.properties`, which was added in the earlier step. The browser will display properties configured in the `application.properties`. The browser should display content similar to this:

```
{"name":"application","profiles":["default"],"label":"master",
  "version":"6046fd2ff4fa09d3843767660d963866ffcc7d28",
  "propertySources":[{"name":"file:///Users/rvlabs
  /config-repo /application.properties","source":
  {"message":"helloworld"}}]}
```

Understanding the Config Server URL

In the previous section, we used `http://localhost:8888/application/default/master` to explore the properties. How do we interpret the given URL?

The first element in the URL is the application name. In the last example, the application name should be `application`. The application name is a logical name given to the application, using the `spring.application.name` property in the `bootstrap.properties` of the Spring Boot application. Each application must have a unique name. The Config Server will use the name to resolve and pick up appropriate properties from the Config Server repository. The application name is also sometimes referred to as service ID. If there is an application with the name `myapp`, then there should a `myapp.properties` in the configuration repository to store all properties related to that application.

The second part of the URL represents the profile. There can be more than one profile configured within the repository for an application. The profiles can be used in various scenarios. The two common scenarios are to segregate different environments such as Dev, Test, Stage, Prod, and so on, or to segregate server configurations such as primary, secondary, and others. The first one represents different environments of an application, whereas the second one represents different servers where an application is deployed.

The profile names are logical names, which will be used for matching the filename in the repository. The default profile is named as `default`. To configure properties for different environments, we have to configure different files, as shown next. In this example, the first file is for the development environment, whereas the second is for the production environment:

```
application-development.properties
application-production.properties
```

These are accessible using the following URLs:

`http://localhost:8888/application/development`

`http://localhost:8888/application/production`

The last part of the URL is the `label`, and is named as `master` by default. The `label` is an optional Git label, which can be used if required.

In short, the URL is based on this pattern:

`http://localhost:8888/{name}/{profile}/{label}`

The configuration can also be accessed by ignoring the profile. In the given example, all the following three URLs point to the same configuration:

```
http://localhost:8888/application/default
```

```
http://localhost:8888/application/master
```

```
http://localhost:8888/application/default/master
```

There is an option to have different Git repositories for different profiles. This makes sense for production systems, since the access to different repositories could be different.

Accessing the Config Server from clients

In the previous section, a Config Server is set up and accessed using a web browser. In this section, the Search microservice will be modified to use the Config Server. The Search microservice will act as a Config Client.

Follow the steps listed next to use the Config Server instead of reading properties from the application.properties file:

1. Add the Spring Cloud Config dependency and the Actuator (if Actuator is not already in place) to pom.xml. The Actuator is mandatory for refreshing the configuration properties:

   ```xml
   <dependency>
     <groupId>org.springframework.cloud</groupId>
     <artifactId>spring-cloud-starter-config</artifactId>
   </dependency>
   ```

2. Since we are modifying the Spring Boot Search microservice from the earlier chapter, we will have to add the following to include the Spring Cloud dependencies. This is not required if the project is created from scratch:

   ```xml
   <dependencyManagement>
     <dependencies>
     <dependency>
   <groupId>org.springframework.cloud</groupId>
   <artifactId>spring-cloud-dependencies</artifactId>
   <version>Dalston.BUILD-SNAPSHOT</version>
   <type>pom</type>
   <scope>import</scope>
   </dependency>
   </dependencies>
   </dependencyManagement>
   ```

3. The following screenshot shows the Cloud starter library selection screen. If the application is built from the ground up, select the libraries as shown here:

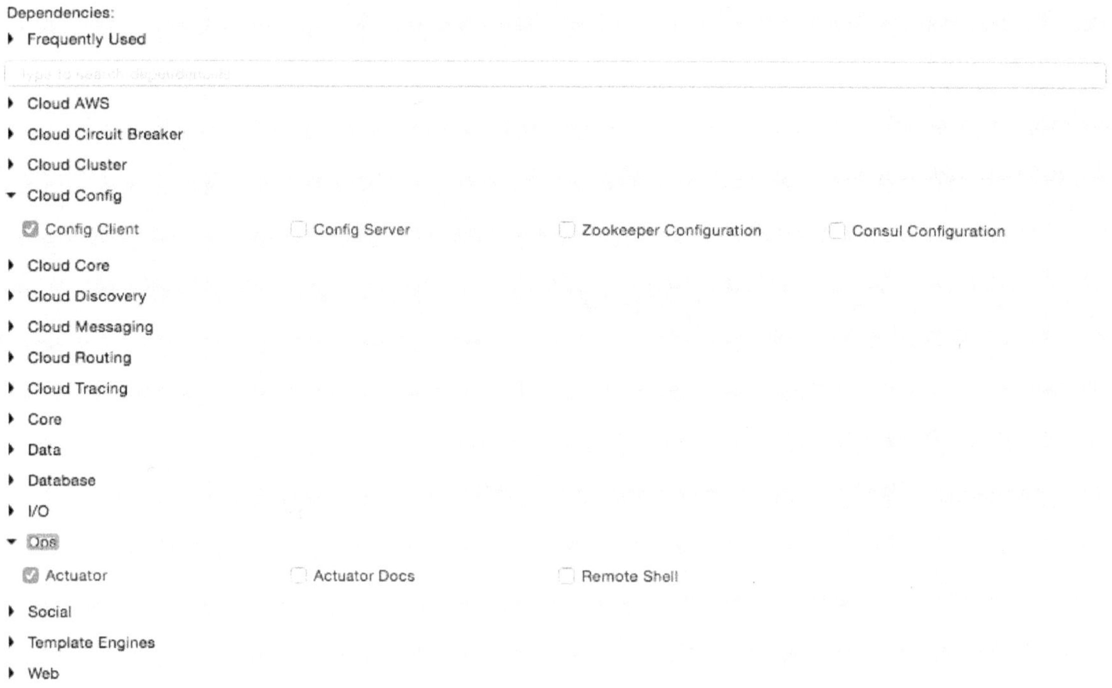

Dependencies:
- ▶ Frequently Used

▶ Cloud AWS
▶ Cloud Circuit Breaker
▶ Cloud Cluster
▼ Cloud Config

| ☑ Config Client | ☐ Config Server | ☐ Zookeeper Configuration | ☐ Consul Configuration |

▶ Cloud Core
▶ Cloud Discovery
▶ Cloud Messaging
▶ Cloud Routing
▶ Cloud Tracing
▶ Core
▶ Data
▶ Database
▶ I/O
▼ Ops

| ☑ Actuator | ☐ Actuator Docs | ☐ Remote Shell |

▶ Social
▶ Template Engines
▶ Web

4. Rename the `application.properties` to `bootstrap.properties`, and add an application name and a configuration server URL. The configuration server URL is not mandatory if the Config Server is running on the default port (`8888`) on the local host.

The new `bootstrap.properties` file will look like this:

```
spring.application.name=search-service
spring.cloud.config.uri=http://localhost:8888
server.port=8090
spring.rabbitmq.host=localhost
spring.rabbitmq.port=5672
spring.rabbitmq.username=guest
spring.rabbitmq.password=guest
```

`search-service` is a logical name given to the Search microservices. This will be treated as the service ID. The Config Server will look for `search-service.properties` in the repository to resolve the properties.

5. Create a new configuration file for `search-service`. Create a new `search-service.properties` under the `config-repo` folder where the Git repository is created. Note that `search-service` is the service ID given to the Search microservice in the `bootstrap.properties` file. Move service-specific properties from `bootstrap.properties` to the new `search-service.properties`. The following properties will be removed from `bootstrap.properties` and added to `search-service.properties`:

```
spring.rabbitmq.host=localhost
spring.rabbitmq.port=5672
spring.rabbitmq.username=guest
spring.rabbitmq.password=guest
```

6. In order to demonstrate the centralized configuration of properties and propagation of changes, add a new application-specific property to the property file. We will add `originairports.shutdown` to temporarily take out an airport from the search. Users will not get any flights when searching with an airport mentioned in the shutdown list:

```
originairports.shutdown=SEA
```

In this preceding example, we will not return any flights when searching with SEA as origin.

7. Commit this new file into the Git repository by executing the following commands:

```
git add -A .
git commit -m "adding new configuration"
```

The final `search-service.properties` file should look like this:

```
spring.rabbitmq.host=localhost
spring.rabbitmq.port=5672
spring.rabbitmq.username=guest
spring.rabbitmq.password=guest
originairports.shutdown:SEA
```

The `chapter7.search` project's `bootstrap.properties` should look like the following:

```
spring.application.name=search-service
server.port=8090
spring.cloud.config.uri=http://localhost:8888
```

8. Modify the Search microservice code to use the configured parameter, `originairports.shutdown`. A `RefreshScope` annotation has to be added at the class level to allow properties to be refreshed when there is a change. In this case, we are adding a refresh scope to the `SearchRestController` class.

   ```
   @RefreshScope
   ```

9. Add the following instance variable as a placeholder for the new property that is just added in the Config Server. The property names in the `search-service.properties` must match:

   ```
   @Value("${originairports.shutdown}")
   private String originAirportShutdownList;
   ```

10. Change the application code to use this property. This is done by modifying the search method as follows:

    ```
    @RequestMapping(value="/get", method = RequestMethod.POST)
    List<Flight> search(@RequestBody SearchQuery query){
      logger.info("Input : "+ query);
      if(Arrays.asList(originAirportShutdownList.split(","))
      .contains(query.getOrigin())){
        logger.info("The origin airport is in shutdown state");
        return new ArrayList<Flight>();
      }
      return searchComponent.search(query);
    }
    ```

    The search method is modified to read the parameter `originAirportShutdownList` and see whether the requested origin is in the shutdown list. If there is a match, instead of proceeding with the actual search, the search method will return an empty flight list.

11. Start the Config Server. Then start the Search microservice. Make sure that the Rabbit MQ server is running.

12. Modify the `chapter7.website` project to match the `bootstrap.properties` content, as follows, to utilize the Config Server:

```
spring.application.name=test-client
server.port=8001
spring.cloud.config.uri=http://localhost:8888
```

13. Change the `CommandLineRunner`'s run method in Application.java to query SEA as origin airport.

```
SearchQuery searchQuery = new SearchQuery(
    "SEA","SFO","22-JAN-18");
```

14. Run the `chapter7.website` project. `CommandLineRunner` will now return an empty flight list. The following message will be printed in the server:

```
The origin airport is in shutdown state
```

Handling configuration changes

The `/refresh` endpoint will refresh the locally cached configuration properties and reload fresh values from the Config Server.

In order to force reloading the configuration properties, call the `/refresh` endpoint of the microservice. This is actually the Actuator's refresh endpoint. The following command will send an empty POST to the `/refresh` endpoint:

```
curl -d {} localhost:8090/refresh
```

Spring Cloud Bus for propagating configuration changes

With the preceding approach, configuration parameters can be changed without restarting the microservices. This is good when there are only one or two instances of the services running. What happens if there are many instances?

For example, if there are five instances, then we have to hit /refresh against each service instance. This is definitely a cumbersome activity.

The following diagram shows the solution using Spring Cloud Bus:

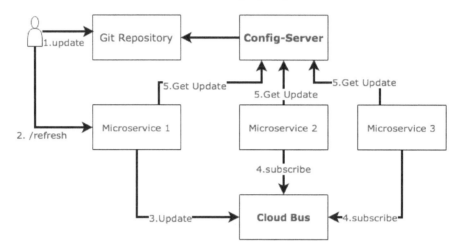

The Spring Cloud Bus provides a mechanism to refresh configurations across multiple instances without knowing how many instances there are, nor their locations. This is particularly handy when there are many service instances of a microservice running, or when there are many microservices of different types running. This is done by connecting all service instances through a single message broker. Each instance subscribes for change events and refreshes its local configuration when required. This refresh is triggered by making a call to any one instance by hitting the /bus/refresh endpoint, which then propagates the changes through the cloud bus and the common message broker.

Setting up high availability for the Config Server

The previous sections explored how to setup the Config Server, allowing real-time refresh of configuration properties. However, the Config Server is a single point of failure in this architecture.

There are three single points of failure in the default architecture established in the previous section. One of them is the availability of the Config Server itself, the second one is the Git repository, and the third one is the RabbitMQ server.

The following diagram shows a high-availability architecture for the Config Server:

The architecture mechanisms and rationale are explained as follows:

The Config Server requires high availability, since the services won't be able to bootstrap if the Config Server is not available. Hence, redundant Config servers are required for high availability. However, the applications can continue to run if the Config Server is unavailable after the services are bootstrapped. In this case, services will run with the last-known configuration state. Hence, the Config Server availability is not at the same critical level as the microservices availability.

In order to make the Config Server highly available, we need multiple instances of the Config servers. Since the Config Server is a stateless HTTP service, multiple instances of configuration servers can be run in parallel. Based on the load on the configuration server, a number of instances have to be adjusted. The `bootstrap.properties` is not capable of handling more than one server address. Hence, multiple configuration servers should be configured to run behind a load balancer or behind a local DNS with failover and fallback capabilities. The load balancer or DNS server URL will be configured in the microservices `bootstrap.properties`. This is with the assumption that the DNS or the load balancer is highly available and capable of handling failovers.

In a production scenario, it is not recommended to use a local-file-based Git repository. The configuration server should be typically backed with a highly available Git service. This is possible by either using an external high available Git service or a highly available internal Git service. SVN can also be considered.

Having said that, an already bootstrapped Config Server is always capable of working with a local copy of the configuration. Hence, we need a highly available Git only when the Config Server needs to be scaled. Therefore, this too is not as critical as the microservices availability or the Config Server availability.

 The GitLab example for setting up high availability is available at the following link: `https://about.gitlab.com/high-availability/`

RabbitMQ also has to be configured for high availability. The high availability for RabbitMQ is needed only to push configuration changes dynamically to all instances. Since this is more of an offline, controlled activity, it does not really require the same high availability as required by the components.

Rabbit MQ high availability can be achieved by either using a cloud service or a locally configured highly available Rabbit MQ service.

 Setting up high availability for Rabbit MQ is documented at the link `https://www.rabbitmq.com/ha.html`.

Monitoring Config Server health

The Config Server is nothing but a Spring Boot application, and is, by default, configured with an Actuator. Hence, all Actuator endpoints are applicable for the Cloud Server. The health of the server can be monitored using the following Actuator URL:

```
http://localhost:8888/health
```

Config Server for configuration files

We may run into scenarios where we need a complete configuration file to be externalized, such as `logback.xml`. The Config Server provides a mechanism to configure and store such files. This is achievable by using the URL format as follows:

```
/{name}/{profile}/{label}/{path}
```

The `name`, `profile`, and `label` has the same meaning as explained earlier. The path indicates the filename, such as `logback.xml`.

Completing changes to use Config Server

In order to build this capability to the complete BrownField Airline's PSS, we have to make use of the configuration server for all services.

 All microservices in our `chapter7.*` examples need to make similar changes to look to the Config Server for getting the configuration parameters.

We are not externalizing the queue names used in the Search, Booking, and Check-in services at the moment. Later in this chapter, these will be changed to use Spring Cloud Streams.

Eureka for registration and discovery

So far, we have achieved externalizing configuration parameters, as well as load balancing across many service instances.

Ribbon-based load balancing is sufficient for most of the microservices requirements. However, this approach falls short in these scenarios:

- If there is a large number of microservices, and if we want to optimize infrastructure utilization, we will have to dynamically change the number of service instances and associated servers. It is not easy to predict and preconfigure the server URLs in a configuration file.
- When targeting cloud deployments for highly scalable microservices, static registration and discovery is not a good solution considering the elastic nature of the cloud environment.
- In cloud deployment scenarios, IP addresses are not predictable and will be difficult to statically configure in a file. We will have to update the configuration file every time there is a change in address.

The Ribbon approach partially addresses this issue. With Ribbon, we can dynamically change the service instances, but whenever we add new service instances or shut down instances, we will have to manually go and update the Config Server. Though the configuration changes will be automatically propagated to all required instances, manual configuration changes will not work with large-scale deployments. When managing large deployments, automation, wherever possible, is paramount.

To fix this gap, the microservices should self-manage their life cycle by dynamically registering service availability and provision-automated discovery for consumers.

Understanding dynamic service registration and discovery

Dynamic registration is primarily from the service provider's point of view. With dynamic registration, when a new service is started, it automatically enlists its availability in a central service registry. Similarly, when a service goes out of service, it is automatically delisted from the service registry. The registry always keeps up-to-date information of the services available, as well as their metadata.

Dynamic discovery is applicable from the service consumer's point of view. Dynamic discovery is where clients look for the service registry to get the current state of the services topology and then invoke the services accordingly. In this approach, instead of statically configuring the service URLs, the URLs are picked up from the service registry.

The clients may keep a local cache of the registry data for faster access. Some registry implementations allow clients to keep a watch on the items they are interested in. In this approach, the state changes in the registry server will be propagated to the interested parties to avoid using stale data.

There are a number of options available for dynamic service registration and discovery. Netflix Eureka, Zookeeper, and Consul are available as part of Spring Cloud, as shown in the `start.spring.io` screenshot that follows. Etcd is another service registry available outside of Spring Cloud to achieve dynamic service registration and discovery. In this chapter, we will focus on the Eureka implementation:

Cloud Discovery

Eureka Discovery
Service discovery using spring-cloud-netflix and Eureka

Eureka Server
spring-cloud-netflix Eureka Server

Zookeeper Discovery
Service discovery with Zookeeper and spring-cloud-zookeeper-discovery

Cloud Foundry Discovery
Service discovery with Cloud Foundry

Consul Discovery
Service discovery with Hashicorp Consul

Understanding Eureka

Spring Cloud Eureka also comes from the Netflix OSS. The Spring Cloud project provides a Spring-friendly declarative approach for integrating Eureka with Spring-based applications. Eureka is primarily used for self-registration, dynamic discovery, and load balancing. The Eureka internally uses Ribbon for load balancing.

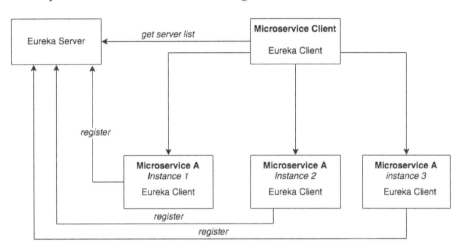

As shown in the preceding diagram, Eureka consists of a server component and a client-side component. The server component is the registry in which all microservices register their availability. The registration typically includes service identity and its URLs. The microservices use the **Eureka Client** for registering their availability. The consuming components will also use the **Eureka Client** for discovering the service instances.

When a microservice is bootstrapped, it reaches out to the **Eureka Server** and advertises its existence with the binding information. Once registered, the service endpoint sends ping requests to the registry every 30 seconds to renew its lease. If a service endpoint cannot renew its lease for a few times, that service endpoint is taken out of the service registry. The registry information is replicated to all Eureka clients so that the clients need to go to the remote **Eureka Server** for each and every request. Eureka clients fetch the registry information from the server and cache it locally. After that, the clients use that information to find other services. This information is updated periodically (every 30 seconds) by getting the delta updates between the last fetch cycle and the current one.

When a client wants to contact a microservice endpoint, the **Eureka Client** provides a list of currently available services based on the requested service ID. The **Eureka Server** is zone-aware. Zone information can also be supplied when registering a service.

When a client requests for a services instance, the Eureka service tries to find the service running in the same zone. The Ribbon client then load balances across these available service instances supplied by the **Eureka Client**. The communication between the **Eureka Client** and **Eureka Server** uses REST and JSON.

Setting up the Eureka Server

In this section, we will run through the steps required for setting up the Eureka Server.

 The full source code of this section is available under the `chapter7.eurekaserver` project in the code files under `https://github .com/rajeshrv/Spring5Microservice`. Note that the Eureka Server registration and refresh cycles takes up to 30 seconds. Hence, when running services and clients, wait for 40-50 seconds.

Start a new Spring Starter project and select **Config Client**, **Eureka Server**, and **Actuator**, as shown in the following screenshot:

▶ Cloud AWS			
▶ Cloud Circuit Breaker			
▶ Cloud Cluster			
▼ Cloud Config			
☑ Config Client	☐ Config Server	☐ Zookeeper Configuration	☐ Consul Configuration
▶ Cloud Core			
▼ Cloud Discovery			
☐ Eureka Discovery	☑ Eureka Server	☐ Zookeeper Discovery	☐ Cloud Foundry Discovery
☐ Consul Discovery			
▶ Cloud Messaging			
▶ Cloud Routing			
▶ Cloud Tracing			
▶ Core			
▶ Data			
▶ Database			
▼ I/O			
☐ Batch	☐ Integration	☐ Activiti	☐ JMS (Artemis)
☐ JMS (HornetQ)	☐ AMQP	☐ Mail	
▼ Ops			
☑ Actuator	☐ Actuator Docs	☐ Remote Shell	
▶ Social			
▶ Template Engines			
▶ Web			

The project structure of the Eureka server is shown in the following screenshot:

Note that the main application is named `EurekaserverApplication.java`.

Rename `application.properties` to `bootstrap.properties`, as this is using the Config Server. As we have done earlier, configure the details of the Config Server in the `bootsratp.properties` so that it can locate the Config Server instance. The `bootstrap.properties` will look like this:

```
spring.application.name=eureka-server1
server.port:8761
spring.cloud.config.uri=http://localhost:8888
```

The Eureka Server can be set up in a standalone mode or in a clustered mode. We will start with the standalone mode. By default, the Eureka Server itself is another Eureka Client. This is particularly useful when there are multiple Eureka servers running for high availability. The client component is responsible for synchronizing the state from other Eureka servers. The Eureka Client is taken to its peers by configuring the `eureka.client.serviceUrl.defaultZone` property.

In the standalone mode, we will point the `eureka.client.serviceUrl.defaultZone` back to the same standalone instance. Later, we will see how we can run Eureka servers in a clustered mode.

Perform the following steps to set up Eureka server:

1. Create a `eureka-server1.properties` file and update it in the Git repository. `eureka-server1` is the name of the application given in the applications `bootstrap.properties` in the previous step. As shown next, the `serviceUrl` points back to the same server. Once the following properties are added, commit the file to the Git repository:

   ```
   spring.application.name=eureka-server1
   eureka.client.serviceUrl.defaultZone:http:
     //localhost:8761/eureka/
   eureka.client.registerWithEureka:false
   eureka.client.fetchRegistry:false
   ```

2. Change the default `Application.java`. In this example, the package is renamed as `com.brownfield.pss.eurekaserver` and the class name is also changed to `EurekaserverApplication`. In `EurekaserverApplication`, add `@EnableEurekaServer`:

   ```
   @EnableEurekaServer
   @SpringBootApplication
   public class EurekaserverApplication {
   ```

3. We are now ready to start the Eureka Server. Ensure the Config Server is also started. Right-click on the application and `Run As`, `Spring Boot App`. Once the application starts, open the following link in a browser to see the Eureka console:

   ```
   http://localhost:8761
   ```

4. In the console, note that there is no instance registered under the instances currently registered with Eureka. Since there are no services started with the Eureka Client enabled, the list is empty at this point.

5. Making a few changes to our microservices will enable dynamic registration and discovery using the Eureka service. To do this, first we have to add Eureka dependencies in `pom.xml`. If the services are being built up fresh using the Spring Starter project, then select **Config Client**, **Actuator**, **Web**, as well as the **Eureka Discovery** client, as shown in the following screenshot:

▸ Cloud AWS

▸ Cloud Circuit Breaker

▸ Cloud Cluster

▾ Cloud Config

  ☑ Config Client   ☐ Config Server   ☐ Zookeeper Configuration   ☐ Consul Configuration

▸ Cloud Core

▾ Cloud Discovery

  ☑ Eureka Discovery   ☐ Eureka Server   ☐ Zookeeper Discovery   ☐ Cloud Foundry Discovery

  ☐ Consul Discovery

▸ Cloud Messaging

▸ Cloud Routing

▸ Cloud Tracing

▸ Core

▸ Data

▸ Database

▸ I/O

▾ Ops

  ☑ Actuator   ☐ Actuator Docs   ☐ Remote Shell

▸ Social

▸ Template Engines

▾ Web

  ☑ Web   ☐ Websocket   ☐ WS   ☐ Jersey (JAX-RS)

  ☐ Ratpack   ☐ Vaadin   ☐ Rest Repositories   ☐ HATEOAS

  ☐ Rest Repositories HAL Browser   ☐ Mobile   ☐ REST Docs

6. Since we are modifying all our microservices, add the following additional dependency to all the microservices in their `pom.xml` files:

```
<dependency>
  <groupId>org.springframework.cloud</groupId>
  <artifactId>spring-cloud-starter-eureka</artifactId>
</dependency>
```

The following property has to be added to all the microservices in their respective configuration files under `config-repo`. This will help the microservices to connect to the Eureka Server. Commit to Git once the updates are completed:

```
eureka.client.serviceUrl.defaultZone:
  http://localhost:8761/eureka/
```

7. Add `@EnableDiscoveryClient` to all the microservices in their respective Spring Boot main classes. This will ask Spring Boot to register these services at startup to advertise its availability.

8. Instead of `RestTemplate`, we will use `@FeignClient` in this example by introducing a `FareServciesProxy`, as shown next:

```
@FeignClient(name="fares-service")
public interface FareServiceProxy {
  @RequestMapping(value = "fares/get",
  method=RequestMethod.GET)
  Fare getFare(@RequestParam(value="flightNumber")
  String flightNumber, @RequestParam(value="flightDate")
  String flightDate);
}
```

9. In order to do this, we have to add a Feign dependency:

```
<dependency>
  <groupId>org.springframework.cloud</groupId>
  <artifactId>spring-cloud-starter-feign</artifactId>
</dependency>
```

10. Start all services except website service.

11. If you go to the Eureka URL, you can see that all three instances are up and running:

```
http://localhost:8761
```

Instances currently registered with Eureka

Application	AMIs	Availability Zones	Status
BOOK-SERVICE	n/a (1)	(1)	UP (1) - 192.168.0.102:book-service:8060
CHECKIN-SERVICE	n/a (1)	(1)	UP (1) - 192.168.0.102:checkin-service:8070
FARES-SERVICE	n/a (1)	(1)	UP (1) - 192.168.0.102:fares-service:8080
SEARCH-SERVICE	n/a (1)	(1)	UP (1) - 192.168.0.102:search-service:8090

12. Change the website project `bootstrap.properties` to make use of Eureka rather than connecting directly to the service instances. We will use the load-balanced `RestTemplate`. Commit these changes to the Git repository:

```
spring.application.name=test-client
eureka.client.serviceUrl.defaultZone:
  http://localhost:8761/eureka/
```

13. Add `@EnableDiscoveryClient` to the Application class to make the client Eureka aware.

14. Edit both `Application.java` as well as `BrownFieldSiteController.java`. Add `RestTemplate` instances. This time, we annotate them with `@Loadbalanced` to ensure that we are using the load balancing features using Eureka and Ribbon. `RestTemplate` cannot be automatically injected. Hence, we have to provide a configuration entry, as follows:

```
@Configuration
class AppConfiguration {
  @LoadBalanced
  @Bean
  RestTemplate restTemplate() {
    return new RestTemplate();
  }
}
@Autowired
RestTemplate restClient;
```

15. We will use these `RestTemplate` instances to call the microservices. We will replace the hard-coded URLs with service IDs, which are registered in the Eureka Server. In the following code, we use the service names `search-service`, `book-service` and `checkin-service` instead of explicit host names and ports:

```
Flight[] flights = searchClient.postForObject(
  "http://search-service/search/get",
   searchQuery, Flight[].class);=

  long bookingId = bookingClient.postForObject(
    "http://book-service/booking/create", booking, long.class);

  long checkinId = checkInClient.postForObject(
  "http://checkin- service/checkin/create", checkIn,
   long.class);
```

16. We are now ready to test. Run the website project. If everything is fine, the website project's `CommandLineRunner` will successfully perform search, book, and check-in.

17. The same can also be tested using the browser by pointing the browser to `http://localhost:8001`.

High availability for Eureka

In the previous example, there was only one Eureka Server in the standalone mode. This is not good enough for a real production system.

The Eureka Client connects to the server, fetches registry information, and stores it locally in a cache. The client always works with this local cache. The Eureka Client checks the server periodically for any state changes. In case of a state change, it downloads the changes from the server and updates the cache. If the Eureka Server is not reachable, then the Eureka Client can still work with the last known state of the servers based on the data available in the client cache. However, this could lead to stale state issues quickly.

This section will explore high availability of the Eureka Server. The high availability architecture is shown in this diagram:

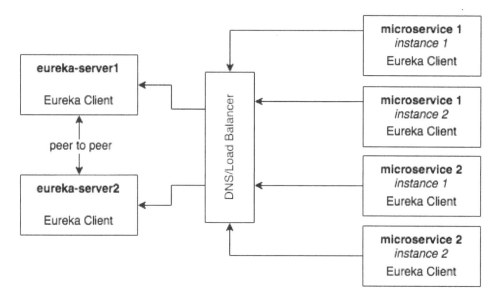

The Eureka Server is built with a peer-to-peer data synchronization mechanism. The run-time state information is not stored in a database, but managed using an in-memory cache. The high availability implementation favors availability and partition tolerance in the CAP theorem, leaving out consistency. Since the Eureka Server instances are synchronized with each other using asynchronous mechanism, the states may not always match between server instances. Peer-to-peer synchronization is done by pointing service URLs to each other. If there is more than one Eureka Server, each one has to be connected to at least one of the peer servers. Since the state is replicated across all peers, Eureka clients can connect to any one of the available Eureka servers.

The best way to achieve high availability for Eureka is to cluster multiple Eureka servers and run them behind a load balancer or a local DNS. The clients always connect to the server using the DNS or load balancer. At runtime, the load balancer will take care of selecting the appropriate servers. This load balancer address will be provided to the Eureka clients.

This section will showcase how to run two Eureka servers in a cluster for high availability. For this, define two property files--`eureka-server1` and `eureka-server2`. These are peer servers--if one fails, the other one will take over. Each of these servers will also act as a client for the other so that they can sync their states. The two property files defined are defined next. Upload and commit these properties to the Git repository. In the following configurations, the client URLs are pointing to each other, forming a peer network:

```
#eureka-server1.properties
eureka.client.serviceUrl.defaultZone:http://localhost:8762/eureka/
eureka.client.registerWithEureka:false
eureka.client.fetchRegistry:false

#eureka-server2.properties
eureka.client.serviceUrl.defaultZone:http://localhost:8761/eureka/
eureka.client.registerWithEureka:false
eureka.client.fetchRegistry:false
```

Update `bootstrap.properties` of Eureka and change the application name to `eureka`. Since we are using two profiles, the Config Server will look for either `eureka-server1` or `eureka-server2` based on the active profile supplied at startup:

```
spring.application.name=eureka
spring.cloud.config.uri=http://localhost:8888
```

Start two instances of the Eureka servers--`server1` on `8761` and `server2` on `8762`:

```
java -jar -Dserver.port=8761 -Dspring.profiles.active=server1
  demo-0.0.1-SNAPSHOT.jar

java -jar -Dserver.port=8762 -Dspring.profiles.active=server2
  demo-0.0.1-SNAPSHOT.jar
```

All our services are still pointing to the first server, server1. Open both the browser windows.

```
http://localhost:8761
http://localhost:8762
```

Start all microservices. The one which opened 8761 will immediately reflect the changes, whereas the other one will take 30 seconds to reflect the states. Since both the servers are in a cluster, the state is synchronized between these two servers. If we keep these servers behind a load balancer or DNS, then the client will always connect to one of the available servers.

After completing this exercise, switch back to the standalone mode for the remaining exercises.

Zuul proxy as the API Gateway

In most microservices implementations, internal microservices endpoints are not exposed outside. They are kept as private services. A set of public services will be exposed to the clients using an API Gateway. There are many reasons to do this, some of which are listed as follows:

- Only a selected set of microservices are required by the clients.
- If there are client-specific policies to be applied, it is easy to apply them in a single place rather than in multiple places. An example of such a scenario is the cross-origin access policy.
- It is hard to implement client-specific transformations at the service endpoint.
- If there is data aggregation required, especially to avoid multiple client calls in a bandwidth restricted environment, then a gateway is required in the middle.

Zuul is a simple gateway service or edge service, which well suits such situations. Zuul also came from the Netflix family of microservices products. Unlike many enterprise API gateway products, Zuul provides complete control to developers to configure or program based on specific requirements.

The following diagram shows Zuul acting as a proxy and load balancer for **Microservice A**:

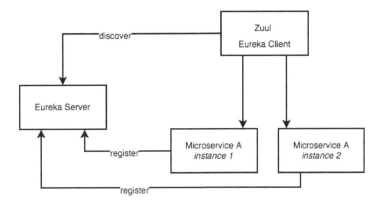

The Zuul proxy internally uses the **Eureka Server** for service discovery, and Ribbon for load balancing between service instances.

The Zuul proxy is also capable of routing, monitoring, managing resiliency, security, and so on. In simple terms, we can consider Zuul as a reverse proxy service. With Zuul, we can even change the behaviors of the underlying services by overriding them at the API layer.

Setting up Zuul

Unlike the Eureka Server and the Config Server, in typical deployments, Zuul is specific to a microservice. However, there are deployments in which one API Gateway covers many microservices. In this case, we are going to add Zuul for each of our microservices--Search, Booking, Fare, and Check-In.

 The full source code of this section is available under the `chapter7.*-apigateway` project in the code files.

Perform the following steps for setting up Zuul:

1. Convert the microservices one by one. Start with the Search API Gateway. Create a new Spring Starter project and select **Zuul**, **Config Client**, **Actuator**, and **Eureka Discovery**:

▸ Cloud Circuit Breaker

▸ Cloud Cluster

▾ Cloud Config

☑ Config Client   ☐ Config Server   ☐ Zookeeper Configuration   ☐ Consul Configuration

▸ Cloud Core

▾ Cloud Discovery

☑ Eureka Discovery   ☐ Eureka Server   ☐ Zookeeper Discovery   ☐ Cloud Foundry Discovery

☐ Consul Discovery

▸ Cloud Messaging

▾ Cloud Routing

☑ Zuul   ☐ Ribbon   ☐ Feign

▸ Cloud Tracing

▸ Core

▸ Data

▸ Database

▸ I/O

▾ Ops

☑ Actuator   ☐ Actuator Docs   ☐ Remote Shell

▸ Social   API documentation for the Actuator endpoints

▸ Template Engines

▾ Web

☐ Web   ☐ Websocket   ☐ WS   ☐ Jersey (JAX-RS)

☐ Ratpack   ☐ Vaadin   ☐ Rest Repositories   ☑ HATEOAS

☑ Rest Repositories HAL Browser   ☐ Mobile   ☐ REST Docs

The project structure for the `search-apigateway` is shown in this screenshot:

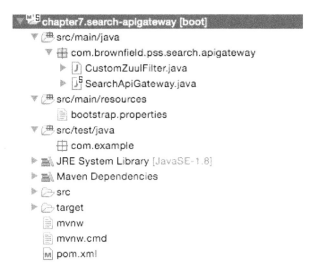

2. The next step is to integrate the API Gateway with Eureka and the Config Server. Create a `search-apigateway.property` file with the contents as given next, and commit to the Git repository.

   This configuration also sets a rule on how to forward traffic. In this case, any request coming on the `/api` endpoint of the API Gateway should be sent to the search-service:

   ```
   spring.application.name=search-apigateway
   zuul.routes.search-apigateway.serviceId=search-service
   zuul.routes.search-apigateway.path=/api/**
   eureka.client.serviceUrl.defaultZone:
   http://localhost:8761/eureka/
   ```

   The `search-service` is the service ID of Search service, and it will be resolved using the Eureka Server.

3. Update `bootstrap.properties` of `search-apigateway` as follows. There is nothing new in this configuration--a name to the service, port, and the Config Server URL:

   ```
   spring.application.name=search-apigateway
   server.port=8095
   spring.cloud.config.uri=http://localhost:8888
   ```

4. Edit `Application.java`. In this case, the package name and the class name also change to `com.brownfield.pss.search.apigateway` and `SearchApiGateway` respectively. Also add `@EnableZuulProxy` to tell Spring Boot that this is a Zuul proxy:

```
@EnableZuulProxy
@EnableDiscoveryClient
@SpringBootApplication
public class SearchApiGateway {
```

5. Run this as Spring Boot app. Before that, ensure that the Config Server, the Eureka Server, and the Search microservice are running.

6. Change the website project's CommandLineRunner, as well as `BrownFieldSiteController`, to make use of the API Gateway:

```
Flight[] flights = searchClient.postForObject(
  "http://search-apigateway/api/search/get",
  searchQuery, Flight[].class);
```

In this case, the Zuul proxy acts as a reverse proxy, which proxies all microservice endpoints to consumers. In the preceding example, the Zuul proxy does not add much value, as we just pass through the incoming requests to the corresponding backend service.

Zuul is particularly useful when we have one or more requirements like these:

- Enforcing authentication and other security policies at the gateway instead of doing that on every microservice endpoint. The gateway can handle security policies, token handling, and so on before passing the request to the relevant services behind. It can also do basic rejections based on some business policies, such as blocking requests coming from certain black-listed users.

- Business insights and monitoring can be implemented at the gateway level. Collect real-time statistical data and push it to an external system for analysis. This will be handy, as we can do this at one place rather than applying it across many microservices.

- API gateways are useful in scenarios where dynamic routing is required based on fine-grained controls. For example, send requests based on certain specific business values such as gold customer to a different service instances. For example, all requests coming from a region to be sent to one group of service instances. Another example--all requests requesting for a particular product have to be routed to a group of service instances.

- Handling the load shredding and throttling requirements is another scenario where API gateways are useful. This is when we have to control load based on set thresholds such as number of requests in a day. For example, control requests coming from a low-value third-party online channel.
- The Zuul gateway is useful for fine-grained load balancing scenarios. Zuul, Eureka Client, and Ribbon together provide fine-grained controls over load balancing requirements. Since the Zuul implementation is nothing but another Spring Boot application, the developer has full control of the load balancing.
- The Zuul gateway is also useful in scenarios where data aggregation requirements are in place. If the consumer wants higher-level coarse-grained services, then the gateway can internally aggregate data by calling more than one service on behalf of the client. This is particularly applicable when the clients are working in low-bandwidth environments.

Zuul also provides a number of filters. These filters are classified under pre-filters, routing filters, post filters, and error filters. As the names indicate, these are applied at different life cycle stages of a service call. Zuul also provides an option for developers to write custom filters. In order to write a custom filter, extend from the abstract ZuulFilter, and implement methods shown as follows:

```
public class CustomZuulFilter extends ZuulFilter{
public Object run(){}
public boolean shouldFilter(){}
public int filterOrder(){}
public String filterType(){}
```

Once a custom filter is implemented, add that class to the main context. In our example case, add this to the SearchApiGateway class as follows:

```
@Bean
public CustomZuulFilter customFilter() {
  return new CustomZuulFilter();
}
```

As mentioned earlier, the Zuul proxy is a Spring Boot service. We can customize the gateway programmatically in the way we want. As shown in the following code, we can add custom endpoints to the gateway, which in turn can call the backend services:

```
@RestController
class SearchAPIGatewayController {
  @RequestMapping("/")
  String greet(HttpServletRequest req){
```

```
    return "<H1>Search Gateway Powered By Zuul</H1>";
  }
}
```

In the preceding case, it just adds a new endpoint, and returns a value from the gateway. We can further use the `@Loadbalanced` RestTemplate to call a backend service. Since we have full control, we can do transformations, data aggregation, and so on. We can also use the Eureka APIs to get the server list and implement completely independent load balancing or traffic shaping mechanisms instead of the out-of-the-box load balancing features provided by Ribbon.

High availability of Zuul

Zuul is just a stateless service with an HTTP endpoint, hence, we can have as many Zuul instances as we need. There is no affinity or stickiness required. However, the availability of Zuul is extremely critical, as all the traffic from the consumer to the provider flows through the Zuul proxy. However, the elastic scaling requirements are not as critical as the backend microservices, where all the heavy lifting is happening.

The high availability architecture of Zuul is determined by the scenario in which we are using Zuul. The typical usage scenarios are as follows:

- When a client-side java script MVC such as Angular JS accesses Zuul services from a remote browser
- Another microservice or non-microservice accesses services via Zuul

In some cases, the client may not have capabilities to use the Eureka Client libraries, such as a legacy application written on PL/SQL. In some cases, organization policies do not allow Internet clients to handle client-side load balancing. In the case of browser-based clients, there are third-party Eureka JavaScript libraries available.

It all boils down to whether the client is using Eureka Client libraries or not. Based on this, there are two ways we can set up Zuul for high availability.

High availability of Zuul when the client is also a Eureka Client

In this case, since the client is also another Eureka Client, Zuul can be configured just like other microservices. Zuul itself registers to Eureka with a service ID. The clients then use Eureka and the service ID to resolve Zuul instances.

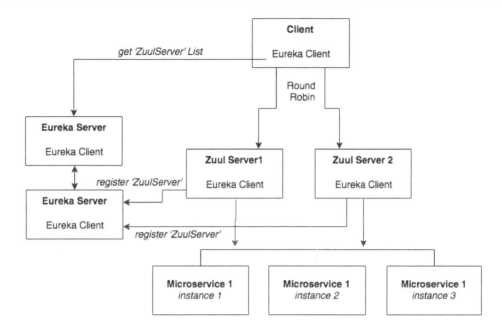

As shown in the preceding diagram, Zuul services register themselves with Eureka with a service ID, `search-apigateway` in our case. The **Eureka Client** will ask for the server list with the ID `search-apigateway`. The **Eureka Server** returns the list of servers based on the current Zuul topology. The **Eureka Client**, based on this list, picks up one of the servers, and initiates the call.

As we saw earlier, the client will use the service ID to resolve the Zuul instance. In the following case, `search-apigateway` is the Zuul instance ID registered with Eureka:

```
Flight[] flights = searchClient.postForObject(
    "http://search-apigateway/api/search/get",
    searchQuery, Flight[].class);
```

High availability when client is not a Eureka Client

In this case, the client is not capable of handling the load balancing by using the Eureka Server. As shown in the following diagram, the client sends the request to a load balancer, which, in turn, identifies the right Zuul service instance.

The Zuul instances, in this case, will be running behind a load balancer such as HAProxy, or a hardware load balancer like NetScaler:

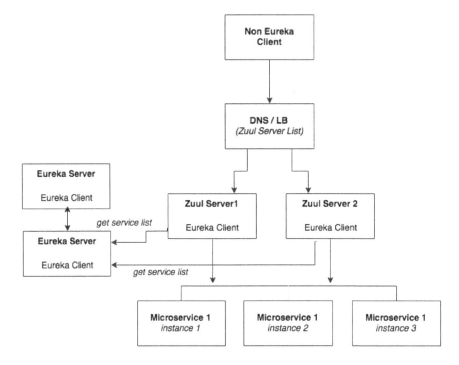

The microservices will still be load balanced by Zuul using the Eureka Server.

Completing Zuul for all other services

In order to complete this exercise, add an API Gateway for all our microservices. The following steps are required to achieve this task:

1. Create new property files per service and check in to Git repositories.
2. Change `application.properties` to `bootstrap.properties` and add the required configurations.
3. Add `@EnableZuulProxy` in the application.
4. `@EnableDiscoveryClient` in all applications.
5. Optionally, change the default generated package names and the filenames.

In the end, we will have the following API Gateway projects:

- `chapter7.fares-apigateway`
- `chapter7.search-apigateway`
- `chapter7.checkin-apigateway`
- `chapter7.book-apigateway`

Streams for reactive microservices

Spring Cloud Streams provides an abstraction over the messaging infrastructure. The underlying messaging implementation can be RabbitMQ, Redis, or Kafka. Spring Cloud Streams provides a declarative approach for sending and receiving messages.

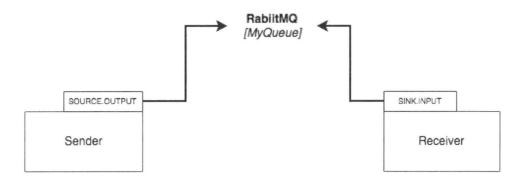

As shown in the preceding diagram, the Cloud Streams work with the concept of a Source and a Sink. The Source represents the sender perspective of the messaging, and Sink represents the receiver perspective of the messaging.

In the given example, the **Sender** defines a logical queue called `Source.OUTPUT` to which the **Sender** sends messages. The **Receiver** defines a logical queue called `Sink.INPUT` from which the **Receiver** retrieves messages. The physical binding of `OUTPUT` to `INPUT` is managed through the configuration. In this case, both link to the same physical queue, `MyQueue` on RabbitMQ. So, at one end, `Source.OUTPUT` will be pointed to `MyQueue`, and on the other end, `Sink.INPUT` will be pointed to the same `MyQueue`.

Spring Cloud offers the flexibility to use multiple messaging providers in one application, such as connecting an input stream from the Kafka to a Redis output stream without managing the complexities. Spring Cloud Streams is the basis for message-based integration. The Cloud Stream Modules sub-project is another Spring Cloud library that provides many endpoint implementations.

As the next step, rebuild the inter-microservice messaging communication with the Cloud Streams. As shown in the diagram, we will define a `SearchSink` connected to `InventoryQ` under the Search microservice. Booking will define a `BookingSource` for sending inventory change messages connected to `InventoryQ`. Similarly, Checkin defines a `CheckinSource` for sending check-in messages. Booking defines a sink `BookingSink` for receiving messages, both bound to the `CheckinQ` queue on Rabbit MQ.

The following diagram shows the example setup using stream based architecture:

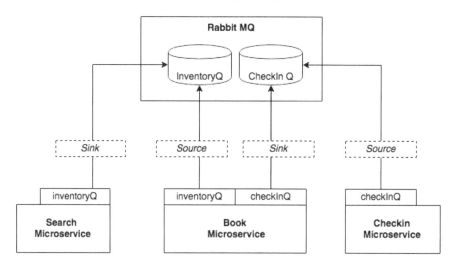

In this example, we will use RabbitMQ as the message broker. Perform the following steps:

1. Add the following Maven dependency to Booking, Search, and Check-in, as these are the three modules using messaging:

```xml
<dependency>
  <groupId>org.springframework.cloud</groupId>
  <artifactId>spring-cloud-starter-stream-rabbit</artifactId>
</dependency>
```

2. Add the following two properties to `booking-service.properties`. These properties bind the logical queues, `inventoryQ` to the physical `inventoryQ`, and the logical `checkinQ` to physical `checkinQ`.

```
spring.cloud.stream.bindings.inventoryQ.destination=inventoryQ
spring.cloud.stream.bindings.checkInQ.destination=checkInQ
```

3. Add the following property to `search-service.properties`. This property binds the logical queue `inventoryQ` to the physical `inventoryQ`:

```
spring.cloud.stream.bindings.inventoryQ.destination=inventoryQ
```

4. Add this next property to the `checkin-service.properties`. This property binds the logical queue `checkinQ` to the physical `checkinQ`:

```
spring.cloud.stream.bindings.checkInQ.destination=checkInQ
```

5. Commit all files to the Git repository.

6. The next step is to edit the code. The Search microservice consumes messages from the Booking microservice. In this case, Booking is the source and Search is the sink.

7. Add `@EnableBinding` to the `Sender` class of the Booking service. This enables the Cloud Stream to work on auto-configurations based on the message broker library available in the class path. In our case, it is RabbitMQ. The parameter, `BookingSource` defines the logical channels to be used for this configuration:

```
@EnableBinding(BookingSource.class)
public class Sender {
```

In this case, `BookingSource` defines a message channel called `inventoryQ`, which is physically bound to the Rabbit MQ `inventoryQ`, as configured in the configuration. `BookingSource` uses an annotation, `@Output`, to indicate that this is of the type output--a message that is outgoing from a module. This information will be used for the auto-configuration of the message channel:

```
interface BookingSource {
  public static String InventoryQ="inventoryQ";
  @Output("inventoryQ")
  public MessageChannel inventoryQ();
}
```

8. Instead of defining a custom class, we can also use the default `Source` class that comes with Spring Could Streams, if the service has only one source and sink:

```
public interface Source {
  @Output("output")
  MessageChannel output();
}
```

9. Define a message channel in the sender based on `BookingSource`. The following code will inject an output message channel with the name inventory, which is already configured in `BookingSource`:

```
@Output (BookingSource.InventoryQ)
@Autowired
private MessageChannel messageChannel;
```

10. Reimplement the send message method in the Booking sender:

```
public void send(Object message){
  messageChannel.send(
  MessageBuilder.withPayload(message).build());
}
```

11. Now add the following to the Search `Receiver` class the same way we did it for the Booking service:

```
@EnableBinding(SearchSink.class)
public class Receiver {
```

12. In this case, the `SearchSink` interface will look like the following. This will define the logical sink queue it is connected with. The message channel in this case is defined as `@Input` to indicate that this message channel is to accept messages:

```
interface SearchSink {
  public static String INVENTORYQ="inventoryQ";

  @Input("inventoryQ")
  public MessageChannel inventoryQ()
}
```

13. Amend the Search service to accept this message:

```
public void accept(Map<String,Object> fare){
    searchComponent.updateInventory(
    (String)fare.get("FLIGHT_NUMBER"),
    (String)fare.get("FLIGHT_DATE"),
    (int)fare.get("NEW_INVENTORY"));}
```

14. We will still need the RabbitMQ configurations that we have in our configuration files to connect to the message broker:

```
spring.rabbitmq.host=localhost
spring.rabbitmq.port=5672
spring.rabbitmq.username=guest
spring.rabbitmq.password=guest
server.port=8090
```

15. Run all the services, and run the website project. If everything is fine, the website project successfully executes the search, book, and check-in functions. The same can also be tested using the browser by pointing to `http://localhost:8001`.

Protecting microservices with Spring Cloud Security

In a monolithic web application, once the user is logged in, user-related information will be stored in an HTTP session. All subsequent requests will be validated against the HTTP session. This is simple to manage, since all requests will be routed through the same session, either through the session affinity or offloaded, shared session store.

In the case of microservices, it is harder to protect from unauthorised access, especially, when many services are deployed and accessed remotely. A typical or rather simple pattern for microservices is to implement perimeter security by using gateways as security watchdogs. Any request coming to the gateway will be challenged and validated. In this case, it is then important to ensure that all requests to downstream microservices are funneled through the API Gateway. Generally, the load balancer sitting in the front will be the only client that sends requests to the gateway. In this approach, downstream microservices processes all requests, assuming they are trusted, without authenticating. It means all microservice endpoints will be open for all.

However, this solution may not be acceptable for enterprise cyber security. One of the ways to eliminate this concern is to create network segregation and zones so that the services are exposed only for the gateways to access. In order to simplify this landscape, a common pattern is to set up consumer-driven gateways, which combine multiple microservices access instead of the one-to-one gateways we have used in our example.

Another way of accomplishing this is through token relay, as shown in this diagram:

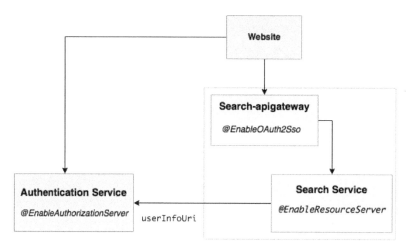

In this case, each microservice will also act as a resource server with a central server for authentication. The API Gateway will forward the request with the token to the downstream microservices for authentication.

Summarising the BrownField PSS architecture

The next diagram shows the overall architecture that we have created with the Config Server, Eureka, Feign, Zuul, and Cloud Streams.

The architecture also includes high availability of all the components. In this case, we are assuming that the client is using the Eureka Client libraries:

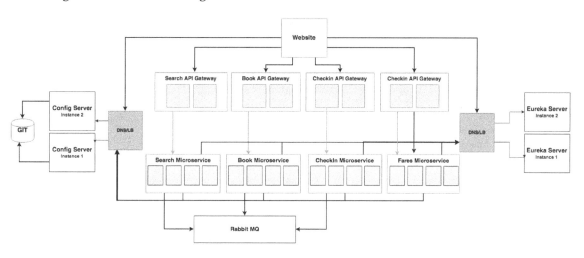

The summary of the projects and the port they are listening to is given in the following table:

Microservice	Projects	Port
Book Microservice	`chapter7.book`	8060-8064
Check In Microservice	`chapter7.checkin`	8070-8074
Fare Microservice	`chapter7.fares`	8080-8084
Search Microservice	`chapter7.search`	8090-8094
Website Client	`chapter7.website`	8001
Spring Cloud Config Server	`chapter7.configserver`	8888 / 8889
Spring Cloud Eureka Server	`chapter7.eurekaserver`	8761 / 8762
Book API Gateway	`chapter7.book-apigateway`	8095-8099
Check In API Gateway	`chapter7.checkin-apigateway`	8075-8079
Fares API Gateway	`chapter7.fares-apigateway`	8085-8089
Search API Gateway	`chapter7.search-apigateway`	8065-8069

Follow these steps to do a final run:

1. Run RabbitMQ.
2. Build all projects using `pom.xml` at the root level:

   ```
   mvn -Dmaven.test.skip=true clean install
   ```

3. Run the following projects from the respective folders. Note that you should wait for 40-50 seconds before starting the next service. This will ensure that the dependent services are registered and are available before we start a new service.

   ```
   java -jar target/config-server-1.0.jar
   java -jar target/eureka-server-1.0.jar
   java -jar target/fares-1.0.jar
   java -jar target/fares-1.0.jar
   java -jar target/search-1.0.jar
   java -jar target/checkin-1.0.jar
   java -jar target/book-1.0.jar
   java -jar target/fares-apigateway-1.0.jar
   java -jar target/search-apigateway-1.0.jar
   java -jar target/checkin-apigateway-1.0.jar
   java -jar target/book-apigateway-1.0.jar
   java -jar target/website-1.0.jar
   ```

4. Open the browser window, and point to `http://localhost:8001`. Follow the steps mentioned in `Chapter 6`, *Microservices Evolution – A Case Study*, Running and Testing Projects section.

Summary

In this chapter, we learned how to scale Twelve-Factor Spring Boot microservices using the Spring Cloud project. Our learnings were applied on the BrownField Airline's PSS microservice, which we developed in the previous chapter.

We explored the Spring Config Server for externalizing microservices configurations, and how to deploy the Config Server for high availability. We also learned Eureka for load balancing, dynamic service registration, and discovery. Implementation of an API Gateway was examined by implementing Zuul. Finally, we concluded with the reactive style integration of microservices using Spring Cloud Streams.

The BrownField Airline's PSS microservices are now deployable for Internet scale. Other Spring Cloud components such as Hyterix, Sleuth, and others will be covered in the next chapter.

8
Logging and Monitoring Microservices

One of the biggest challenges due to the very distributed nature of internet-scale microservices deployment is the logging and monitoring of individual microservices. It is difficult to trace end-to-end transactions by correlating logs emitted by different microservices. Like monolithic applications, there is no single pane of glass for monitoring microservices. This is important, especially when we deal with enterprise-scale microservices with a number of technologies, as discussed in the previous chapter.

This chapter will cover the necessity and importance of logging and monitoring in microservice deployments. This chapter will further examine the challenges and solutions to address logging and monitoring with a number of potential architectures and technologies.

By the end of this chapter, you will have learned about the following:

- The different options, tools, and technologies for log management
- The use of **Spring Cloud Sleuth** for tracing microservices
- The different tools for end-to-end monitoring of microservices
- The use of **Spring Cloud Hystrix** and **Turbine** for circuit monitoring
- The use of **Data Lake** for enabling business data analysis

Understanding log management challenges

Logs are nothing but streams of events coming from a running process. For traditional JEE applications, a number of frameworks and libraries are available for logging. **Java Logging (JUL)** is an option off-the-shelf from Java itself. Log4j, Logback, and SLF4J are some of the other popular logging frameworks available. These frameworks support both UDP as well as TCP protocols for logging. The applications send log entries to the console or the filesystem. File recycling techniques are generally employed to avoid logs filling up all disk space.

One of the best practices for log handling is to switch off most of the log entries in production due to the high cost of disk IOs. The disk IOs not only slow down the application, but can also severely impact the scalability. Writing logs into the disk also requires a high disk capacity. Running out of the disk space scenario can bring down the application. Logging frameworks provide options to control logging at runtime to restrict what has to be printed and what not. Most of these frameworks provide fine-grained controls over the logging controls. It also provides options for changing these configurations at runtime.

On the other hand, logs may contain important information and have a high value if properly analyzed. Therefore, restricting log entries essentially limits our ability to understand the application behavior.

When moved from traditional deployment to cloud deployment, applications are no longer locked to a particular, predefined machine. Virtual machines and containers are not hardwired with an application. The machines used for deployment can change from time to time. Moreover, containers such as Docker are ephemeral. This essentially means one cannot rely on the persistent state of the disk. Logs written to the disk will be lost once the container is stopped and restarted. Therefore, we cannot rely on the local machine's disk to write log files.

As we discussed in `Chapter 2`, *Related Architecture Styles and Use Cases*, one of the principles of the Twelve-Factor application is to avoid routing or storing log files by the application itself. In the context of microservices, they will be running on isolated physical or virtual machines, resulting in fragmented log files. In this case, it would be almost impossible to trace end-to-end transactions that span across multiple microservices.

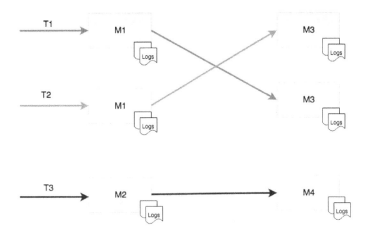

As shown in the preceding diagram, each microservice emits logs to a local file system. In this case, transaction **T1** calls **M1** followed by **M3**. Since **M1** and **M3** runs on different physical machines, both of them writes respective logs to different log files. This makes it harder to correlate and understand the end-to-end transactions flow. Also, since two instances of **M1** and **M3** are running on two different machines, log aggregation at service level is hard to achieve.

Centralized logging solution

In order to address the earlier stated challenges, traditional logging solutions require serious rethinking. The new logging solution, in addition to addressing the preceding challenges, is also expected to support the capabilities summarized here:

- Ability to collect all log messages and run analytics on top of the log messages
- Ability to correlate and track transactions end-to-end
- Ability to keep log information for longer time periods for trending and forecasting
- Ability to eliminate dependency on the local disk system
- Ability to aggregate log information coming from multiple sources, such as network devices, operating system, microservices, and so on

The solution to these problems is to centrally store and analyze all log messages, irrespective of the source of the log. The fundamental principle employed in the new logging solution is to detach log storage and processes from the service execution environments. Big data solutions are better suited for storing and processing a large amount of log messages more effectively than storing and processing them in the microservice execution environments.

In the centralized logging solution, log messages will be shipped from the execution environment to a central big data store. Log analysis and processing will be handled using big data solutions.

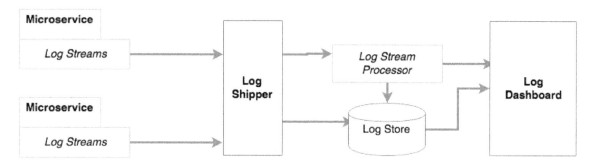

As shown in the preceding logical diagram, there are a number of components in the centralized logging solution. These are explained as follows:

- **Log streams**: These are streams of log messages coming out of the source systems. The source system can be microservices, other applications, or even network devices. In typical Java-based systems, these are equivalent to streaming the Log4j log messages.
- **Log shippers**: These are responsible for collecting the log messages coming from different sources or endpoints. The log shippers then send these messages to another set of endpoints, such as writing to a database, pushing to a dashboard, or sending it to a stream processing endpoint for further real-time processing.
- **Log store**: This is the place where all log messages will be stored for real-time analysis, trending, and so on. Typically, the log store will be a NoSQL database, such as HDFS, capable of handling large data volumes.
- **Log stream processor**: This is capable of analyzing real-time log events for quick decision making. Stream processors take actions such as sending information to a dashboard, sending alerts, and so on. In the case of self-healing systems, stream processors can even take action to correct the problems.

- **Log dashboard**: This dashboard is a single pane of glass for displaying log analysis results, such as graphs and charts. These dashboards are meant for operational and management staff.

The benefits of this centralized approach is that there are no local IOs or blocking disk writes. It is also not using the local machine's disk space. This architecture is fundamentally similar to Lambda architecture for big data processing.

 Follow this link to read more on Lambda architecture:
`http://lambda-architecture.net`

It is important to have each log message, a context, message and a correlation ID. The context typically will have the timestamp, IP address, user information, process details (such as service, class, functions), log type, classification, and so on. The message will be plain and simple free text information. The correlation ID will be used to establish the link between service calls so that calls spanning across microservices can be traced.

Selection of logging solutions

There are a number of options available for implementing a centralized logging solution. These solutions use different approaches, architectures, and technologies. It is important to understand the capabilities required and select the right solution that meets the needs.

Cloud services

There are a number of cloud logging services available as SaaS solution. **Loggly** is one of the most popular cloud-based logging service. The Spring Boot microservices can use the Loggly's Log4j and Logback appenders to directly stream log messages into the Loggly service.

If the application or service is deployed in AWS, the AWS **CloudTrail** can be integrated with Loggly for log analysis.

Papertrial, **Logsene**, **Sumo Logic**, **Google Cloud Logging**, and **Logentries** are examples of other cloud-based logging solutions. Some of the tools in the **Security Operations Center** (**SOC**) are also qualified for centralized log management.

The cloud logging services take away the overhead of managing complex infrastructures and large storage solutions by providing them as simple to integrate services. However, latency is one of the key factors to be considered when selecting cloud logging as a service.

Off-the-shelf solutions

There are many purpose-built tools to provide end-to-end log management capabilities that are installable locally on an on-premise data center or in the cloud.

Graylog is one of the popular open source log management solutions. It uses Elasticsearch for log storage and MongoDB as a metadata store. It also uses GELF libraries for Log4j log streaming.

Splunk is one of the popular commercial tools available for log management and analysis. It uses the log file shipping approach compared to log streaming used by other solutions for collecting logs.

Best of the breed integration

The last approach is to pick and choose the best of the breed components and build a custom logging solution.

Log shippers

There are log shippers that can be combined with other tools to build an end-to-end log management solution. The capabilities differ between different log shipping tools.

Logstash is a powerful data pipeline tool that can be used for collecting and shipping log files. It acts as a broker that provides a mechanism to accept streaming data from different sources and sinks them to different destinations. Log4j and Logback appenders can also be used to send log messages directly from Spring Boot microservices to Logstash. The other end of the Logstash will be connected to Elasticsearch, HDFS, or any other databases.

Fluentd is another tool that is very similar to Logstash. Logspout is another similar tool to Logstash, but it is more appropriate in a Docker container-based environment.

Log stream processors

Stream processing technologies are optionally used for processing log streams on the fly. For example, if a 404 error is continuously received as a response to a particular service call, it means there is something wrong with the service. Such situations have to be handled as soon as possible. Stream processors are pretty handy in such cases, as they are capable of reacting to certain streams of events compared to traditional reactive analysis.

A typical architecture used for stream processing is a combination of **Flume** and **Kafka** together, with either **Storm** or **Spark Streaming**. Log4j has Flume appenders that are useful for collecting log messages. These messages will be pushed into distributed Kafka message queues. The stream processors collect data from Kafka and process it on the fly before sending it to Elasticsearch and other log stores.

Spring Cloud Stream, **Spring Cloud Stream modules**, and **Spring Cloud Data Flow** can also be used to build the log stream processing.

Log storage

Real-time log messages are typically stored in Elasticsearch, which allows clients to query based on the text-based indexes. Apart from Elasticsearch, HDFS is also commonly used to store archived log messages. MongoDB or Cassandra are used to store summary data, such as monthly aggregated transaction counts. Offline log processing can be done using Hadoop map reduce programs.

Dashboards

The last piece required in the central logging solution is a dashboard. The most commonly used dashboard for log analysis is **Kibana** on top of an Elasticsearch data store. **Graphite** and **Grafana** are also used to display log analysis reports.

Custom logging implementation

The tools mentioned in the preceding section can be leveraged to build a custom end-to-end logging solution. The most commonly used architecture for custom log management is a combination of **Logstash**, **Elasticsearch**, and **Kibana**, also known as the **ELK** stack.

The full source code of this chapter is available under the `chapter8` projects in the code files under `https://github.com/rajeshrv/Spring5M icroservice`. Copy `chapter7.configserver`, `chapter7.eurekaserver`, `chapter7.search`, `chapter7.search-apigateway`, and `chapter7.website` into a new STS workspace and rename `chapter8.*`.

Note: Even though Spring Cloud Dalston SR1 officially supports Spring Boot 1.5.2.RELEASE, there are a few issues around Hystrix. In order to run the Hystrix examples, it is advised to upgrade the Spring Boot version to 1.5.4.RELEASE.

The following diagram shows the log monitoring flow:

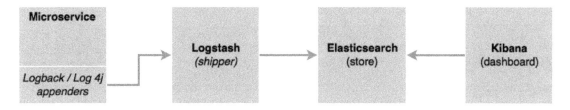

In this section, a simple implementation of a custom logging solution using the ELK stack will be examined.

Follow these steps to implement the ELK stack for logging:

1. Download and install Elasticsearch, Kibana, and Logstash from `https://www.ela stic.co`.

2. Update the Search microservice (`chapter8.search`). Review and ensure that there are some log statements in `Application.java` of the Search microservice. The log statements are nothing special but simple log statements using slf4j as shown in the following code snippet:

```
import org.slf4j.Logger;
import org.slf4j.LoggerFactory;
//other code goes here
private static final Logger logger = LoggerFactory
  .getLogger(SearchRestController.class);

//other code goes here

logger.info("Looking to load flights...");
```

```
for (Flight flight : flightRepository
  .findByOriginAndDestinationAndFlightDate
  ("NYC", "SFO", "22-JAN-18")) {
    logger.info(flight.toString());
}
```

3. Add the Logstash dependency to integrate `logback` to `logstash` in the Search service's `pom.xml`:

```
<dependency>
  <groupId>net.logstash.logback</groupId>
  <artifactId>logstash-logback-encoder</artifactId>
  <version>4.6</version>
</dependency>
```

4. Override the default `logback` configuration. This can be done by adding a new `logback.xml` under `src/main/resources`. A sample log configuration is shown as follows:

```
<?xml version="1.0" encoding="UTF-8"?>
<configuration>
  <include resource="org/springframework/boot/logging
    /logback/defaults.xml"/>
  <include resource="org/springframework/boot/logging
    /logback/console-appender.xml" />
  <appender name="stash"
    class="net.logstash.logback.appender
    .LogstashTcpSocketAppender">
    <destination>localhost:4560</destination>
    <!-- encoder is required -->
    <encoder class="net.logstash.logback.encoder
    .LogstashEncoder" />
  </appender>
  <root level="INFO">
   <appender-ref ref="CONSOLE" />
   <appender-ref ref="stash" />
  </root>
</configuration>
```

The preceding configuration overrides the default `logback` configuration by adding a new TCP socket appender, which streams all log messages to a Logstash service that is listening on port `4560`. It is important to add an encoder, as mentioned in the preceding configuration.

5. Create a configuration, as shown next, and store it in a `logstash.conf` file. The location of this file is irrelevant, since it will be passed as an argument when starting Logstash. This configuration will take input from the socket, listening on port `4560` and send the output to Elasticsearch running on port `9200`. The `stdout` is optional and set for debugging:

```
input {
  tcp {
    port => 4560
    host => localhost
  }
}
output {
  elasticsearch { hosts => ["localhost:9200"] }
  stdout { codec => rubydebug }
}
```

6. Run Logstash, Elasticsearch, and Kibana from their respective installation folders:

```
./bin/elasticsearch
./bin/kibana
./bin/logstash -f logstash.conf
```

7. Run the Search microservice. This will invoke the unit test cases and result in printing the log statements mentioned earlier. Ensure that RabbitMQ, Config Server, and Eureka servers are running.

8. Go to a browser and access Kibana:

```
http://localhost:5601
```

Go to settings and configure an index pattern, as shown in the following screenshot:

Configure an index pattern

In order to use Kibana you must configure at least one index pattern. Index patterns are used to identify the Elasticsearch index to run search and analytics against. They are also used to configure fields.

☑ **Index contains time-based events**
☐ **Use event times to create index names**

Index name or pattern

Patterns allow you to define dynamic index names using * as a wildcard. Example: logstash-*

logstash-*

Time-field name ❶ refresh fields

@timestamp

Create

9. Go to discover menu to see the logs. If everything is successful, we will see the following Kibana screenshot. Note that the log messages are displayed in the Kibana screen.

Kibana provides out-of-the-box features to build summary charts and graphs using log messages.

The Kibana UI will look like the following screenshot:

Distributed tracing with Spring Cloud Sleuth

The previous section addressed the microservices distributed and fragmented the logging issue by centralizing the log data. With the central logging solution, we have all the logs in central storage. However, still, it is almost impossible to trace end-to-end transactions. In order to do end-to-end tracking, transactions spanning across microservices need to have a correlation ID.

Twitter's **Zipkin**, Cloudera's **HTrace**, and Google's **Dapper** are examples of distributed tracing systems. The Spring Cloud provides a wrapper component on top of these using the Spring Cloud Sleuth library.

Distributed tracing works with the concepts of **Span** and **Trace**. Span is a unit of work, such as **calling a service**, identified by a 64-bit span ID. A set of spans form a tree-like structure called trace. Using the trace ID, a call can be tracked end-to-end as shown in the following diagram:

As shown in the preceding diagram, **Microservice 1** calls **2**, and **2** calls **3**. In this case, as shown in the diagram, the same **Trace-id** will be passed across all microservices, which can be used to track transactions end-to-end.

In order to demonstrate this, we will use the Search API Gateway and Search microservices. A new endpoint has to be added in the Search API Gateway (`chapter8.search-apigateway`), which internally calls the Search service to return data. Without the trace ID, it is almost impossible to trace or link calls coming from a website to `search-apigateway` to the Search microservice. In this case, it only involves two to three services; whereas, in a complex environment, there can be many interdependent services.

Follow these steps to create an example using Sleuth:

1. Update Search and Search API Gateway. Before that, the Sleuth dependency has to be added to the respective pom files:

    ```
    <dependency>
      <groupId>org.springframework.cloud</groupId>
      <artifactId>spring-cloud-starter-sleuth</artifactId>
    </dependency>
    ```

2. Add the Logstash dependency to the Search service as well as the `logback` configuration, as shown in the previous example.

3. The next step is to add the service name `property` in the `logback` configuration of the respective microservices:

```
<property name="spring.application.name"
  value="search-service"/>
<property name="spring.application.name"
  value="search-apigateway"/>
```

4. Add a new endpoint to the Search API Gateway, which will call the Search service, as follows. This is to demonstrate the propagation of the trace ID across multiple microservices. This new method in the gateway returns the operating hub of the airport by calling the search service. Note--the Rest Template (with `@Loadbalanced`) and Logger details also need to be added to the `SearchAPIGateway.java` class:

```
@RequestMapping("/hubongw")
String getHub(HttpServletRequest req){
  logger.info("Search Request in API gateway
   for getting Hub, forwarding to search-service ");
  String hub = restTemplate.getForObject("http://search-
    service/search/hub", String.class);
  logger.info("Response for hub received,  Hub "+ hub);
  return hub;
}
```

5. Add another endpoint in the Search service, as follows:

```
@RequestMapping("/hub")
String getHub(){
  logger.info("Searching for Hub, received from
    search-apigateway ");
  return "SFO";
}
```

6. Once added, run both services. Hit the gateway's new hub on the gateway (`/hubongw`) endpoint using a browser. Copy and paste the following link:

```
http://localhost:8095/hubongw
```

As mentioned earlier, the Search API Gateway service is running on `8095` and the Search service is running on `8090`.

7. Notice the console logs to see the trace ID and span IDs printed. The following print is from the Search API Gateway:

```
2017-03-31 22:30:17.780  INFO [search-
apigateway,9f698f7ebabe6b83,9f698f7ebabe6b83,false]
47158 --- [nio-8095-exec-1]
c.b.p.s.a.SearchAPIGatewayController: Response for hub
received,  Hub SFO
```

The following log is coming from the Search service:

```
2017-03-31 22:30:17.741 INFO [search-
service,9f698f7ebabe6b83,3a63748ac46b5a9d,false]
47106---[nio-8090-exec-
1]c.b.p.s.controller.SearchRestController  : Searching
for Hub, received from search-apigateway
```

Note that the trace IDs are the same in both cases.

8. Open the Kibana console and search for the trace ID using the trace ID printed in the console. In this case, it is `9f698f7ebabe6b83`. As shown in the following screenshot, with a trace ID, one can trace service calls that span across multiple services:

Monitoring microservices

Microservices are truly distributed systems with fluid deployment topology. Without a sophisticated monitoring in place, the operations team may run into trouble managing large-scale microservices. Traditional monolithic application deployments are limited to a number of known services, instances, machines, and so on. This is easier to manage as compared to a large number of microservices instances potentially running across different machines. To add more complications, these services dynamically change its topologies. The centralized logging capability only addresses part of the issue. It is important for the operations team to understand the runtime deployment topology, and also the behavior of the systems. This demands more than centralized logging can offer.

In general, application monitoring is more of a collection of metrics and aggregation and validating them against certain baseline values. If there is a service-level breach, then monitoring tools generate alerts and send to administrators. With hundreds and thousands of interconnected microservices, traditional monitoring does not really offer true value. A one-size-fits-all approach to monitoring, or monitoring everything with a single pane of glass is not easy to achieve in large-scale microservices.

One of the main objectives of microservice monitoring is to understand the behaviors of the system from the user experience point of view. This will ensure that the end-to-end behavior is consistent and in line with what is expected by users.

Monitoring challenges

Similar to the fragmented logging issue, the key challenge in monitoring microservices is that there are many moving parts in a microservice ecosystem.

Typical issues are summarized as follows:

- The statistics and metrics are fragmented across many services, instances, and machines.
- Heterogeneous technologies may be used to implement microservices, making things even more complex. A single monitoring tool may not give all required monitoring options.
- Microservices deployment topologies are dynamic, making it impossible to preconfigure servers, instances, and monitoring parameters.

Many of the traditional monitoring tools are good for monitoring monolithic applications, but fall short in monitoring large-scale distributed and interlinked microservice systems. Many of the traditional monitoring systems are agent-based, preinstall agents on the target machines or application instances. This poses the following two challenges:

- If the agents require deep integration with the services or operating systems, then this will be hard to manage in a dynamic environment
- If these tools impose overheads when monitoring or instrumenting the application, they can hinder performance issues

Many traditional tools need baseline metrics. Such systems work with preset rules, such as if the CPU utilization goes above 60% and remains at that level for two minutes, then send an alert to the administrator. It is extremely hard to preconfigure these values in large internet-scale deployments.

New generation monitoring applications self learn the application behavior and set automatic threshold values. This frees up the administrators from performing this mundane task. Automated baselines are sometimes more accurate than human forecasts.

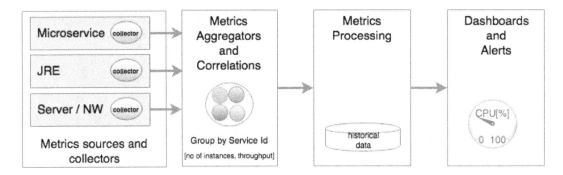

As shown in the preceding diagram, key areas of microservices monitoring are as follows:

- **Metrics sources and data collectors**: The metrics collection at the source will be done by either the server pushing metrics information to a central collector or by embedding lightweight agents to collect information. The data collectors collect monitoring metrics from different sources, such as network, physical machines, containers, software components, application, and so on. The challenge is to collect this data using auto-discovery mechanisms instead of static configurations.

  This will be done by either running agents on the source machines, streaming data from the sources, or polling at regular intervals.

- **Aggregation and correlation of metrics**: The aggregation capability is required to aggregate metrics collected from different sources, such as user transaction, service, infrastructure, network, and so on. Aggregation can be challenging, as it requires some level of understanding of the applications behaviors, such as service dependencies, service grouping, and so on. In many cases, these are automatically formulated based on the metadata provided by the sources.

  Generally, this will be done by an intermediary that accepts the metrics.

- **Processing metrics and actionable insights**: Once the data is aggregated, then the next step is to take measurements. Measurements are typically done by using set thresholds. In the new generation monitoring systems, these thresholds are automatically discovered. The monitoring tools then analyze the data and provide actionable insights.

  These tools may use big data and stream analytics solutions.

- **Alerting, actions and dashboards**: As soon as issues are detected, they have to be notified to the relevant people or systems. Unlike traditional systems, the microservices monitoring systems should be capable of taking actions on a real-time basis. Proactive monitoring is essential to achieving self-healing. Dashboards are used to display SLAs, KPIs, and so on.

  Dashboards and alerting tools are capable of handling these requirements.

Microservice monitoring is typically done with three approaches. A combination of them is really required for effective monitoring:

- **Application Performance Monitoring** (**APM**) (sometimes referred to as **Digital Performance Monitoring** or **DPM**) is is more of a traditional approach of system metrics collection, processing, alerting, and rendering dashboards. These are more from the system's point of view. Application topology discovery and visualization are new capabilities implemented by many of the APM tools. The capabilities vary between different APM providers.
- **Synthetic monitoring** is is a technique that is used to monitor system behavior using end-to-end transactions with a number of test scenarios in a production or production-like environment. Data will be collected to validate the system behavior and potential hotspots. Synthetic monitoring helps us understand system dependencies as well.

- **Real user monitoring** (**RUM**) or user experience monitoring is typically a browser-based software that records real user statistics, such as response times, availability, and service levels. With microservices, with a more frequent release cycle and dynamic topology, users experience that monitoring is more important.

Monitoring tools

There are many tools available for monitoring microservices. There are also overlaps between many of these tools. Selection of monitoring tools really depends upon the ecosystem that needs to be monitored. In most cases, more than one tool is required to monitor the overall microservice ecosystem.

The objective of this section is to familiarize a number of common microservices-friendly monitoring tools:

- **AppDynamics**, **Dynatrace** and **New Relic** are top commercial vendors in the APM space, as per Gartner magic quadrant 2015. These tools are microservice-friendly and support microservice monitoring effectively in a single console. **Ruxit**, **Datadog**, and **Dataloop** are other commercial offerings that are purpose-built for distributed systems that are essentially microservices-friendly. Multiple monitoring tools can feed data to Datadog using plugins.
- Cloud vendors come with their own monitoring tools, but, in many cases, these monitoring tools alone may not be sufficient for large-scale microservices monitoring. For instance, AWS uses **CloudWatch** and Google Cloud Platform uses **Cloud Monitoring** to collect information from various sources.
- Some of the data collecting libraries, such as **Zabbix**, **statd**, **collectd**, **jmxtrans**, and so on, operate at a lower level in collecting runtime statistics, metrics, gauges, and counters. Typically, this information will be fed into data collectors and processors, such as **Riemann**, **Datadog**, and **Librato**, or dashboards, such as **Graphite**.
- Spring Boot **Actuator** is one of the good vehicles for collecting microservices metrics, gauges, and counters, as we saw in `Chapter 3`, *Building Microservices with Spring Boot*. Netflix's **Servo** is a metric collector similar to Actuator. **QBit** and **Dropwizard** metrics also fall in the same category of metric collectors. All these metrics collectors need an aggregator and dashboard to facilitate full-sized monitoring.

- Monitoring through logging is popular, but a less effective approach in microservices monitoring. In this approach, as discussed in the previous section, log messages will be shipped from various sources, such as microservices, containers, networks, and so on, to a central location. Then, use the log files to trace transactions, identify hotspots, and so on. **Loggly**, **ELK**, **Splunk**, and **Trace** are candidates in this space.

- **Sensu** is a popular choice for microservice monitoring from the open source community. **Weave scope** is another tool, primarily targeting containerized deployments. SimianViz (formerly **Spigo)** is one of the purpose-built microservices, monitoring the system closely aligned with the Netflix stack. Cronitor is also another useful tool.

- **Pingdom**, **New Relic synthetic**, **Runscope**, **Catchpoint**, and so on, provide options for synthetic transaction monitoring and user experience monitoring on live systems.

- **Circonus** is classified more towards DevOps monitoring tools, but can also do microservices monitoring. **Nagios** is a popular open source monitoring tool, but it falls more into the traditional monitoring systems.

- **Prometheus** provides a time series database and visualization GUI useful for building custom monitoring tools.

Monitoring microservice dependency

When there are a large number of microservices with dependencies, it is important to have a monitoring tool that can show the dependencies between microservices. It is not a scalable approach to statically configure and manage these dependencies. There are many tools that are useful for monitoring microservice dependencies.

Mentoring tools, such as **AppDynamics**, **Dynatrace**, and **New Relic**, can draw dependencies between microservices. End-to-end transaction monitoring can also trace transaction dependencies. Other monitoring tools such as Spigo are also useful for microservices dependency management.

CMDB tools, such as **Device42**, or purpose-built tools, such as **Accordance**, are useful for managing dependency of microservices. **Vertias Risk Advisor** (**VRA**) is also useful for infrastructure discovery.

A custom implementation with a Graph database such as Neo4j can also be used. In this case, microservices has to be preconfigured with its direct and indirect dependencies. At the startup of the service, it publishes and cross-checks its dependencies with this Neo4j database.

Spring Cloud Hystrix for fault-tolerant microservices

This section will explore the Spring Cloud Hystrix as a library for fault-tolerant and latency-tolerant microservice implementation. The Hystrix is based on fail-fast and rapid recovery principles. If there is an issue with a service, Hystrix helps isolate the issue. It helps to fail-fast quickly by falling back to another preconfigured fallback service. It is another battle-tested library from Netflix and is based on the **Circuit Breaker** pattern.

 Read more about the Circuit Breaker pattern at `https://msdn.microsoft` `.com/en-us/library/dn589784.aspx`.

In this section, we will build a circuit breaker with the Spring Cloud Hystrix. Follow these steps to change the Search API Gateway service to integrate with the Hystrix. Update the Search API Gateway service.

Add the Hystrix dependency to the service, as follows:

```
<dependency>
  <groupId>org.springframework.cloud</groupId>
  <artifactId>spring-cloud-starter-hystrix</artifactId>
</dependency>
```

If developing from scratch, select the following libraries:

▶ Cloud AWS

▼ Cloud Circuit Breaker

- ☑ Hystrix   ☑ Hystrix Dashboard   ☐ Turbine   ☐ Turbine AMQP
- ☐ Turbine Stream

▶ Cloud Cluster

▶ Cloud Config

▶ Cloud Core

▶ Cloud Data Flow

▶ Cloud Discovery

▶ Cloud Messaging

▶ Cloud Routing

▶ Cloud Tracing

▶ Core

▶ Data

▶ Database

▶ I/O

▼ Ops

- ☑ Actuator   ☐ Actuator Docs   ☐ Remote Shell

▶ Social

▶ Template Engines

▼ Web

- ☑ Web   ☐ Websocket   ☐ WS   ☐ Jersey (JAX-RS)
- ☐ Ratpack   ☐ Vaadin   ☐ Rest Repositories   ☐ HATEOAS
- ☐ Rest Repositories HAL Browser   ☐ Mobile   ☐ REST Docs

In the Spring Boot Application class (`SearchAPIGateway`), add `@EnableCircuitBreaker`. This command will tell Spring Cloud Hystrix to enable circuit breaker for this application. It also exposes the `/hystrix.stream` endpoint for metrics collection.

Add a component class to the Search API Gateway service with a method; in this case; `getHub` annotated with `@HystrixCommand`. This tells Spring that this method is prone to failure. The Spring Cloud libraries wrap these methods to handle fault-tolerance and latency-tolerance by enabling circuit breaker. The `HystrixCommand` typically follows with a `fallbackMethod`. In case of failure, Hystrix automatically enables the `fallbackMethod` mentioned and diverts the traffic to the `fallbackMethod`. As shown in the following code, in this case, `getHub` will fall back to `getDefaultHub`:

```
@Component
class SearchAPIGatewayComponent {
```

```
@LoadBalanced
@Autowired
RestTemplate restTemplate;
@HystrixCommand(fallbackMethod = "getDefaultHub")
public String getHub(){
  String hub = restTemplate
    .getForObject("http://search-service/search/hub",
    String.class);
  return hub;
}

public String getDefaultHub(){
  return "Possibily SFO";
}
}
```

The getHub method of SearchAPIGatewayController calls the getHub method of SearchAPIGatewayComponent:

```
@RequestMapping("/hubongw")
String getHub(){
  logger.info("Search Request in API gateway for getting Hub,
    forwarding to search-service ");
  return component.getHub();
}
```

The last part of this exercise is to build a Hystrix dashboard. For this, build another Spring Boot application. Include **Hystrix**, **Hystrix Dashboard**, and **Actuator** when building this application.

In the Spring Boot Application class, add the @EnableHystrixDashboard annotation.

Start the Search service, Search API Gateway, and Hystrix Dashboard applications. Point the browser to the Hystrix dashboard application's URL. In this example, the Hystrix dashboard is started on port 9999.

Open the following URL:
http://localhost:9999/hystrix

A screen as shown in the following screenshot will be displayed. In the **Hystrix Dashboard**, enter the URL of the service to be monitored.

In this case, the Search API Gateway is running on the `8095` port. Hence the `hystrix.stream` URL will be `http://localhost:8095/hytrix.stream`:

Hystrix Dashboard

http://localhost:8095/hystrix.stream

Cluster via Turbine (default cluster): http://turbine-hostname:port/turbine.stream
Cluster via Turbine (custom cluster): http://turbine-hostname:port/turbine.stream?cluster=[clusterName]
Single Hystrix App: http://hystrix-app:port/hystrix.stream

Delay: ms   Title: SearchAPIGateway

Monitor Stream

The Hystrix dashboard will be displayed as follows:

Hystrix Stream: SearchAPIGateway

Circuit   Sort: Error then Volume | Alphabetical | Volume | Error | Mean | Median | 90 | 99 | 99.5

Success | Short-Circuited | Timeout | Rejected | Failure | Error %

getHub

	6	0	0.0 %
	0	0	
		0	

Host: **0.6/s**
Cluster: **0.6/s**
Circuit Closed

Hosts	1	90th	16ms
Median	12ms	99th	19ms
Mean	12ms	99.5th	19ms

Thread Pools   Sort: Alphabetical | Volume |

SearchAPIGatewayComponent

Host: **0.6/s**
Cluster: **0.6/s**

Active	0	Max Active	1
Queued	0	Executions	6
Pool Size	10	Queue Size	5

Note that at least one transaction has to be executed to see the display. This can be done by hitting `http://localhost:8095/hubongw`.

Create a failure scenario by shutting down the Search service. Note that the fallback method will be called when hitting the following URL:
`http://localhost:8095/hubongw`

If there are continuous failures, then the circuit status will be changed to open. This can be done by hitting the preceding link a number of times. In the open state, the original service will no longer be checked. The Hystrix dashboard will show the status of the circuit as **Open**, as shown in the following screenshot. Once the circuit is opened, periodically, the system will check for the original service status for recovery. When the original service is back, the circuit breaker falls back to the original service and the status will be set to **Closed**:

Hystrix Stream: SearchAPIGateway

Circuit

Sort: Error then Volume | Alphabetical | Volume | Error | Mean | Median | 90 | 99 | 99.5

Success | Short-Circuited | Timeout | Rejected | Failure | Error %

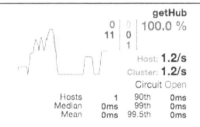

getHub

0	0	100.0 %
11	0	
	1	

Host: **1.2/s**
Cluster: **1.2/s**
Circuit Open

Hosts	1	90th	0ms
Median	0ms	99th	0ms
Mean	0ms	99.5th	0ms

Thread Pools

Sort: Alphabetical | Volume |

SearchAPIGatewayComponent

Host: **0.1/s**
Cluster: **0.1/s**

Active	0	Max Active	1
Queued	0	Executions	1
Pool Size	10	Queue Size	5

The following Hystrix Wiki URL shows the meaning of each of these parameters:
`https://github.com/Netflix/Hystrix/wiki/Dashboard`

Aggregate Hystrix streams with Turbine

In the previous example, the /hystrix.stream endpoint of our microservice was given in the Hystrix dashboard. Hystrix dashboard can only monitor one microservice at a time. If there are many microservices, then the Hystrix dashboard pointing to the service has to be changed every time when switching the microservices to the monitor. Looking into one instance at a time is tedious, especially when there are many instances of a microservice or multiple microservices.

We have to have a mechanism to aggregate data coming from multiple /hystrix.stream instances, and consolidate them into a single dashboard view. Turbine does exactly the same. It is another server that collects the Hystrix streams from multiple instances and consolidates them into one /turbine.stream. Now the Hystrix dashboard can point to /turbine.stream to get the consolidated information. Take a look at the following diagram:

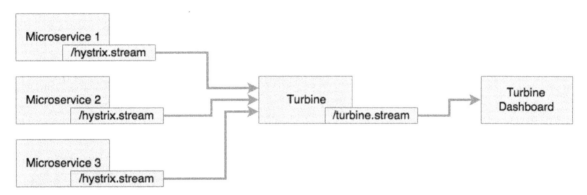

Turbine works only with different host names. Each instance has to run on separate hosts. If testing multiple services locally on the same host, update the host file (/etc/hosts) to simulate multiple hosts. Once done, the bootstrap.properties have to be configured as follows:
eureka.instance.hostname: localdomain2.

The following example showcases how to use Turbine to monitor circuit breakers across multiple instances and services. We will use the Search service and Search API Gateway in this example. Turbine internally uses Eureka to resolve service IDs that are configured for monitoring.

Follow these steps to build and execute this example.

1. The Turbine server can be created as just another Spring Boot application using Spring Boot Starter. Select **Turbine** to include the Turbine libraries.

2. Once the application is created, add `@EnableTurbine` to the main Spring Boot Application class. In this example, both the Turbine and the Hystrix dashboard are configured to run on the same Spring Boot Application. This is possible by adding the following annotations to the newly created Turbine application:

```
@EnableTurbine
@EnableHystrixDashboard
@SpringBootApplication
public class TurbineServerApplication {
```

3. Add the following configuration to the `yaml` or property file to point to instances that we are interested in `monitor.spring`:

```
application:
  name : turbineserver
turbine:
  clusterNameExpression: new String('default')
  appConfig : search-service,search-apigateway
  server:
    port: 9090
    eureka:
  client:
    serviceUrl:
      defaultZone: http://localhost:8761/eureka/
```

4. The preceding configuration instructs the Turbine server to look up the Eureka server to resolve the `search-service` and `search-apigateway` services. The `search-service` and `search-apigateways` services are the service IDs used to register services with Eureka. Turbine will use these names to resolve the actual service host and port by checking with the Eureka server. It then uses this information to read `/hystrix.stream` from each of these instances. Turbine then reads all individual Hystrix streams, aggregates all of them together, and exposes them under the Turbine server's `/turbine.stream` URL.

   The cluster name expression points to the default cluster, since there is no explicit cluster configurations done in this example. If clusters are manually configured, then the following configuration has to be used:

```
turbine:
  aggregator:
    clusterConfig: [comma separated clusternames]
```

5. Change the Search service and `SearchComponent` to add another circuit breaker:

```
@HystrixCommand(fallbackMethod = "searchFallback")
public List<Flight> search(SearchQuery query){
```

6. Also add `@EnableCircuitBreaker` to the main class in the Search service.
   In this example, we will run two instances of `search-apigateway`--One on
   `localdomain1:8095` and another one on `localdomain2:8096`. We will also
   run one instance of `search-service` on `localdomain1:8090`.

7. Run the microservices with command-line overrides to manage different host
   addresses, as follows:

```
java -jar -Dserver.port=
    8096 -Deureka.instance.hostname=localdomain2 -
    Dserver.address=localdomain2
    target/search-apigateway-1.0.jar

java -jar -Dserver.port=
    8095 -Deureka.instance.hostname=localdomain1 -
    Dserver.address=localdomain1
    target/search-apigateway-1.0.jar

java -jar -Dserver.port=
    8090 -Deureka.instance.hostname=localdomain1 -
    Dserver.address=localdomain1
    target/search-1.0.jar
```

8. Open the Hystrix dashboard by pointing the browser to the following URL:
   `http://localhost:9090/hystrix`

9. Instead of giving `/hystrix.stream`, this time, we will point to
   `/turbine.stream`. In this example, the Turbine stream is running on `9090`.
   Hence, the URL to be given in the Hystrix dashboard is as follows:
   `http://localhost:9090/turbine.stream`

10. Fire a few transactions by opening the browser window and hitting
    `http://localhost:8095/hubongw` and `http://localhost:8096/hubongw`.

11. Once this is done, the dashboard page will show the `getHub` service.

12. Run `chapter8.website`. Execute the search transaction using the following
    website:
    `http://localhost:8001`

13. After executing the preceding search, the dashboard page will show `search-service` as well. This is shown in the following screenshot:

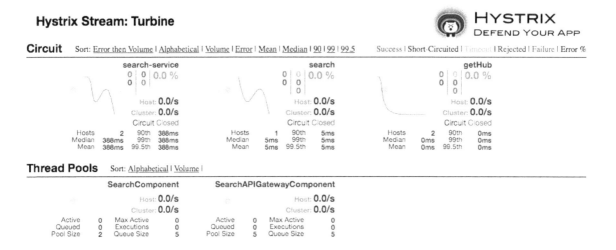

As we can see in the dashboard, `search-service` and `getHub` is coming from the Search API Gateway. Since we have two instances of the Search API Gateway, `getHub` is coming from two hosts, indicted by **Hosts 2**. The search is coming from the Search microservice. Data has been provided by the two components we created--`SearchComponent` in Search microservice and the `SearchAPIGateway` component in the Search API Gateway microservices.

Data analysis using Data Lake

Just like the scenario of fragmented logs and monitoring, fragmented data is another challenge in microservice architecture. Fragmented data poses challenges in data analytics. This data may be used for simple business event monitoring, data auditing, or even for deriving business intelligence out of the data.

Data Lake or a data hub is an ideal solution to handle such scenarios. The event-sourced architecture pattern is generally used to share state and state changes as events with an external data store. When there is a state change, microservices publish the state change as events. Interested parties may subscribe to these events and process them based on their requirements. A central event store can also subscribe to these events and store them in a big data store for further analysis.

One of the commonly followed architectures for such data handling is shown in the following diagram:

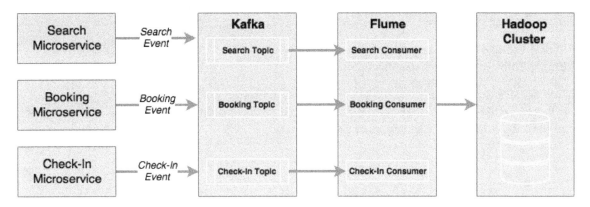

The state change events generated from the microservices, in our case, **Search**, **Booking**, and **Check-In** events, are pushed to a distributed high performance messaging system such as **Kafka**. A data ingestion, such as **Flume**, can subscribe these events and update them to an **HDFS** cluster. In some cases, these messages will be processed in real time by **Spark Streaming**. To handle heterogeneous sources of events, **Flume** can also be used between event sources and **Kafka**.

Spring Cloud Streams, **Spring Cloud Streams modules**, and **Spring Cloud Data Flow** are also useful as an alternative for high velocity data ingestion.

Summary

In this chapter, we learned about the challenges around logging and monitoring when dealing with internet-scale microservices.

We explored the various solutions for centralized logging and also learned how to implement a custom centralized logging using **Elasticsearch**, **Logstash**, and **Kibana** (**ELK**). In order to understand distributed tracing, we upgraded the BrownField microservices using the Spring Cloud Sleuth.

In the second half of this chapter, we went deeper into the capabilities required for microservices monitoring solutions and different approaches for monitoring. Subsequently, we examined a number of tools available for microservices monitoring.

The BrownField microservices were further enhanced with the Spring Cloud Hystrix and Turbine for monitoring latencies and failures in inter-service communications. The examples also demonstrated how to use the Circuit Breaker pattern to fall back to another service in case of failures.

Finally, we also touched upon the importance of Data Lake and how to integrate a Data Lake architecture in a microservice context.

Microservice management is another important challenge we have to tackle when dealing with large-scale microservices deployments. The next chapter will explore how containers can help in simplifying microservice management.

9
Containerizing Microservices with Docker

In the context of microservices, containerized deployment is like the icing on the cake. It helps microservices to be further autonomous by self-containing the underlying infrastructure, thereby making microservices cloud-neutral.

This chapter will introduce the concepts and relevance of virtual machine images and containerized deployments of microservices. Then, this chapter will further familiarize you with how to build Docker images for BrownField PSS microservices developed with Spring Boot and Spring Cloud. Finally, this chapter will also touch base on how to manage, maintain, and deploy Docker images in a production-like environment.

By the end of this chapter, you will have learned about the following:

- The concept of containerization and its relevance in the context of microservices
- How to build and deploy microservices as Docker images and containers
- Using AWS as an example of cloud-based Docker deployments

Understanding gaps in the BrownField PSS microservices

In `Chapter 7`, *Scale Microservices with Spring Cloud Components*, the BrownField PSS microservices were developed using Spring Boot and Spring Cloud. Those microservices are deployed as versioned fat jar files on bare metals, specifically on a local development machine. In `Chapter 8`, *Logging and Monitoring Microservices*, challenges around logging and monitoring were addressed using centralized logging and monitoring solutions.

This is good enough for most implementations. However, there are still a few gaps in our BrownField PSS implementation. So far, the implementation has not used any cloud infrastructure. Dedicated machines, as in the traditional monolithic application deployments, are not the best solution for deploying microservices. Automation such as automatic provisioning, the ability to scale on demand, self service, and payment based on usage are essential capabilities required to manage large-scale microservice deployments efficiently. In general, a cloud infrastructure provides all these essential capabilities. Therefore, a private or public cloud with the capabilities mentioned earlier is better suited for deploying internet-scale microservices.

Additionally, running one microservice instance per bare metal is not cost-effective. Therefore, in most cases, enterprises end up deploying multiple microservices on a single bare metal server. Running multiple microservices on a single bare metal could create a noisy neighbor problem. There will not be any isolation between microservice instances running on the same machine. As a result, the services deployed on a single machine can eat other's space, and, thus, impact the performance of other microservices.

An alternative approach is to run microservices on VMs. However, VMs are heavyweight in nature. Therefore, running many smaller VMs on a physical machine is not resource-efficient. This generally results in resource wastage. In cases of sharing a VM for deploying multiple services, developers will end up facing the same issues of sharing the bare metal, as explained earlier.

In the case of Java-based microservices, sharing a VM or bare metal for deploying multiple microservices also results in sharing the JRE between microservices. This is because the fat jars created in our BrownField PSS abstract only the application code and its dependencies, but not JREs. Any update on the JRE installed on the machine will have implications for all microservices deployed on that machine. Similarly, if there are OS-level parameters, libraries, or tunings that are required for specific microservices, then it will be hard to manage them on a shared environment.

One of the microservice principles insists on being self-contained and autonomous by fully encapsulating its end-to-end runtime environment. In order to align with this principle, all components, such as the OS, JRE, and microservices binaries, have to be self-contained and isolated. The only option to achieve this is to follow the approach of deploying one microservice per VM. However, this will result in under-utilized virtual machines, and, in many cases, extra costs due to this can nullify the benefits of microservices.

What are containers?

Containers are not revolutionary groundbreaking concepts. It has been in action for quite a while. However, the world is witnessing the reentry of containers, mainly due to the wide adoption of cloud computing. The shortcomings of traditional virtual machines in the cloud computing space has also accelerated the use of containers. Container providers, such as Docker, simplified container technologies to a great extent, which also helped the large adoption of container technologies in today's world. The recent popularity of DevOps and microservices also acted as catalysts for the rebirth of container technologies.

So, what are containers? Containers provide private spaces on top of the operating system. This technique is also called operating system virtualization. In this approach, the kernel of the operating system provides isolated virtual spaces. Each of these virtual spaces are called **containers** or **virtual engines** (**VEs**). Containers allow processes to run on an isolated environment, on top of the host operating system. A representation of multiple containers running on the same host is shown in the following figure:

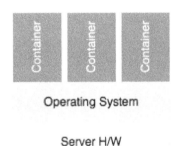

Containers are easy mechanisms to build, ship, and run compartmentalized software components. Generally, containers package all binaries and libraries that are essential for running an application. Containers reserve their own filesystem, IP address, network interfaces, internal processes, name spaces, OS libraries, application binaries, dependencies, and other application configurations.

There are billions of containers used by organizations. Moreover, there are many large organizations heavily investing in container technologies. Docker is, by far, ahead of the competition, supported by many large operating system vendors and cloud providers. **Lmctfy**, **Systemd Nspawn**, **Rocket**, **Drawbridge**, **LXD**, **Kurma**, and **Calico** are some of the other containerization solutions. Open-container specification is also under development.

Difference between VM and containers

Virtual machines such as **Hyper-V**, **VMWare**, and **Zen** were popular choices for data center virtualization a few years back. Enterprises experienced cost savings by implementing virtualization over traditional bare metal usage. It has also helped many enterprises to utilize their existing infrastructure in a much more optimized manner. Since VMs support automation, many enterprises have experienced less management efforts with virtual machines. Virtual machines have also helped organizations to get isolated environments for applications to run.

On prima facie, both virtualization and containerization exhibit exactly the same characteristics. However, in a nutshell, containers, and virtual machines are not the same. Therefore, it is unfair to make an apple-to-apple comparison between VMs and containers. Virtual machines and containers are two different techniques that address different problems of virtualization. This difference is evident in the following diagram:

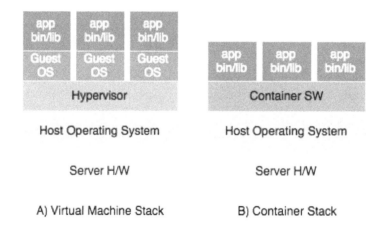

The **Virtual Machine** (**VM**) operates at a much lower level compared to containers. VMs provide hardware virtualization, such as virtualization of CPUs, motherboards, memory, and so on. A VM is an isolated unit with an embedded operating system, generally called a **Guest OS**. VMs replicate the whole operating system and run it within the VM with no dependency on the host operating system environment. Since VMs embed the full operating system environment, these are heavyweight in nature. This is an advantage as well as a disadvantage. The advantage is that VMs offer full isolation to the processes running on the VMs. The disadvantage is that it limits the number of VMs one can spin up in a bare metal due to the resource requirements of VMs. The size of the VMs have a direct impact on the time to start and stop them.

Since starting a VM intern will boot the OS, the start time for it is generally high. VMs are more friendly for the infrastructure teams, since they require low-level infrastructure competency to manage VMs. Processes running inside the VMs are completely isolated from the processes on a different VM running on the same host.

In the container world, containers do not emulate the entire hardware or operating system. Unlike VMs, containers share certain parts of host kernels and the operating system. There is no concept of Guest OS in the case of containers. Containers provide an isolated execution environment directly on top of the host operating system. This is an advantage as well as a disadvantage. The advantage is that it is lighter as well as faster. Since containers on the same machine share the host operating system, the overall resource utilization of containers is fairly small. As a result, many smaller containers can be run on the same machine compared to heavyweight VMs. Since the containers on the same host share the host operating system, there are limitations as well. For example, it is not possible to set iptables firewall rules inside a container. Processes inside the container are completely independent from the processes on different containers running on the same host.

Unlike VMs, container images are publicly available on community portals. This makes the developer's life much easier, as they don't have to build images from scratch, instead, they can now take base images from certified sources and add additional layers of software components on top of the downloaded base image.

The lightweight nature of the containers is also opening up a plethora of opportunities, such as automated build, publishing, downloading, copying, and so on. The ability to download, build, ship, and run containers with few commands make containers more developer-friendly. Building a new container will not consume more than a few seconds. Containers are now a part and parcel of the continuous delivery pipelines as well.

In summary, there are many advantages for containers over VMs, but a VM has its own exclusive strengths. Many organizations use both containers together with VMs; for example, by running containers on top of VMs.

Benefits of containers

We have already seen many benefits of containers over VMs. This section will explain the overall benefits of containers beyond the benefits of VMs.

Some of the benefits of containers are summarized as follows:

- **Self contained**: Containers package essential application binaries and its dependencies together to make sure that there is no disparity between different environments, such as development, testing, or production. This promotes the concept of the Twelve-Factor applications and the concept of immutable containers. The Spring Boot microservices bundles all required application dependencies. Containers stretch this boundary further by embedding the JRE and other operating system-level libraries, configurations, and so on, if any.

- **Lightweight**: Containers, in general, are smaller in size with a lighter footprint. The smallest container, **Alpine**, has a size of only less than 5 MB. The simplest Spring Boot microservices packaged with an Alpine container with **Java 8** will only come at around 170 MB. Though the size is still on the higher side, it is much less than the VM image size, which will generally be in GBs. Smaller footprint of containers not only helps to spin new containers quickly, but also to make building, shipping, and storing easier.

- **Scalability**: Since container images are smaller in size, and there is no OS booting at the startup, containers are generally faster to spin up and shut down. This makes containers a popular choice for cloud-friendly elastic applications.

- **Portability**: Containers provide portability across machines and cloud providers. Once containers are built with all dependencies, they can be ported across multiple machines or multiple cloud providers without relying on the underlying machines. Containers are portable from desktops to different cloud environments.

- **License cost**: Many software license terms are based on the physical core. Since containers share the operating system and are not virtualized at the physical resources level, there is an advantage in terms of the license cost.

- **DevOps**: The lightweight footprint of containers makes them easy for automating builds and publishing and downloading containers from remote repositories. This makes them easy to use in agile and DevOps environments by integrating with automated delivery pipelines. Containers also support the concept of build once by creating immutable containers at build time and moving them across multiple environments. Since containers are not deep into the infrastructure, multi-disciplinary DevOps teams can manage containers as part of their day-to-day life.

- **Version controlled**: Containers support versions by default. This helps build versioned artifacts, just like versioned archive files.

- **Reusable**: Container images are reusable artifacts. If an image is built by assembling a number of libraries for a purpose, it can be reused in similar situations.

- **Immutable containers**: In this concept, the containers are created and disposed of after usage. They are never updated or patched. Immutable containers are used in many environments to avoid complexities in patching deployment units. Patching will result in a lack of traceability and an inability to recreate environments consistently.

Microservices and containers

There is no direct relationship between microservices and containers. Microservices can run without containers and containers can run monolithic applications. However, there is a sweet spot between microservices and containers.

Containers are good for monolithic applications; however, the complexities and the size of the monolith application may kill some of the benefits of containers. For example, spinning new containers quickly may not be easy with monolithic applications. In addition to that, monolithic applications generally have local environment dependencies, such as local disk, stove pipe dependencies with other systems, and more. Such applications are difficult to manage with container technologies. This is where microservices go hand in hand with containers.

The following diagram shows three polyglot microservices running on the same host machine and sharing the same operating system, but abstracts the runtime environment:

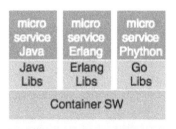

The real advantage of containers is when managing many polyglot microservices. For instance, one microservice in Java is another one in Erlang or some other language. Containers help developers to package microservices written in any language or technology in a uniform fashion. It also helps deployment team to distribute across multiple environments without spending too much attention to configuration of such environments. Containers eliminate the need to have different deployment management tools to handle polyglot microservices. Containers not only abstract the execution environment, but also abstract how to access the services. Irrespective of the technologies used, containerized microservices expose REST APIs. Once the container is up and running, it binds to certain ports and exposes its APIs. Since containers are self-contained and provide full-stack isolation between services, in a single VM or bare metal, one can run multiple heterogeneous microservices and handle them in a uniform way. Containers can really help avoid conflicting situations where dev, test, and prod teams blame each other for their configuration and operating environments.

Introduction to Docker

Previous sections talked about containers and their benefits. Containers have been present in the business for years, but the popularity of Docker has given containers a new outlook. As a result, many container definitions and perspectives have emerged from the Docker architecture. Docker is so popular, that even containerization is referred to as **Dockerization**.

Docker is a platform to build, ship, and run lightweight containers based on Linux kernels. Docker has a default support for Linux platforms. They also have support for Mac and Windows using **Boot2Docker**, which runs on top of Virtual Box.

Amazon **EC2 Container Service** (**ECS**) has out-of-the-box support for Docker on AWS EC2 instances. Docker can be installed on bare metals and also on traditional virtual machines such as VMWare or Hyper-V.

Key components of Docker

The Docker installation has two key components. A **Docker daemon** and a **Docker client**. Both, Docker daemon and Docker client are distributed as a single binary.

The following diagram shows the key components of a Docker installation:

The Docker daemon

The Docker daemon is the server-side component that runs on the host machine responsible for building, running, and distributing the Docker containers. The Docker daemon exposes APIs for the Docker client to interact with the daemon. These APIs are primarily REST-based endpoints. One can imagine the Docker daemon as a controller service running on the host machine. Developers can programmatically use the APIs to build custom clients as well.

The Docker client

The Docker client is a remote command-line program that interacts with the Docker daemon either through a socket or through REST APIs. The CLI can run on the same host as the daemon is running on, or it can run on a completely different host and connect to the daemon remotely using the CLI. The Docker users will use the CLI to build, ship, and run Docker containers.

Docker concepts--The Docker architecture is built around a few concepts, such as images, containers, registry, and Dockerfile.

The Docker image

One of the key concepts of Docker is the image. The Docker image is the read-only copy of the operating system libraries and applications and their libraries. Once an image is created, it is guaranteed to run on any Docker platforms without alterations.

In Spring Boot microservices, a Docker image will package operating systems such as Ubuntu, Alpine, JRE, and the Spring Boot fat application jar file. It also includes instructions to run the application and how to expose services.

Spring Boot
Application Jar

Java Runtime

Operating System

As shown in the preceding diagram, the Docker images are based on a layered architecture, where the base image will be one of the flavors of Linux. Each layer, as shown in the preceding diagram, gets added to the base image layer with the previous image as the parent layer. Docker uses the concept of the union filesystem to combine all these layers into a single image, forming a single filesystem.

In typical cases, developers will not build Docker images from scratch. Images, such as operating system, or other common libraries, such as Java 8 images are publicly available from trusted sources. Developers can start building on top of these base images. The base image in Spring microservices can be JRE 8 rather than starting from a Linux distribution image such as Ubuntu.

Every time we rebuild the application, only the changed layer gets rebuilt and the remaining layers are kept intact. All intermediate layers are cached and, hence, if there is no change, Docker will use the previously cached layer and build it on top. Multiple containers running on the same machine with the same type of base images will reuse the base image, thus reducing the size of the deployment. For instance, in a host, if there are multiple containers running with Ubuntu as the base image, they all reuse the same base image. This is applicable when publishing or downloading images as well.

Write - FS

Spring Boot

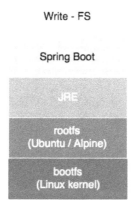

As shown in the preceding figure, the first layer in the image is a boot filesystem called **bootfs**, which is similar to the **Linux kernel** and the boot loader. The boot filesystem acts as a virtual file system for all images.

On top of the boot filesystem, the operating system's filesystem will be placed, which is called **rootfs**. The root filesystem adds the typical operating system directory structure to the container. Unlike in the Linux systems, rootfs, in the case of Docker, will be in read-only mode.

On top of the **rootfs**, other required images will be placed, as per the requirements. In our case, these are **JRE** and the Spring Boot microservice jars. When a container is initiated, a writable filesystem will be placed on top of all other filesystems for the processes to run. Any changes made by the process to the underlying filesystem will not be reflected in the actual container. Instead, these will be written to the writable filesystem. This writable file system is volatile. Hence, the data will be lost once the container is stopped. Due to this reason, Docker containers are ephemeral in nature.

The base operating system packaged inside Docker is generally a minimal copy of just the OS filesystem. In reality, the process running on top may not use the entire OS service. In a Spring Boot microservice, in many cases, the container just initiates a CMD and JVM, and then invokes the Spring Boot fat jar.

The Docker container

Docker containers are the running instances of a Docker image. The containers use the kernel of the host operating system when running. Hence, they share the host kernel with other containers running on the same host. Docker runtime ensures that the container processes are allocated with their own isolated process space using kernel features, such as **cgroups**, and the kernel **namespace** of the operating system. In addition to resource fencing, the containers will get their own filesystem and network configurations as well.

The containers, when instantiated, can have a specific resource allocation, such as memory and CPU. Containers, when initiated from the same image, can have a different resource allocation. The Docker container, by default, gets an isolated **subnet** and **gateway** to the network.

The Docker registry

The Docker registry is a central place where Docker images are published and downloaded from. The central registry provided by Docker is `https://hub.docker.com`. The Docker registry has public images that one can download and use as a base registry. Docker also has private images that are specific to the accounts created in the Docker registry. The Docker registry screenshot is shown as follows:

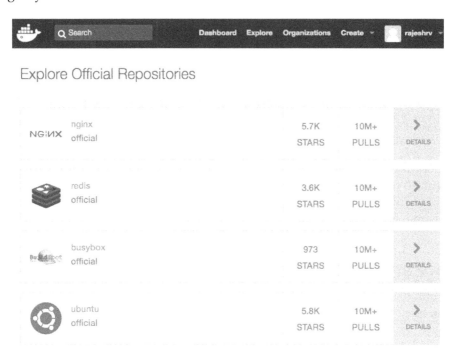

Docker also offers **Docker Trusted Registry** (**DTR**), which can be used to set up registries locally on-premise.

Dockerfile

Dockerfile is a build file or a scripting file that contains instructions to build a Docker image. There can be multiple steps included in a Dockerfile, start with downloading a base image. Dockerfile is a text file generally named `Dockerfile`. The `docker build` command looks up the Dockerfile for instructions for building. One can compare `Dockerfile` as a `pom.xml` file used in the Maven build.

Deploying microservices into Docker

This section will operationalize our learning by showcasing how to build containers for our BrownField PSS microservices.

 The full source code of this chapter is available under the `chapter9` projects, in the code files under `https://github.com/rajeshrv/Spring5M icroservice`. Copy `chapter6.*` into a new STS workspace and rename `chapter9.*`.

Follow these steps to build Docker containers for the BrownField microservices:

1. Install Docker from the official Docker site (`https://www.docker.com`).

2. Follow the *Get Started* link for the download and install instructions based on the operating system of choice.

3. Once installed, run `Docker.app` and then use the following command to verify the installation:

```
Client:
Version:      17.03.1-ce
API version:  1.27
Go version:   go1.7.5
Git commit:   c6d412e
Built:        Tue Mar 28 00:40:02 2017
OS/Arch:      darwin/amd64
Server:
Version:      17.03.1-ce
API version:  1.27 (minimum version 1.12)
Go version:   go1.7.5
Git commit:   c6d412e
Built:        Fri Mar 24 00:00:50 2017
OS/Arch:      linux/amd64
Experimental: true
```

4. Before we make any changes, we need to edit `application.properties` of all services to change from localhost to the IP address, since localhost is not resolvable from within the Docker containers. In the real world, this will point to a DNS or load balancer. Also, we change the port bindings to reflect the ports mentioned in `Chapter 6`, *Microservices Evolution - A Case Study.*

`application.properties` file looks like as follows:

```
server.port=8090
spring.rabbitmq.host=192.168.0.101
spring.rabbitmq.port=5672
spring.rabbitmq.username=guest
spring.rabbitmq.password=guest
```

 Note: Replace the IP address with the IP address of your machine.

5. Update `Application.java` and `BrownFieldSiteController.java` in the `chapter9.website` project to replace localhost with IP address.

6. Update `BookingComponent.java` under `chapter9.book` to reflect the IP address instead of localhost.

7. Create a Dockerfile under the root directory of all microservices. An example of the Dockerfile to search for a microservice will look like this:

```
FROM frolvlad/alpine-oraclejdk8
VOLUME /tmp
ADD  target/search-1.0.jar search.jar
EXPOSE 8090
ENTRYPOINT ["java","-jar","/search.jar"]
```

8. The following is a quick examination of the contents of the Dockerfile:

- `FROM frolvlad/alpine-oraclejdk8` tells the Docker build to use a specific `alpine-oraclejdk8` version as the basic image for this build. The `frolvlad` indicates the repository to locate the `alpine-oraclejdk8` image. In this case, this is an image built with Alpine Linux and Oracle JDK 8. This will help layer our application on top of this base image without setting up Java libraries ourselves. In this case, since this image is not available on our local image store, the Docker build will go ahead and download this image from the remote Docker Hub registry.

- `VOLUME /tmp` enables access from the container to the directory specified in the host machine. In our case, this is pointing to the `tmp` directory where the Spring Boot application creates working directories for Tomcat. The `tmp` directory is a logical directory for the container that will indirectly point to one of the local directories of the host.

- ADD `target/search-1.0.jar search.jar` adds the application's binary file to the container with the destination file's name specified. In this case, the Docker build copies `target/search-1.0.jar` to the container as `search.jar`.

- EXPOSE `8090` tells the container how to perform port mapping. This will associate `8090` as the external port binding for the internal Spring Boot service.

- ENTRYPOINT `["java","-jar", "/search.jar"]` tells the container which default application to run when it is started. In this case, we are pointing to the Java process and the Spring Boot fat jar file to initiate the service.

9. The next step is to run the `docker build` command from the folder where Dockerfile is stored. This will download the base image and run the entries in the Dockerfile one after the other.

Docker build command for search is shown as follows:

```
docker build -t search:1.0 .
```

The preceding command will result in building a docker image for search. The log is shown as follows:

```
rvslab:chapter9.search rajeshrv$ docker build -t search:1.0 .
Sending build context to Docker daemon 57.01 MB
Step 1/5 : FROM frolvlad/alpine-oraclejdk8
latest: Pulling from frolvlad/alpine-oraclejdk8
627beaf3eaaf: Pull complete
95a531c0fa10: Pull complete
b03e476748e7: Pull complete
Digest: sha256:8ad40ff024bff6df43e3fa7e7d0974e31f6b3f346c666285e275afee72c74fcd
Status: Downloaded newer image for frolvlad/alpine-oraclejdk8:latest
 ---> f656c77f5536
Step 2/5 : VOLUME /tmp
 ---> Running in c816f2b47568
 ---> e6028f6a76bc
Removing intermediate container c816f2b47568
Step 3/5 : ADD target/search-1.0.jar search.jar
 ---> 39f28a242676
Removing intermediate container b4463e6220fc
Step 4/5 : EXPOSE 8090
 ---> Running in 2c25a35d20ea
 ---> d0738b1fb63a
Removing intermediate container 2c25a35d20ea
Step 5/5 : ENTRYPOINT java -jar /search.jar
 ---> Running in 095e60d75f13
 ---> a9f2ae1252c2
Removing intermediate container 095e60d75f13
Successfully built a9f2ae1252c2
```

10. Repeat the preceding step for all microservices.

11. Once the images are created, they can be verified by typing the following command. This command will list the images and their details, including the size of the image files:

```
docker images
```

The preceding command will show all images as follows:

```
rvslab:chapter9.website rajeshrv$ docker images
REPOSITORY              TAG               IMAGE ID          CREATED           SIZE
book                    1.0               8c0dbbe5ffc4      11 minutes ago    203 MB
checkin                 1.0               2ee2d759fecd      12 minutes ago    209 MB
fares                   1.0               13275668b4ea      12 minutes ago    202 MB
website                 1.0               b4b3c7d59ff8      13 minutes ago    187 MB
search                  1.0               8f42cd4d1f86      13 minutes ago    203 MB
```

12. Next, we will run the Docker container. This can be done using the following command. This command will load and run the container. Upon starting, container calls the Spring Boot executable jar to start the microservice:

```
docker run -p 8090:8090 -t search:1.0
docker run -p 8080:8080 -t fares:1.0
docker run -p 8060:8060 -t book:1.0
docker run -p 8070:8070 -t checkin:1.0
docker run -p 8001:8001 -t website:1.0
```

The preceding command starts the Search and Search API Gateway microservices and the website.

Once all the services are fully started, verify with the `docker ps` command:

```
rvslab:chapter9.website rajeshrv$ docker ps
CONTAINER ID    IMAGE          COMMAND               CREATED         STATUS          PORTS                     NAMES
9a11b3478e28    book:1.0       "java -jar /book.jar" 36 seconds ago  Up 34 seconds   0.0.0.0:8060->8060/tcp    hardcore_booth
2e629addd32b    website:1.0    "java -jar /websit..."12 minutes ago  Up 12 minutes   0.0.0.0:8001->8001/tcp    boring_mcclintock
bf0b4436a387    checkin:1.0    "java -jar /checki..."12 minutes ago  Up 12 minutes   0.0.0.0:8070->8070/tcp    angry_darwin
02d9c291b8b8    fares:1.0      "java -jar /fares.jar"13 minutes ago  Up 13 minutes   0.0.0.0:8080->8080/tcp    affectionate_sinoussi
8a40e771dbe2    search:1.0     "java -jar /search..."14 minutes ago  Up 14 minutes   0.0.0.0:8090->8090/tcp    loving_edison
```

The next step is to point the browser to the following URL. This will open the BrownField website:

```
http://localhost:8001
```

Running RabbitMQ on Docker

Since our example also uses RabbitMQ, let's explore how to set up RabbitMQ as a Docker container. The following command pulls the RabbitMQ image from the Docker Hub and starts RabbitMQ:

```
docker run rabbitmq
```

Using the Docker registry

The Docker Hub provides a central location to store all Docker images. The images can be stored as public as well as private. In many cases, organizations deploy their own private registries on-premise due to security related concerns.

Follow these steps to set up and run a local registry:

1. The following command will start a registry that will bind the registry on port `5000`:

   ```
   docker run -d -p 5000:5000 --restart=always --name registry
     registry:latest
   ```

2. Tag `search:1.0` to the registry:

   ```
   docker tag search:1.0 localhost:5000/search:1.0
   ```

3. Push the image to the registry:

   ```
   docker push localhost:5000/search:1.0
   ```

4. Pull the image back from the registry:

   ```
   docker pull localhost:5000/search:1.0
   ```

Setting up the Docker Hub

In the previous chapter, we played with a local Docker registry. This section will show us how to set up and use the Docker Hub to publish the Docker containers. This is a convenient mechanism to globally access the Docker images. Later in this chapter, the Docker images will be published to the Docker Hub from the local machine and downloaded from the EC2 instances.

Perform the steps mentioned in the following link for setting up a public Docker Hub account and a repository:

`https://docs.docker.com/engine/installation/`

The registry, in this case, act as the microservices repository where all the Dockerized microservices will be stored and accessed. This is one of the capabilities explained in the microservices capability model.

Publish microservices to the Docker Hub

In order to push the Dockerized services to the Docker Hub, follow these steps. The first step below tags the Docker image and the second command push the Docker image to the Docker hub repository:

```
docker tag search:1.0 brownfield/search:1.0
docker push brownfield/search:1.0
```

To verify whether the container images are published, go to the Docker Hub repository using the following URL:

`https://hub.docker.com/u/brownfield`

Replace `brownfield` with the repository name used in the previous section.

Repeat this step for all the other microservices as well. At the end of this step, all the services will be published to the Docker Hub.

Microservices on Cloud

One of the capabilities mentioned in the microservices capability model is the use of the Cloud infrastructure for microservices. Earlier in this chapter, we also explored the necessity of using Cloud for microservices deployments. So far, we have not deployed anything to the Cloud. Once we have many microservices, it will be hard to run all of them on the local machine.

In the rest of this book, we will operate using AWS as the Cloud platform for deploying the BrownField PSS microservices.

Installing Docker on AWS EC2

In this section, we will install Docker on the EC2 instance. Follow these steps to install Docker.

This example assumes that you are familiar with AWS and an account has already been created on AWS:

Follow these steps to set up Docker on EC2:

1. Launch a new EC2 instance. In this case, if we have to run all instances together, we may need a large instance. The example uses `t2.large`.

    In this example, the following Ubuntu AMI is used.
   Ubuntu Server 16.04 LTS (HVM), SSD Volume Type - ami-a58d0dc5

2. Connect to the EC2 instance and run the following commands:

```
sudo apt-get update
sudo apt-get install docker.io
```

3. The preceding command will install Docker on the EC2 instance. Verify the installation with the following command:

```
sudo docker version
```

Running BrownField services on EC2

In this section, we will set up BrownField microservices on the EC2 instances created. In this case, the build is set up in the local desktop machine and the binaries will be deployed into AWS.

Follow these steps to set up services on the EC2 instance:

1. Change all IP addresses in `*.properties` to reflect the IP address of the EC2 instance.

2. Change the Java files mentioned earlier under `chapter9.book` and `chapter9.website` to reflect the IP addresses.

3. On the local machine, recompile all projects and create Docker images for all microservices. Push all of them to the Docker Hub registry.

4. Set up Java 8 on the EC2 instance.
5. Execute the following commands in sequence:

```
sudo docker run --net=host rabbitmq:3
sudo docker run -p 8090:8090 rajeshrv/search:1.0
sudo docker run -p 8001:8001 rajeshrv/website:1.0
```

6. Validate whether all services are working by opening the URL of the website and execute search. Note that we will be using the public IP of the EC2 instance in this case.

The URL for the website application is as follows:

```
http://54.165.128.23:8001
```

Future of containerization

Containerization is still evolving, but the number of organizations adopting containerization techniques has gone up in recent times. In addition to Docker, Microsoft has already invested in Windows containers. While many organizations are aggressively adopting Docker and other container technologies, the downside of these techniques are still the size of the containers and security concerns. Container portability and standardization is another challenge.

Currently, the Docker images are, in general, heavy. In an elastic-automated environment, where containers are created and destroyed quite frequently, size is still an issue. A larger size indicates more code, and more code means they are more prone for security vulnerabilities.

The future is definitely in small-footprint containers. Docker is working on unikernels, a lightweight kernel or cloud operating system that can run Docker even on low-powered IoT devices. Unikernels are not full-fledged operating systems, but they provide the basic necessary libraries to support deployed applications. Unikernels offer better speed, scalability, a smaller size, and enhanced security.

Many organizations are moving toward hybrid cloud solutions to avoid vendor locking. This leads to work with a safe distance from the vendor, that helps organizations quickly build containers and deploy across various environments. There are efforts gone into standardizing container runtimes as well as container images such as **Open Container Initiative** (**OCI**). Many container vendors have already been adopted as OCI standards.

Security concerns and security issues are much-discussed and debated on containers. Key security issues are around the user namespace segregation or user ID isolation. If a container is on root (by default), it can gain root privilege of the host. Using container images from untrusted sources is another security concern. The attacking surface is wider in the case of large-scale containers, as each container may expose endpoints.

Docker is closing these gaps as quickly as possible, but there are many organizations that use a combination of VMs and containers to circumvent some of the security concerns. Tools such as Docker Security Scanning could identify vulnerabilities associated with images automatically. There are other security control tools such as Docker Bench, Clair by CoreOS, and Twistlock.

Summary

In this chapter, we learned about the need to have a cloud environment when dealing with internet-scale microservices.

We explored the concept of containers and compared them with traditional virtual machines. We also learned the basics of Docker and were explained the concepts of Docker images, containers, and registry. The importance and benefits of containers were explained in the context of microservices.

This chapter then switched to a hands-on example by Dockerizing the BrownField microservices. We demonstrated how to deploy the Spring Boot microservices developed earlier on Docker. We learned the concept of registry by exploring a local registry, as well as the Docker Hub for pushing and pulling Dockerized microservices.

As a last step, we explored how to deploy Dockerized BrownField microservices in the AWS cloud environment.

10
Scaling Dockerized Microservices with Mesos and Marathon

In order to leverage full power of a cloud-like environment, the dockerized microservice instances should also be capable of scaling out and shrinking automatically, based on the traffic patterns. However, this could lead to another problem. Once there are many microservices, it is not easy to manually manage thousands of dockerized microservices. It is essential to have an infrastructure abstraction layer and a strong container orchestration platform to successfully manage internet-scale dockerized microservice deployments.

This chapter will explain the basic scaling approaches and the need and use of Mesos and Marathon as an infrastructure-orchestration layer to achieve optimized resource usage in a cloud-like environment when deploying microservices at scale. This chapter will also provide a step-by-step approach to setting up Mesos and Marathon in a cloud environment. Finally, this chapter will demonstrate how to manage dockerized microservices into the Mesos and Marathon environment.

By the end of this chapter, we will have learned about the following:

- Options to scale containerized Spring Boot microservices
- The need to have an abstraction layer and a container orchestration software
- An understanding Mesos and Marathon from the context of microservices
- How to manage dockerized BrownField Airline's PSS microservices with Mesos and Marathon

Scaling microservices

At the end of Chapter 7, *Scale Microservices with Spring Cloud Components*, we discussed two options for scaling either using Spring Cloud components or dockerized microservices using Mesos and Marathon. In Chapter 7, *Scale Microservices with Spring Cloud Components*, you learned how to scale the Spring Boot microservices using the Spring Cloud components.

The two key concepts of Spring Cloud that we have implemented are self-registration and self-discovery. These two capabilities enable automated microservices deployments. With self-registration, microservices can automatically advertise the service availability by registering service metadata to a central service registry as soon as the instances are ready to accept traffic. Once microservices are registered, consumers can consume newly registered services from the very next moment by discovering service instances using the registry service. In this model, registry is at the heart of this automation.

The following diagram shows the Spring Cloud method for scaling microservices:

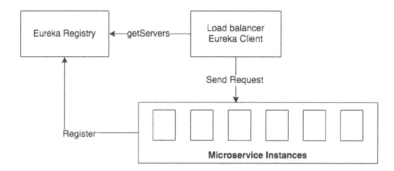

In this chapter, we will focus on the second approach, scaling dockerized microserices using Mesos and Marathon. It also provides us with one additional capability that you didn't learn about in Chapter 7, *Scale Microservices with Spring Cloud Components*. When there is a need for an additional microservice instance, a manual task is required to kick off a new instance. Similarly, when there is not enough traffic, there should be an option to turn off unused instances. In an ideal scenario, the start and stop of microservices instances also require automation. This is especially relevant when services are running on a pay as per usage cloud environment.

Understanding autoscaling

Autoscaling is an approach to automatically scale out instances based on the resource usage to meet agreed SLAs by replicating the services to be scaled.

The system automatically detects an increase in traffic, spins up additional instances, and makes them available for traffic handling. Similarly, when the traffic volumes go down, the system automatically detects and reduces the number of instances by taking active instances back from the service. It is also required to ensure that there is a set number of instances always up and running. In addition to this, the physical or virtual machines also need a mechanism to automatically provision machines. The latter part is much more easy to handle using APIs provided by different cloud providers.

Autoscaling can be done by considering different parameters and thresholds. Some of them are easy to handle whereas some of them are complex to handle. The following are the points that summarizes some of the commonly followed approaches:

- **Scale with resource constraints**: This approach is based on real-time service metrics collected through monitoring mechanisms. Generally, the resource scaling approach makes decisions based on the CPU, memory, or the disk of machines. It can also be done by looking at the statistics collected on the service instances itself, such as heap memory usage.
- **Scale during specific time periods**: Time-based scaling is an approach to scale services based on certain periods of the day, month, or year to handle seasonal or business peaks. For example, some services may experience higher number of transactions during office hours, and considerably less number of transactions outside office hours. In this case, during the day time, services autoscale to meet the demand and automatically downsizes during the off office hours.
- **Scale based on message queue length**: This is particularly useful when the microservices are based on asynchronous messaging. In this approach, new consumers will be automatically added when the messages in the queue goes beyond certain limits.
- **Scale based on business parameters**: In this case, adding instances will be based on certain business parameters. For example, spinning up a new instance just before handling sales, closing transactions. As soon as the monitoring service receives a preconfigured business event, such as sales closing minus 1 hour, a new instance will be brought up in anticipation of large volumes of transactions. This will provide fine grained controls on scaling based on business rules.

- **Predictive autoscaling**: This is a new paradigm of autoscaling, which is different from the traditional real-time metrics-based autoscaling. A prediction engine will take multiple inputs, such as historical information, current trends, and more, to predict possible traffic patterns. Autoscaling will be done based on these predictions. Predictive autoscaling helps in avoiding hardcoded rules and time windows. Instead, the system can automatically predict such time windows. In more sophisticated deployments, the predictive analysis may use cognitive computing mechanisms to predict autoscaling.

The missing pieces

In order to achieve autoscaling as mentioned previously, it requires a lot of scripting at the operating system level. Docker is a good step toward achieving this as it provides a uniform way of handling the containers, irrespective of the technologies used by the microservices. It also helped us in isolating microservices to avoid resource stealing by nosy neighbors.

However, Docker and scripting only address the issues partially. In the context of large-scale Docker deployments, some of the key questions to be answered are as follows:

- How do we manage thousands of containers?
- How do we monitor them?
- How do we apply rules and constraints when deploying artifacts?
- How do we ensure that we utilize containers properly to gain resource efficiency?
- How do we ensure that at least a certain number of minimal instances are running at any point in time?
- How do we ensure that dependent services are up and running?
- How do we do rolling upgrades and graceful migrations?
- How do we rollback faulty deployments?

All these preceding questions point to the need of having a solution to address the following two key capabilities:

- A container abstraction layer that provides a uniform abstraction over many physical or virtual machines
- A container orchestration and init system to manage deployments intelligently on top of the cluster abstraction

The rest of this chapter focuses on addressing these two points.

Container orchestration

Container orchestration tools provide a layer of abstraction for developers and infrastructure teams to deal with large-scale containerized deployments. The features offered by the container orchestration tools vary between providers. However, common denominators are provision, discovery, resource management, monitoring, and deployments.

Why is container orchestration is important

Since microservices break applications into different micro applications, many developers request more server nodes for deployment. In order to manage microservices properly, developers tend to deploy one microservice per VM, which further drives down the resource utilization. In many cases, this results in over-allocation of CPUs and memory.

In many deployments, the high availability requirements of microservices force engineers to add more and more service instances for redundancy. In reality, although it provides the required high availability, this will result in under-utilized server instances.

In general, microservices deployment requires more infrastructure compared to monolithic application deployments. Due to the increase in cost of the infrastructure, many organizations fail to see the value of microservices.

The following diagram shows dedicated VMs for each microservices:

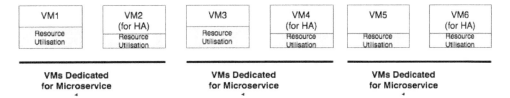

In order to address the issue stated in the preceding image, we need a tool that is capable of the following:

- Automating a number of activities such as allocation of containers to infrastructure efficiently, which are transparent to the developers and administrators
- Providing a layer of abstraction for the developers so that they can deploy their application against a data center without knowing which machine is to be used for hosting their applications

- Setting rules or constraints against deployment artifacts
- Offering higher levels of agility, with minimal management overheads for developers and administrators, perhaps with minimal human interactions
- Building, deploying, and managing applications cost effectively by driving maximum utilization of the available resources

Containers solve an important issue in this context. Any tools that we select with these capabilities can handle containers in a uniform way, irrespective of the undelaying microservice technologies.

What does container orchestration do?

Typical container orchestration tools help virtualize a set of machines and manage them as a single cluster. The container orchestration tools also help move the workload or containers across machines transparent to the consumer. Technology evangelists and practitioners use different terminologies, such as container orchestration, cluster management, data center virtualization, container schedulers, container life cycle management, data center operating system, and so on.

Many of these tools are currently supporting both Docker-based containers as well as non-containerized binary artifact deployments, such as the standalone Spring Boot application. The fundamental function for these container orchestration tools are to abstract the actual server instance from the application developers and administrators.

Container orchestration tools help self-service and provisioning of infrastructure rather than requesting the infrastructure teams to allocate the required machines with a predefined specification. In this automated container orchestration approach, machines are no longer provisioned upfront and preallocated to the applications. Some of the container orchestration tools also help virtualize the data centers across many heterogeneous machines, or even across data centers, and create an elastic private cloud-like infrastructure. There is no standard reference model for container orchestration tools. Therefore, the capabilities vary between vendors.

Some of the key capabilities of the container orchestration software are summarized as follows:

- **Cluster management**: This manages a cluster of VMs and physical machines as a single large machine. These machines could be heterogeneous in terms of resource capabilities, but, by and large, machines with Linux as the operating system. These virtual clusters can be formed on cloud, on premises, or a combination of both.

- **Deployments**: These handle automatic deployments of applications and containers with a large set of machines. It support multiple versions of the application containers, and also support rolling upgrades across a large number of cluster machines. These tools are also capable of handling a rollback of faulty promotes.
- **Scalability**: This handles automatic and manual scalability of application instances as and when required with optimized utilization as a primary goal.
- **Health**: This manages the health of the cluster, nodes, and applications. It removes faulty machines and application instances from the cluster.
- **Infrastructure abstraction**: This abstracts the developers from the actual machine where the applications are deployed. The developers need not worry about the machines, capacity, and so on. It is entirely the container orchestration software's decision to see how to schedule and run the applications. These tools also abstract the machine details, their capacity, utilization, and location from the developers. For application owners, these are equivalent to a single large machine with almost unlimited capacity.
- **Resource optimizations**: The inherent behavior of these tools is to allocate the container workloads across a set of available machines in an efficient way, thereby reducing the cost of ownership. Simple to extremely complicated algorithms can be used effectively to improve utilization.
- **Resource allocations**: These allocate servers based on resource availability and constraints set by the application developers. The resource allocation will be based on these constraints, affinity rules, port requirements, application dependencies, health, and so on.
- **Service availability**: This ensures that the services are up and running somewhere in the cluster. In case of a machine failure, container orchestration automatically handle failures by restarting those services on some other machine in the cluster.
- **Agility**: Agility tools are capable of quickly allocating workloads to available resources or move the workload across machines if there is change in resource requirements. Also, constraints can be set to realign resources based on business criticality, business priority, and more.

- **Isolation**: Some of these tools provide resource isolation out-of-the-box. Hence, even if the application is not containerized, resource isolation can be achieved.

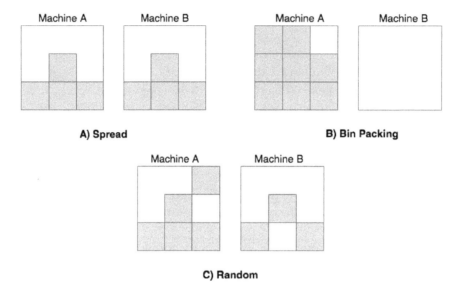

A variety of algorithms are used for resource allocation ranging from simple algorithms to complex algorithms with machine learning and artificial intelligence. The common algorithms used are **Random**, **Bin Packing**, and **Spread**. Constraints set against applications will override the default algorithms based on resource availability.

The preceding diagram shows how these algorithms fill the available machines with deployments. In this case, it is demonstrated with two machines.

Three common strategies of resource allocation are explained as follows:

- **Spread**: This equally distributes the allocation of workloads across available machines., which is shown in diagram **A**.
- **Bin packing**: This tries to fill machine by machine and ensure the maximum utilization of machines. Bin packing is especially good when using cloud services in a pay as you use style. This is shown in diagram **B**.
- **Random**: This algorithm randomly chooses machines and deploys containers on randomly selected machines, which is shown in diagram **C**.

There are possibilities of using cognitive computing algorithms such as machine learning and collaborative filtering to improve efficiency. Techniques such as **oversubscriptions** allow for better utilization of resources by utilizing under-utilized resources allocated for high priority tasks, including revenue generating services for best effort tasks such as analytics, video, image processing, and more.

Relationship with microservices

The infrastructure for microservices, if not properly provisioned, can easily result in over-sized infrastructures, and, essentially, higher cost of ownership. As discussed in the previous sections, a cloud-like environment with a container orchestration tool is essential to realize the cost benefits when dealing with large-scale microservices.

The Spring Boot microservices turbo, charged with the Spring Cloud project, is the ideal candidate workload to leverage container orchestration tools. Since the Spring Cloud based microservices are location unaware, these services can be deployed anywhere in the cluster. Whenever services come up, it automatically registers to the service registry and advertises its availability. On the other hand, consumers always look for the registry to discover available service instances. This way the application supports a full fluid structure without preassuming deployment topology. With Docker, we are able to abstract the runtime so that the services could run on any Linux-based environments.

Relationship with virtualization

The container orchestration solutions are different from server virtualization solutions in many aspects. Container orchestration solutions run on top of the VMs or physical machines as an application component.

Container orchestration solutions

There are many container orchestration software tools available. It is unfair to do an apple to apple comparison between them. Even though there are no one-to-one components, there are many areas of overlap in capabilities between them. In many situations, organizations use a combination of one or more of these tools to fulfill their requirements.

The following diagram shows the position of container orchestration tools from the microservices context:

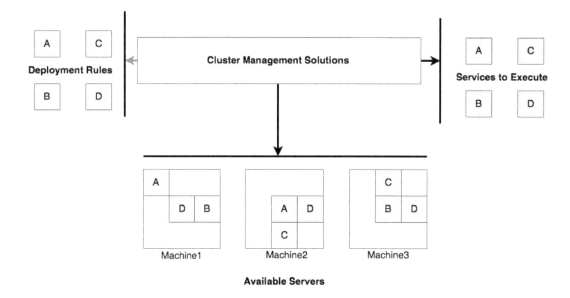

Available Servers

As shown in the preceding diagram, the container management or orchestration tools take a set of deployable artifacts in the form of containers (**Services to Execute**) and a set of constraints or rules as deployment descriptors then find the most optimal compute infrastructure for deployment which are available and fragmented across multiple machines.

In this section, we will explore some of the popular container orchestration solutions available in the market.

Docker Swarm

Docker Swarm is Docker's native container orchestration solution. Swarm provides native and deeper integration with Docker and exposes APIs that are compatible with Docker's remote APIs. It logically groups a pool of Docker hosts and manages them as a large single Docker virtual host. Instead of application administrators and developers deciding on which host the container is to be deployed, this decision making will be delegated to the Docker Swarm. It will decide which host to be used based on bin packing and spread algorithms.

Since the Docker Swarm is based on Docker's remote APIs, the learning curve for existing Docker users is much less compared to any other container orchestration tools. However, the Docker Swarm is a relatively new product in the market and it only supports the Docker containers.

Docker Swarm works with the concept of **manager** and **nodes**. The manager is the single point for administrations to interact and schedule the Docker containers for execution. The nodes are where the Docker containers are deployed and run.

Kubernetes

Kubernetes (**k8s**) is coming from Google's engineering, is written in Go language, and is battle tested for large-scale deployments at Google. Similar to Swarm, Kubernetes helps to manage containerized applications across a cluster of nodes. It helps to automate container deployments and scheduling and scalability of containers. It supports a number of useful out-of-the-box features, such as automatic progressive rollouts, versioned deployments, and container resiliency if containers fail for some reason.

Kubernetes architecture has the concept of **master**, **nodes**, and **pods**. The master and nodes together are called a Kubernetes cluster. The master node is responsible for allocating and managing the workload across a number of nodes. Nodes are nothing but a VM or a physical machine. Nodes are further subsegmented as pods. A node can host multiple pods. One or more containers are grouped and executed inside a pod. Pods are also helpful to manage and deploy co-located services for efficiency. Kubernetes also support the concept of labels as key-value pairs to query and find containers. Labels are user-defined parameters to tag certain types of nodes that perform common types of workloads, such as frontend web servers. The services deployed on the cluster will get a single IP/DNS to access the service.

Kubernetes has out-of-the-box support for Docker; however, Kubernetes' learning curve will be more compared to Docker Swarm. Red Hat offers commercial support for Kubernetes as part of its OpenShift platform.

Apache Mesos

Mesos is an open source framework originally developed by the University of California at Berkeley and is used by Twitter at scale. Twitter used Mesos primarily to manage a large Hadoop ecosystem.

Mesos is slightly different from the previous solutions. It is more of a resource manager that relies on other frameworks to manage workload execution. It sits between the operating system and the application, providing a logical cluster of machines.

Mesos is a distributed system kernel that logically groups and virtualizes many computers to a single large machine. It is capable of grouping a number of heterogeneous resources to a uniform resource cluster on which applications can be deployed. For these reasons, Mesos is also known as a tool for building a private cloud in a data center.

Mesos has the concept of the **master** and **slave** nodes. Similar to the earlier solutions, master nodes are responsible for managing the cluster, whereas slaves run the workloads. It internally uses **ZooKeeper** for cluster coordination and storage. It also supports the concept of frameworks. These frameworks are responsible for scheduling and running non-containerized applications and containers. **Marathon**, **Chronos**, and **Aurora** are popular frameworks for the scheduling and execution of applications. Netflix's **Fenzo** is another open source Mesos framework. Interestingly, Kubernetes also can be used as a Mesos framework.

Marathon supports the Docker container, as well as the non-containerized applications. The Spring Boot can be directly configured in Marathon. Marathon provides a number of out-of-the-box capabilities, such as support application dependencies, grouping of applications for scaling and upgrading services, start and shutdown of healthy and unhealthy instances, rolling promotes, rollback failed promoted, and so on.

Mesosphere offers commercial support for Mesos and Marathon as part of their DCOS platform.

HashiCorp Nomad

Nomad is from **HashiCorp**, another container orchestration software. Nomad is a container orchestration system that abstracts lower-level machine details and their locations. It has a simpler architecture compared to other solutions explored earlier. It is also lightweight. Similar to other container orchestration solutions, it will take care of resource allocations and the execution of applications. Nomad also accepts user-specific constraints and allocates resources based on that.

Nomad has the concept of servers where all jobs are managed. One server will act as the **leader** and others will act as **followers**. It has the concept of **tasks**, which are the smallest units of work. Tasks are grouped into **task groups**. A task group will have tasks that are to be executed in the same location. One or more task groups or tasks are managed as **jobs**.

Nomad supports many workloads, including Docker out of the box. Nomad also supports across data center deployments and is region data center aware.

CoreOS Fleet

Fleet is a container orchestration system from CoreOS. Feet runs on a lower level and works on top of the `systemd`. It can manage application dependencies and make sure that all required services are running somewhere in the cluster. If a service fails, it restarts the service on another host. Affinity and constraint rules are possible to supply when allocating resources.

Fleet has the concept of **engine** and **agents**. There will only be one engine at any point in the cluster with multiple agents. Tasks are submitted to the engine and the agents run these tasks on a cluster machine. Fleet also supports Docker out of the box.

In addition to this, **Amazon EC2 Container Services (ECS)**, **Azure Container Services (ACS)**, Cloud Foundry **Diego**, and **Google Container Engine** provide container orchestration functions as part of their respective cloud platform offerings.

Container orchestration with Mesos and Marathon

As we have seen in the previous section, there are many container orchestration solutions available. Different organizations choose different solutions to address problems based on their environments. Many organizations choose Kubernetes or Mesos with a framework such as Marathon. In most of the cases, Docker is used as a default containerization method to package and deploy workloads.

For the rest of this chapter, we will show how Mesos works with Marathon to provide the required container orchestration capability. Mesos is used by many organizations including Twitter, Airbnb, Apple, eBay, Netflix, Paypal, Uber, Yelp, and many others.

Mesos in details

Mesos can be treated as a data center kernel. Enterprise **DCOS** is the commercial version of Mesos supported by Mesosphere. In order to run multiples tasks on one node, Mesos uses resource isolation concepts. It relies on **cgroups** of the Linux kernel to achieve resource isolation similar to the container approach. It also supports containerized isolation using Docker. Mesos supports both, batch workloads as well as OLTP kind of workloads.

The following diagram shows Mesos logically abstracting multiple machines as a single resource cluster:

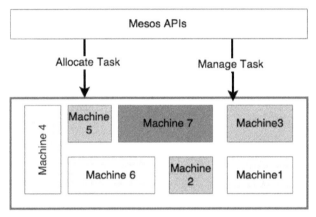

Cluster As A Single Machine

Mesos is an open source top-level Apache project under Apache License. It abstracts lower-level computing resources such as CPU, memory, and storage from the lower-level physical or virtual machines.

Before we examine why we need both Mesos and Marathon, let's understand the Mesos architecture.

Mesos architecture

The following diagram shows the simplest architecture representation of Mesos. The key components of Mesos include a **Mesos Master**, a set of slave nodes, a **ZooKeeper** service, and a Mesos framework. The Mesos framework is further subdivided into two components: a **Scheduler** and an **Executor**.

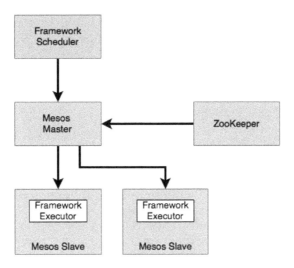

The boxes in the preceding diagram are explained as follows:

- **Master**: The **Mesos Master** is responsible for managing all Mesos slaves. It gets information on the resource availability from all slave nodes and takes responsibility of filling the resources appropriately, based on certain resource policies and constraints. The **Mesos Master** preempts available resources from all slave machines and pools them as a single large machine. Master offers resources to frameworks running on slave machines based on this resource pool.

  For high availability, the **Mesos Master** is supported by the Mesos master **standby** components. Even if the master is not available, existing tasks can be still executed. However, new tasks cannot be scheduled in the absence of a master node. The master standby nodes are nodes that wait for the failure of the active master and takeover the master role in case of a failure. They use **ZooKeeper** for the master leader election. Minimum quorum requirements must be met in this case for leader election.

- **Slave**: The Mesos slaves are responsible for hosting task execution frameworks. Tasks are executed on the slave nodes. Mesos slaves can be started with attributes as key value pairs, such as *datacenter* = *X*. This will be used for constraint evaluations when deploying workloads. Slave machines share resource availability to the **Mesos Master**.

- **ZooKeeper**: This is a centralized coordination server used in Mesos to coordinate activities across the Mesos cluster. Mesos uses **ZooKeeper** for leader election in case of a **Mesos Master** failure.

- **Framework**: The Mesos framework is responsible for understanding the application constraints, accepting resource offers from the master, and, finally, running the tasks on the slave resources offered by the master. The Mesos framework consists of two components: **Framework Scheduler** and **Framework Executor**.
- The **Scheduler** is responsible for registering to Mesos and handles resource offers.
- **Executor** runs the actual program on the Mesos slave nodes.

The framework is also responsible for enforcing certain policies and constraints. For example, a constraint can be, let's say, a minimum of 500 MB of RAM for execution.

The framework is a pluggable component and is replaceable with another framework. Its workflow is depicted in the following diagram:

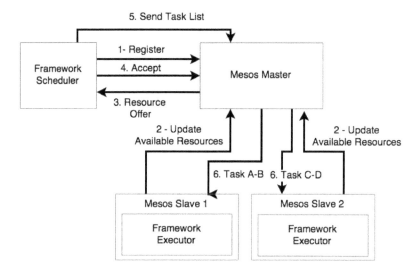

The steps denoted in the preceding workflow diagram are elaborated as follows:

1. The framework registers with the **Mesos Master** and waits for the resource offers. The scheduler may have many tasks in its queue to be executed with different resource constraints (task **A-D** in this example). A task, in this case, is a unit of work that is scheduled. For example, a Spring Boot microservice.
2. The Mesos slave offers available resources to the **Mesos Master**. For example, the slave advertizes the CPU and memory available with the slave machine.

3. **Mesos Master** creates a resource offer based on the allocation policies set and offers it to the scheduler component of the framework. The allocation policies determine to which framework the resources are to be offered and how many. The default policies can be customized by plugging additional allocation policies.

4. Scheduler framework components, based on the constraints, capabilities, and policies may accept or reject the resource offering. For example, the framework rejects the resource offer if the resources are insufficient as per the constraints and policies set.

5. If the scheduler component accepts the resource offer, it submits one or more task details to the **Mesos Master** with resource constraints per tasks. Let's say, in this example, it is ready to submit tasks **A-D**.

6. The **Mesos Master** sends this list of tasks to the slave where the resources are available. The framework executor components installed on the slave machines pick up and run these tasks.

Mesos supports a number of frameworks, such as the following:

- Marathon and Aurora for **long running** processes, such as web applications
- Hadoop, Spark, and Storm for **big data** processing
- Chronos and Jenkins for **batch scheduling**
- Cassandra and Elasticsearch for **data management**

In this chapter, we will use Marathon to run the dockerized microservices.

Marathon

Marathon is one of the Mesos framework implementations that can run both container as well as non-container execution. It is particularly designed for long running applications, such as a web server. It will ensure that the service started with Marathon will continue to be available even if the Mesos slave it is hosted on fails. This will be done by starting another instance.

Marathon is written in Scala and is highly scalable. It offers UI as well as REST APIs to interact with Marathon, such as starting, stopping, scaling, and monitoring applications.

Similar to Mesos, Marathon's high availability is achieved by running multiple Marathon instances pointing to a ZooKeeper instance. One of the Marathon instances will act as a leader and others will be in standby mode. In case the leading master fails, a leader election will take place and the next active master will be determined.

Some of the basic features of Marathon include the following:

- Setting resource constraints
- Scale up, scale down, and instance management of applications
- Application version management
    - Start and kill applications

Some of the advanced features of Marathon include the following:

- Rolling upgrades, rolling restarts, and rollbacks
- Blue-green deployments

Implementing Mesos and Marathon with DCOS

In Chapter 7, *Scale Microservices with Spring Cloud Components*, we discussed Eureka and Zuul for achieving load balancing. With container orchestration tools, load balancing and DNS services come out of the box and are much more simple to use. However, when developers need code-level control for load balancing and traffic routing, such as the business parameter based scaling scenarios mentioned earlier, Spring Cloud components may fit better.

 In order to understand the technologies better, we will use Mesos and Marathon directly in this chapter. However, in all practical scenarios, it is better to go with Mesosphere DCOS rather than playing with plain vanilla Mesos and Marathon.

DCOS offers a number of supporting components on and above plain Mesos and Marathon to manage enterprise-scale deployments.

 The DCOS architecture is well explained in the following link:
https://dcos.io/docs/1.9/overview/architecture

Let's do a side-by-side comparison of the components used for scaling microservices with Spring Cloud components and similar capabilities offered by DCOS.

The following points examines the major differences between Spring Cloud approach and DCOS:

- Configurations are managed using the Spring Cloud Config server when we approach with Spring Cloud for scaling microservices. When using DCOS, configurations can be managed by using one of Spring Cloud Config, Spring Profiles, or tools such as Puppet, Chef, and more.
- The Eureka server was used for managing service discovery and Zuul was used for load balancing with the Spring Cloud approach. DCOS has Mesos DNS, VIPs, and HAProxy based Marathon-lb components to achieve the same.
- Logging and monitoring, explained in `Chapter 8`, *Logging and Monitoring Microservices*, is accomplished using Spring Boot Actuator, Seluth, and Hystrix . DCOS offers various log aggregation and metrics collection features out of the box.

Implementing Mesos and Marathon for BrownField microservices

In this section, the dockerized Brownfield microservices developed in `Chapter 9`, *Containerizing Microservices with Docker*, will be deployed into the AWS cloud, and we will manage them with Mesos and Marathon.

For demonstration purposes, we will cover only two services (search and website deployment) in this chapter. Also, we will use one EC2 instance for the sake of simplicity.

Installing Mesos, Marathon, and related components

Launch a **t2.large** EC2 instance with the Ubuntu 16.04 version AMI, which will be used for this deployment. In this example, we are using another instance to run RabbitMQ; however, this can be done on the same instance as well.

Perform the following steps to install Mesos and Marathon:

- To install Mesos 1.2.0, follow the instructions documented in the following link. This will also install JDK 8:

    https://mesos.apache.org/gettingstarted/.

- To install Docker, perform the following steps:

    ```
    sudo apt-get update
    sudo apt-get install docker.io
    sudo docker version
    ```

- To install Marathon 1.4.3, follow the steps documented in the following link:

    ```
    curl -O http://downloads.mesosphere.com/marathon
      /v1.4.3/marathon-1.4.3.tgz
    tar xzf marathon-1.4.3.tgz
    ```

- To install ZooKeeper, perform the following steps:

    ```
    wget http://ftp.unicamp.br/pub/apache/zookeeper/zookeeper-
      3.4.9/zookeeper-3.4.9.tar.gz
    tar -xzvf zookeeper-3.4.9.tar.gz
    rm -rf zookeeper-3.4.9.tar.gz
    cd zookeeper-3.4.9/
    cp zoo_sample.cfg  zoo.cfg
    ```

Alternatively, you may use the DCOS package distribution on AWS using CloudFormation, which offers a high availability Mesos cluster out of the box.

Running Mesos and Marathon

Perform the following steps to run Mesos and Marathon:

1. Log in to the EC2 instance and run the following commands:

    ```
    ubuntu@ip-172-31-19-249:~/zookeeper-3.4.9
    $ sudo -E bin/zkServer.sh start

    ubuntu@ip-172-31-19-249:~/mesos-1.2.0/build/bin
    $ ./mesos-master.sh --work_dir=/home/ubuntu/mesos-
      1.2.0/build/mesos-server

    ubuntu@ip-172-31-19-249:~/marathon-1.4.3
    ```

```
$ MESOS_NATIVE_JAVA_LIBRARY=/home/ubuntu/mesos-
  1.2.0/build/src/.libs/libmesos.so ./bin/start --master
  172.31.19.249:5050
```

ubuntu@ip-172-31-19-249:~/mesos-1.2.0/build
```
$ sudo ./bin/mesos-agent.sh --master=172.31.19.249:5050 --
  containerizers=mesos,docker --work_dir=/home/ubuntu/mesos-
  1.2.0/build/mesos-agent --resources='ports:[0-32000]'
```

Note that the relative path for a working directory may lead to execution problems. The `--resources` are required only if you want to force the host port to be in a certain range.

2. If you have more slave machines, you may repeat slave commands on those machines to add more nodes to the cluster.

3. Open the following URL to see the Mesos console. In this example, there are three slaves running, connecting to the master:

   ```
   http://ec2-54-68-132-236.us-west-2.compute.amazonaws.com:5050
   ```

You will see the Mesos console similar to the following screenshot:

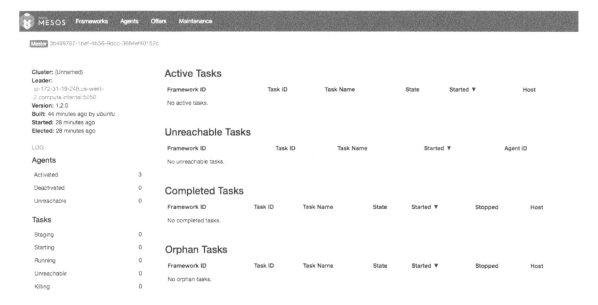

The **Agents** section of the console shows that there are three activated Mesos agents available for execution. It also indicates that there is no **Active Tasks**.

4. Open the following URL to inspect the Marathon UI. Replace the IP address with the public IP address of the EC2 instance:

   `http://ec2-54-68-132-236.us-west-2.compute.amazonaws.com:8080`

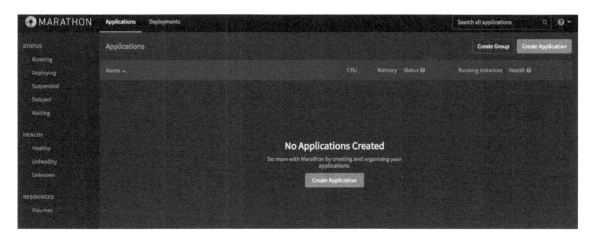

Since there are no applications deployed so far, the **Applications** section of the UI is empty.

Preparing BrownField PSS services

In the previous section, we successfully set up Mesos and Marathon. In this section, we will see how to deploy the BrownField PSS application previously developed using Mesos and Marathon.

The full source code of this chapter is available under the `chapter10` projects in the code files under `https://github.com/rajeshrv/Spring5Microservice`. Copy `chapter9.*` into a new STS workspace and rename it `chapter10.*`.

In this example, we will force the Mesos cluster to bind to fixed ports, but, in an ideal world, we will delegate the Mesos cluster to dynamically bind services to ports. Also, since we are not using a DNS or HA Proxy, we will hardcode the IP addresses. In the real world, a VIP for each service will be defined, and that VIP will be used by the services. This VIP will be resolved by the DNS and Proxy.

Perform the following steps to change the BrownField application to run on AWS:

1. Update search microservices (`application.properties`) to reflect the RabbitMQ IP and port. Also, update the website (`Application.java` and `BrownFieldSiteController.java`) to reflect the IP address of the EC2 machines.

2. Rebuild all microservices using Maven. Build and push the Docker images to the Docker Hub. The working directory has to be switched to the respective directories before executing these commands from the respective folders:

```
docker build -t search-service:1.0 .
docker tag search:1.0 rajeshrv/search:1.0
docker push rajeshrv/search:1.0

docker build -t website:1.0 .
docker tag website:1.0 rajeshrv/website:1.0
docker push rajeshrv/website:1.0
```

Deploying BrownField PSS services

The Docker images are now published to the Docker Hub registry. Perform the following steps to deploy and run the BrownFIeld PSS services:

1. Start the dockerized RabbitMQ:

```
sudo docker run --net=host rabbitmq:3
```

2. At this point, the Mesos Marathon cluster is up and running and is ready to accept deployments. The deployment can be done by creating one JSON file per service, as follows:

```
{
  "id": "search-3.0",
  "container": {
    "type": "DOCKER",
    "docker": {
      "image": "rajeshrv/search:1.0",
      "network": "BRIDGE",
      "portMappings": [
        { "containerPort": 8090, "hostPort": 8090 }
      ]

    }
  },
```

```
    "instances": 1,
    "cpus": 0.5,
    "mem": 512
}
```

3. The preceding JSON will be stored on the `search.json` file. Similarly, create a JSON file for other services as well.

   The JSON structure is explained as follows:

   - `id`: This is a unique `id` of the application and it can be a logical name.
   - `Cpus`, `mem`: This sets the resource constraints for this application. If the resource offer does not satisfy this resource constraint, Marathon will reject that resource offer from the Mesos Master.
   - `instances`: How many instances of this application to start with? In the preceding configuration, by default, it starts one instance as soon as it gets deployed. Marathon will maintain the number of instances mentioned at any point.
   - `container`: This parameter tells the Marathon executor to use the Docker container for execution.
   - `image`: This tells the Marathon scheduler which Docker image has to be used for deployment. In this case, this will download the `search-service:1.0` image from the Docker Hub repository, `rajeshrv`.
   - `network`: This value is used for Docker runtime to advice on the `network` mode to be used when starting the new Docker container. This can be `BRIDGE` or `HOST`. In this case, the `BRIDGE` mode will be used.
   - `portMappings`: The port mapping provides information on how to map internal and external ports. In the preceding configuration, `hostPort`, set as `8090`, tells the Marathon executor to use `8090` when starting the service. Since `containerPort` is set as `0`, the same host port will be assigned to the container. Marathon picks up random ports if the `hostPort` value is `0`.

4. Once this JSON is created and saved, deploy this to Marathon using the Marathon REST APIs as follows:

   ```
   curl -X POST http://54.85.107.37:8080/v2/apps
     -d @search.json -H "Content-type: application/json"
   ```

5. Alternatively, use the Marathon console for deployment as follows:

```json
New Application                                          JSON Mode ⬤

 1  {
 2    "id": "search-3.0",
 3    "container": {
 4      "type": "DOCKER",
 5      "docker": {
 6        "image": "rajeshrv/search:1.0",
 7        "network": "BRIDGE",
 8        "portMappings": [
 9          {   "containerPort": 8090, "hostPort": 8090 }
10        ]
11
12      }
13    },
14    "instances": 1,
15    "cpus": 0.5,
16    "mem": 512
17  }
18
```

Cancel   **Create Application**

6. Repeat this step for the website as well.

7. Open the Marathon UI. As shown in the following diagram, the UI shows that both the applications are deployed and are in the **Running** state. It also indicates that a **1 of 1** instance is in the **Running** state.

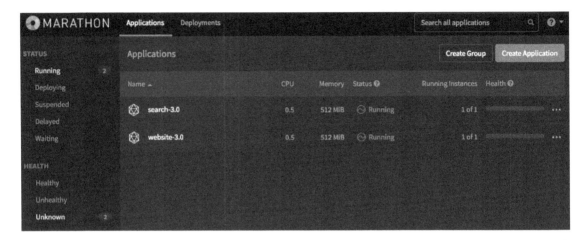

8. If you inspect the search service, it shows `ip` and the port it is bound to:

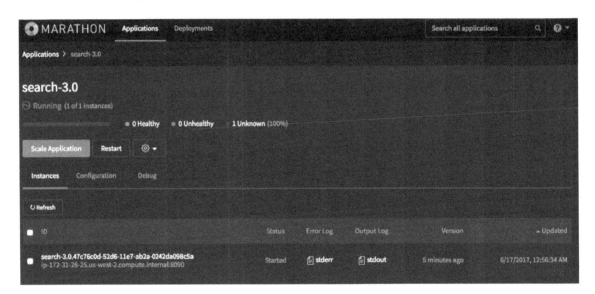

9. Open the following URL in a browser to verify the website application:

```
http://ec2-34-210-109-17.us-west-2.compute.amazonaws.com:8001
```

Summary

In this chapter, we learned the different aspects of autoscaling applications and the importance of a container orchestration to efficiently manage dockerized microservices at scale.

We explored the different container orchestration tools before deep diving into Mesos and Marathon. We also implemented Mesos and Marathon in the AWS cloud environment to demonstrate how to manage dockerized microservices developed for the BrownField PSS.

So far, we have seen all the core and supporting technology capabilities required for a successful microservices implementation. A successful microservice implementation also requires processes and practices beyond technology. In the next chapter, the last in the book, we will cover the process and practice perspectives of microservices.

11
Microservice Development Life Cycle

Similar to the **software development life cycle** (**SDLC**), it is important to understand the aspects around the microservice development life cycle processes for a successful implementation of microservice architecture.

This final chapter will focus on the development process and practice of microservices with the help of the BrownField Airline's PSS microservices example. Furthermore, this chapter will describe the best practices to structure development teams, development methodologies, automated testing, and continuous delivery of microservices, in line with the DevOps practices. Finally, this chapter will conclude by shedding light on the importance of reference architecture in a decentralized governance approach for microservices.

By the end of this chapter, we will have learned about the following:

- Reviewing a number of practice points that are useful when developing microservices
- Best practices around automating development, testing, and deployment of internet-scale microservices

Practice points for microservice development

For a successful microservice delivery, a number of development to delivery practices need to be considered, including the DevOps philosophy. In the previous chapters, you learned about the different architecture capabilities of microservices. In this section, we will explore the non-architectural aspects of microservice developments.

Understanding business motivation and value

Microservices should not be used for the sake of implementing a niche architecture style. It is extremely important to understand the business value and business KPIs before selecting microservices as an architectural solution for a given problem. A good understanding of the business motivation and business value will help the engineers focus on achieving those goals in a cost-effective way.

The business motivation and value should justify the selection of microservices. Also, by using microservices, the business value should be realizable from a business point of view. This will avoid situations where IT invests in microservices, but there is no appetite from the business to leverage any of the benefits microservices can bring to the table. In such cases, a microservices-based development will be an overhead to the enterprise.

Change the mindset from project to product development

As discussed in `Chapter 1`, *Demystifying Microservices*, microservices are more aligned to product development. Business capabilities that are delivered using microservices should be treated as products.

The mindsets for project and product development are different. The product team will always have a sense of ownership and take responsibility of what they produce. As a result, the product team always tries to improve the quality of the product. The product team is not only responsible for delivering the software, but also for the production support and maintenance of the product.

The product teams are generally linked directly to a business department for which they are developing the product. In general, product teams will have both an IT and a business representative. As a result, product thinking will be closely aligned with the actual business goals. At every moment, the product teams understand the value they are adding to the business to achieve the business goals. The success of the product directly lies with the business value gained out of the product.

Because of the high velocity release cycles, the product teams always get a sense of satisfaction in their delivery, and they always try to improve on that. This will bring a lot more positive dynamics within the team.

In many cases, typical product teams are funded for a long term, and they remain intact. As a result, the product teams will become more cohesive in nature. Since they are small in size, such teams focus on improving their process from their day-to-day learning.

Choosing the right development philosophy

Different organizations take different approaches to develop microservices, be it a migration or a new development. It is important to choose an approach that suits the organization. There are many approaches available, such as design thinking, agile, and startup models. It is important to choose an approach that avoids the long development cycle, which is essential for microservices development.

Using the concept of minimum viable product (MVP)

Irrespective of the development philosophy explained earlier, it is essential to identify a **minimum viable product** (**MVP**) when developing microservice systems for speed and agility.

Eric Ries, pioneering the lean startup movement, defined MVP as follows:

> *A Minimum Viable Product is that version of a new product which allows a team to collect the maximum amount of validated learning about customers with the least effort.*

The objective of the MVP approach is to quickly build a piece of software that showcases the most important aspects of the software. The MVP realizes the core concept of an idea, and, perhaps, chooses those features that add maximum value to the business. MVP will help you get an early feedback, and then correct as necessary before building a heavy product.

MVP may be a full-fledged service addressing limited user groups or partial services addressing wider user groups. The feedback from customers is extremely important in the MVP approach. Therefore, it is important to release MVP to the real users.

Overcoming the legacy hotspot

It is important to understand the environment and political challenges in the organization before embarking on the microservices development.

It is common in microservices to have dependencies to other legacy applications, directly or indirectly. A common issue with direct legacy integrations are the slow development cycles of the legacy application. For example, an innovative railway reservation system relaying on an age old **transaction processing facility** (**TPF**) for some of the core backend features, such as reservation. This is especially common when migrating legacy monolithic applications to microservices. In many cases, legacy systems will continue to undergo development in a non-agile way with larger release cycles. In such cases, the microservices development teams may not be able to move so quickly, because of the coupling with legacy systems. The integration points might drag the microservices developments heavily. Organizational political challenges make things even worse.

There is no silver bullet for solving this issue. The cultural difference and process difference could be an ongoing issue. Many enterprises ring-fence such legacy systems with focused attention and investments to support fast moving microservices. Targeted C-level interventions on those legacy platforms could reduce the overhead.

Establishing self-organizing teams

One of the most important activities in microservices development is to establish the right teams for development. As recommended in many DevOps processes, a small focused team will always deliver the best results.

As shown in the following diagram, there may be one team per microservices, or one team for a group of related microservices depending on the size of microservices:

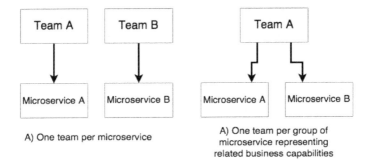

A) One team per microservice

A) One team per group of microservice representing related business capabilities

Since microservices are aligned with business capabilities and are fairly loosely-coupled products, it is ideal to have a dedicated team per microservice. There could be cases where the same team owns multiple microservices from the same business area, representing related capabilities. These are generally decided by the coupling and size of the microservices.

The team size is an important aspect of setting up effective teams for microservices development. A general notion is that the team size should not exceed 10 people. The recommended size for optimal delivery is between four-seven. The founder of *Amazon.com*, Jeff Bezos, coined the theory of two pizza teams. Jeff's theory says the team will face communication issues if the size gets bigger. Larger teams work with consensus, which results in increased wastage. Large teams also lose ownership and accountability. A yardstick is that the product owner should get enough time to speak to the individuals in the team to make them understand the value of what they are delivering.

The teams are expected to take full ownership in ideating, analyzing, developing, and supporting the services. Werner Vogels from *Amazon.com* calls this approach **you build it and you run it**. As per Werner's theory, developers pay more attention to develop quality code to avoid unexpected support calls. The members in the team will consist of full stack developers and operational engineers. The team will be fully aware of all the areas. The developers will understand operations as well as the operations teams understand applications. This not only reduces the changes of throwing the mud across teams, but it also improves the quality.

Teams should have multidisciplinary skills to satisfy all capabilities required to deliver the service. The team ideally should not rely on external teams to deliver components of the service. Instead, the team should be self-sufficient. However, in most of the organizations, the challenge is on specialized skills, which are rare. For example, there may not be many experts in the organization on a graph database. One common solution to this problem is to use the concepts of consultants. Consultants are SMEs and will be engaged to get expertise on specific problems faced by the team. Some organizations also use shared teams or platform teams to deliver some common capabilities.

The team members will have a full understanding of the product, not only from the technical standpoint, but also from the business case and the business KPIs. The team will have a collective ownership in delivering the product as well as in achieving the business goals together.

Self-organizing teams act as a cohesive unit and find ways to achieve their goals as a team. The team will automatically align themselves and distribute the responsibilities. The members in the team are self-managed and empowered to make decisions on their day-to-day work. Communication and transparency are extremely important in such teams. This emphasizes the need for colocation and collaboration, with high bandwidth for communication.

In the preceding diagram, both **Microservice A** and **Microservice B** represents related business capabilities. Self-organizing teams treat everyone in the team equally, without too many hierarchies and management overheads within the team. The management will be thin in such cases. There won't be many designated vertical skills in the team, such as team lead, UX manager, development manager, testing manager, and so on. In a typical microservice development, a shared product manager, architect, and people manager are good enough to manage the different microservice teams. In some organizations, architects also take up the delivery responsibility.

Self-organizing teams will have some level of autonomy and are empowered to take decisions in a quick and agile mode, rather than having to wait for long running bureaucratic decision making processes that exist in many enterprises. In many of these cases, enterprise architecture and security are seen as an afterthought. However, it is important to have them on board from the beginning. While empowering the teams with maximum freedom for developers in decision making capabilities, it is equally important to have fully automated QA and compliance, so as to ensure that deviations are captured at the earliest.

Communication between teams is important. However, in an ideal world, it should be limited to interfaces between microservices. Integrations between teams ideally has to be handled through **Consumer-Driven Contracts** in the form of test scripts rather than having large interface documents describing various scenarios. Teams will use mock service implementations when services are not available.

Building the self-service cloud

One of the key aspects one should consider before embarking on microservices is to build a cloud environment. When there are only a few services, it is easy to manage them by manually assigning them to a certain predesignated set of virtual machines.

However, what microservice developers need is more than just an IaaS cloud platform. Neither the developers, nor the operations engineers in the team should worry about where the application is deployed and how optimally it is deployed. They also should not worry about how the capacity is managed.

This level of sophistication requires a cloud platform with self-service capabilities, such as what we have seen in Chapter 10, *Scaling Dockerized Microservices with Mesos and Marathon*, with the Mesos and Marathon cluster management solutions. Containerized deployment, discussed in Chapter 9, *Containerizing Microservices with Docker*, is also important in managing an end to-end-automation. Building this self-service cloud ecosystem is a prerequisite for microservice development.

Building a microservices ecosystem

As we have seen in Chapter 4, *Applying Microservices Concepts*, under the capability model, microservices require a number of other capabilities. All these capabilities should be in place before implementing microservices at scale.

These capabilities include service registration, discovery, API gateways, and externalized configuration services and more; these are all provided by the Spring Cloud project. Capabilities such as centralized logging, monitoring, and more are also required as a prerequisite for microservices development.

DevOps as a life cycle process

DevOps is the best suited practice for microservices development. Organizations already practicing DevOps do not need another practice for microservices development.

In this section, we will explore the life cycle of microservices development. Rather than reinventing a process for microservices, we will explore the DevOps processes and practices from the microservice perspective.

Before we explore the DevOps processes, let's iron out some of the common terminologies used in the DevOps world:

- **Continuous Integration** (**CI**) is automating the application build and quality checks continuously in a designated environment, either in a time-triggered manner or on developer commits. CI also publishes code metrics to a central dashboard as well as binary artifacts to a central repository. CI is popular in agile development practices.
- **Continuous Delivery** (**CD**) is automating the end-to-end software delivery practice, ranging from ideas to production. In a non-DevOps model, this used to be known as **Application Lifecycle Management** (**ALM**). One of the common interpretations of CD is that it is the next evolution of CI, which adds the QA cycles into the integration pipeline and makes the software ready to release to production. A manual action is required to move to production.
- **Continuous Deployment** is an approach to automate deploying application binaries into one or more environments by managing binary movement and associated configuration parameters. A second interpretation of continuous deployment is the next evolution of CD by automatic release to production into the CD pipeline.

- **Application Release Automation** (**ARA tools**) are tools that help monitor and manage end-to-end delivery pipelines. The ARA tools use CI and CD tools and manage additional steps of release management approvals. ARA tools are also capable of rolling out releases to different environments and rolling them back in case of a failed deployment. ARA provides a fully-orchestrated workflow pipeline, implementing delivery life cycles by integrating many specialized tools for repository management, quality assurance, deployment, and so on. XL Deploy and Automic are some of the ARA tools.

The following diagram shows the DevOps process for microservices development:

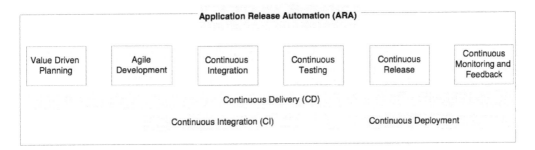

Let's now further explore these life cycle stages of microservices development.

Value driven planning

Value driven planning is a term used in agile development practices. Value driven planning is extremely important in the microservices development. In value driven planning, we will identify which microservices to develop. The most important aspect is to identify those requirements that have the highest value to the business and those that have the lowest risks. The MVP philosophy will be used when developing microservices from the ground-up. In the case of monolithic to microservices migration, we will use the guidelines provided in Chapter 6, *Microservices Evolution – A Case Study*, to identify which services have to be taken first. The selected microservices are expected to precisely deliver the expected value to the business. Business KPIs for measuring this value have to be identified as part of the value driven planning.

Continuous monitoring and feedback

The continuous monitoring and feedback phase is the most important phase in agile microservices development. In an MVP scenario, this phase gives feedback on the initial acceptance of the MVP and also evaluates the value of the service developed. In a feature addition scenario, this further gives an insight into how that new feature is accepted by users. Based on the feedback, the services will be adjusted and the same cycle is then repeated.

Automating development cycle

In the previous section, we saw the life cycle of microservices development. The life cycle stages can be altered by organizations based on their organizational needs, but also based on the nature of the application. In this section, we will see a sample continuous delivery pipeline, as well as tools set to implement a sample pipeline.

There are many tools available to build end-to-end pipelines, both in the open source and the commercial space. Organizations can select the products of their choice to connect the pipeline tasks.

 Refer to the Xebialabs periodic table (`https://xebialabs.com/periodic-table-of-devops-tools/`) for tool references to build continuous delivery pipelines.

The pipelines may initially be expensive to set up, as it requires many tool sets and environments. Organizations may not realize an immediate cost benefit in implementing the delivery pipeline. Also, building a pipeline needs high power resources. Large build pipelines may involve hundreds of machines. It also takes hours to move changes through the pipeline from one end to the other. Hence, it is important to have different pipelines for different microservices. This will also help to decouple between releases of different microservices.

Within a pipeline, parallelism should be employed to execute tests on different environments. It is also important to parallelize the execution of test cases as much as possible. Hence, designing the pipeline based on the nature of the application is important. There is no one size fit for all scenarios.

The key focus in the pipeline is on the end-to-end automation, ranging from development to production, and on failing fast, if something goes wrong.

The following pipeline is an indicative one for microservices, and explores different capabilities that one should consider when developing a microservices pipeline:

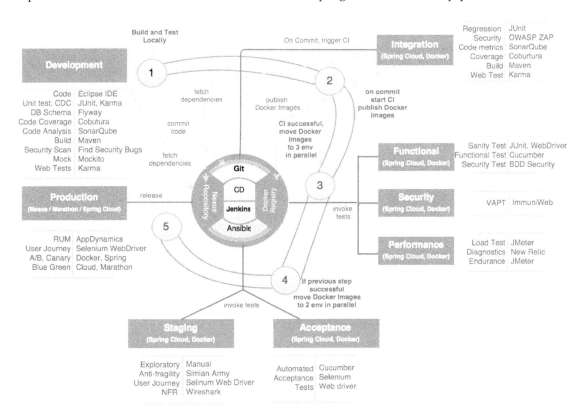

The continuous delivery pipeline stages are explained next.

Development

The development stage will have the following activities from a development perspective. This section also indicates some of the tools that can be used in the development stage. These tools are in addition to the planning, tracking, and communication tools, such as Agile Jira, Slack, and more, used by the agile development teams:

- **Source code**: The development team requires an IDE or a development environment to cut source code. In most organizations, developers get the freedom to choose the IDEs they want. Having said that, the IDEs can be integrated with a number of tools to detect violations against guidelines. Generally, the Eclipse IDEs have plugins for static code analysis and code matrices. **SonarQube** is one example that integrates other plugins, such as **Checkstyle** for code conventions, **PMD** for detecting bad practices, **FindBugs** for detecting potential bugs, and **Cobertura** for code coverage. It is also recommended to use Eclipse plugins, such as **ESVD**, **Find Security Bugs**, **SonarQube security rules**, and more, to detect security vulnerabilities.

- **Unit test cases**: The development team will also produce unit test cases using **JUnit**, **NUnit**, **TestNG**, and more. The unit test cases will be written against components, repository, services, and more. These unit test cases will be integrated with the local maven builds. The unit test cases targeting the microservice endpoints (service test) will serve as the regression test pack. Web UI, if written on Angular JS, can be tested using **Karma**.

- **Consumer driven contracts**: Developers are also to write CDCs to test integration points with other microservices. Contract test cases will be generally written as JUnit, NUnit, TestNG, and more, and will be added to the service tests pack mentioned in the earlier steps.

- **Mock testing**: Developers also write mocks to simulate the integration endpoints to execute the unit test cases. **Mockito**, **PowerMock**, and more are generally used for mock testing. It is a good practice to deploy a mock service based on the contract as soon as the service contract is identified. This will act as a simple mechanism for service virtualization for the subsequent phases.

- **Behavior driven design (BDD)**: The agile team also writes BDD scenarios using one of the BDD tools, such as Cucumber. Typically, these scenarios will be targeted against the microservices contract or the user interface, which is exposed by a microservice-based web application. Cucumber with JUnit and Cucumber with **Selenium WebDriver** respectively will be used on these scenarios. Different scenarios will be used for functional testing, user journey testing, as well as acceptance testing.

- **Source code repository**: A source control repository is a part and parcel of the development. Developers check-in their code to a central repository, mostly with the help of IDE plugins. One microservice per repository is a common pattern used by many organizations. This will disallow other microservice developers from modifying other microservices or writing code based on internal representations of other microservices. **Git** and **Subversion** are the popular choices used as a source code repository.

- **Build tool**: A build tool such as **Maven** or **Gradle** is used to manage dependencies and build target artifacts; in this case, Spring Boot services. There are many cases, such as basic quality checks, security checks, unit test cases, code coverage, and more that will be integrated as part of the build itself. These are similar to the IDE, especially when the IDEs are not used by developers. The tools that we have examined as part of the IDEs are also available as maven plugins. The development team will not use containers such as Docker until the CI phase of the project. All the artifacts will have to be versioned properly for every change.

- **Artifact repository**: The artifact repository plays a pivotal role in the development process. It is where all build artifacts are stored. It could be **Artifactory**, **Nexus**, or any similar product.

- **Database schemas**: **Liquibase** and **Flyway** are commonly used to manage, track, and apply database changes. The maven plugins allow interactions with the Liquibase or Flyway libraries. The schema changes will be versioned and maintained, just like in the source code.

Integration

Once the code is committed to the repository, the next phase, continuous integration, will automatically start. This is done by configuring a CI pipeline. This phase will build the source code with a repository snapshot and generate deployable artifacts. Different organizations use different events to kick-start the build. A CI start event may be on every developer commit or may be based on a time window, such as daily, weekly, and more.

The CI workflow is the key aspect of this phase. Continuous integration tools, such as **Jenkins**, **Bamboo**, and more, play the central role of orchestrating the build pipeline. The tool will be configured with a workflow of activities to be invoked. The workflow automatically executes the configured steps, such as build, deploy, and QA. On the developer commit or on a set frequency, the CI will kick-start the workflow.

The following activities will take place in a continuous integration workflow:

- **Build and QA**: The workflow will listen to the Git webhooks for any commits. Once it detects a change, the first activity will be to download the source code from the repository. A build will be executed on the downloaded snapshot source code. As part of the build, a number of QA checks will be automatically performed, which are similar to the QA check executed in the development environment. These include code quality checks, security checks, and code coverage. Many of the QAs will be done with tools, such as SonarQube, and the IDE plugins mentioned under the development section earlier. It also collects code metrics, such as code coverage and more, and publishes it to a central database for analysis. Additional security checks will be executed using **OWASP ZAP Jenkins'** plugins. As a part of the build, it also executes the JUnit, or similar tools used to write test cases. If the web application supports Karma for UI testing, Jenkins is also capable of running web tests written on Karma. If the build or QA fails, then it sends out the alarms as configured in the system.
- **Packaging**: Once build and QA are passed, the CI will create a deployable package. In our microservices case, it generates the Spring Boot standalone jar. It is recommended to build Docker images as a part of the integration build. This is the one and only place where we build the binary artifacts. Once the build is complete, it pushes the immutable Docker images to a **Docker registry**. This could be on Docker Hub or to a private Docker registry. It is important to properly version control the containers at this stage itself.
- **Integration tests**: The Docker image will be moved to the integration environment, where regression tests (service tests) and the likes will be executed. This environment will have other dependent microservices capabilities, such as Spring Cloud, logging, and more, in place. All dependent microservices will also be there in this environment. If an actual dependent service is not yet deployed, service virtualization tools, such as **MockServer**, will be used. Alternately, a base version of the service will be pushed to the Git by the respective development teams. Once successfully deployed, Jenkins will trigger service tests (JUnits against services), a set of end-to-end sanity tests written in Selenium WebDriver (in the case of the web), and security tests with **OWASP ZAP**.

Testing

There are many types of testing to be executed as part of the automated delivery process before declaring the build as ready for production. The testing may happen by moving the application across multiple environments. Each environment will be designated for a particular testing, such as acceptance testing, performance testing, and more. These environments will be adequately monitored to gather respective metrics.

In a complex microservices environment, testing should not be seen as a last minute gate check; rather, testing should be considered as a way to improve the software quality as well as to avoid last minute failures. Shift left testing is an approach for shifting tests as early as possible in the release cycle. Automated testing will turn software development to every day development, every day testing mode. By automating test cases, we will avoid manual errors as well as the effort required to complete the testing.

The CI or ARA tools will be used to move the Docker images across multiple test environments. Once deployed in an environment, test cases will be executed based on the purpose of the environment. By default, a set of sanity tests will be executed to verify the test environment.

In this section, we will cover all types of tests that are required in the automated delivery pipeline, irrespective of the environment. We have already seen some types of tests as a part of the development and integration environment. Later in this section, we will also map test cases against the environments in which they are executed. There are different types of tests that we can automate.

Sanity tests

When moving from one environment to another, it is advisable to run a few sanity tests to make sure that all basic things are working. This will be created as a test pack using JUnit service tests, Selenium WebDriver, or a similar tool. It is important to carefully identify and script all critical service calls. Especially if the microservices are integrated using synchronous dependencies, it is better to consider those scenarios to ensure that all dependent services are also up and running.

Regression testing

Regression tests will ensure that the changes in the software are not breaking the system. In a microservices context, the regression tests could be at the service level (Rest API or message endpoints), and written using JUnit or a similar framework, as explained earlier. The service virtualizations will be used when dependent services are not available. Karma and Jasmine can be used for web UI testing. In cases where the microservices are used behind web applications, Selenium WebDriver or a similar tool will be used to prepare regression test packs and tests will be conducted at the UI level rather than focusing on the service endpoints. Alternately, BDD tools, such as Cucumber with JUnit or Cucumber with Selenium WebDriver, can also be used to prepare the regression test packs. CI tools, such as Jenkins or ARA, will be used to automatically trigger the regression test packs. There are other commercial tools, such as TestComplete, that can also be used to build regression test packs.

Functional testing

The functional test cases will be generally targeted at the UIs that are consuming the microservices. These are business scenarios based on the user stories or features. These functional tests will be executed on every build to ensure that the microservice is performing as expected. BDD will be generally used in developing functional test cases. Typically, in BDD, the business analysts write test cases in plain English. The developers then add scripts to execute those scenarios. Automated web testing tools, such as Selenium WebDriver, will be useful in such scenarios together with BDD tools, such as Cucumber, JBehave, Spec Flow, and more. JUnit test cases will be used in the case of headless microservices. There are pipelines that combine both, regression testing and functional testing as one step with the same set of test cases.

Acceptance testing

This is similar to the preceding functional test cases. In many cases, the automated acceptance tests generally use the screenplay or journey pattern, and are applied at the web application level. The customer perspective will be used in building the test cases rather than features or functions. These tests will mimic user flows. The BDD tools, such as Cucumber, JBehave, and SpecFlow, are generally used in these scenarios together with JUnit or Selenium WebDriver, as discussed in the previous scenario. The nature of the test cases will be different in functional and acceptance testing. Automation of acceptance test packs will be achieved by integrating them with Jenkins. There are many other specialized automatic acceptance testing tools available in the market. FitNesse is one such tool.

Performance testing

It is important to automate performance testing as part of the delivery pipeline. This will position performance testing from a gate check model to integral part of the delivery pipeline. By doing so, bottlenecks can be identified at the very early stages of the build cycles. In some organizations, performance tests will be conducted only for major releases, but, in others, performance tests are a part of the pipeline. There are multiple options for performance testing. Tools such as JMeter, Gatling, Grinder, and more can be used for load testing. These tools can be integrated into the Jenkins workflow for automation. Tools such as BlazeMeter can then be used for test reporting. Application Performance Management tools, such as AppDynamics, New Relic, Dynatrace, and more, provide quality metrics as part of the delivery pipeline. This can be done using these tools as part of the performance testing environment. In some pipelines, these are integrated into the functional testing environment to get better coverage. Jenkins has plugins in to fetch measurements.

Real user flow simulation or Journey testing

This is another form of tests, typically used in staging and production environments. These tests will be continuously running in staging and production environments to ensure that all critical transactions are performing as expected. This is much more useful than the typical URL ping monitoring mechanism. Generally, similar to the automated acceptance testing, these test cases will simulate user journeys as they happen in the real world. These are also useful to check whether the dependent microservices are up and running. These test cases could be a carved-out subset of acceptance test cases or test packs created using Selenium WebDriver.

Security testing

It is extremely important to make sure that the automation is not violating the security policies of the organization. Security is most important and compromising it for speed is not desirable. Hence, it is important to integrate security testing as part of the delivery pipeline. Some of the security evaluations are already integrated in the local build environment as well as in the integration environment, such as SonarQube, Find Security Bugs, and more. Some security aspects will be covered as part of the functional test cases. Tools such as BDD-Security, Mittn, and Gauntlt are other security test automation tools following the BDD approach. VAPT can be done using tools such as ImmuniWeb. OWASP ZAP, and Burp Suite, which are other useful tools for security testing.

Exploratory testing

Exploratory testing is a manual testing approach done by the testers or the business users to validate specific scenarios that they think the automated tools may not capture. The testers interact with the system in any manner they want without any prejudgment. They use their intellect to identify scenarios that they think some special users may explore. They also do exploratory testing by simulating certain user behavior.

A/B testing, Canary testing, and blue-green deployments

When moving applications to production, A/B testing, blue-green deployments, and Canary testing are generally applied. A/B testing is primarily used to review the effectiveness of a change and how the market reacts to the change. The new features will be rolled out to a certain set of users. A Canary release is moving a new product or feature to a certain community before fully rolling out to all customers. Blue-green is a deployment strategy from an IT point of view to test the new version of a service. In this model, both blue and green will be up and running at some point of time and then gracefully migrate from one to the other.

Other non-functional tests

High availability and anti-fragility testing (Failure Injection tests) are also important to execute before production. This will help developers unearth unknown errors that may occur in a real production scenario. This is generally done by breaking components of the system to understand their failover behavior. This is also helpful to test the circuit breakers and fallback services in the system. Tools such as Simian Army are useful in these scenarios.

Testing in production (TiP)

Testing in production is as important as all the other environments, as we can only simulate to a certain extent. There are two types of tests generally executed against production. The first approach is running real user flows or journey tests in a continuous manner simulating various user actions. This will be automated using one of the **Real User Monitoring** (**RUM**) tools, such as AppDynamics. The second approach is to wiretap messages from production and execute them in a staging environment, then compare the results in production with those in the staging environment.

Antifragility testing

Antifragility testing is generally conducted in a preproduction environment identical to production, or even in a production environment, by creating chaos in the environment to see how the application responds and recovers from those situations. Over a period of time, the application gains the ability to automatically recover from most of these failures. Simian Army is one such tool from Netflix. It is a suite of products built for the AWS environment. Also, it is for disruptive testing using a set of autonomous monkeys that can create chaos in the preproduction or production environments. Chaos Monkey, Janitor Monkey, and Conformity Monkey are some of the components of Simian Army.

Deployment

Continuous deployment is the process of deploying applications to one or more environments, and configuring and provisioning those environments accordingly. As discussed in `Chapter 9`, *Containerizing Microservices with Docker*, the infrastructure provisioning and automation tools will facilitate the deployment automation.

From the deployment perspective, the released Docker images will be moved to production automatically once all quality checks are successfully completed. The production environment, in this case, has to be cloud based with a cluster management tool such as Mesos or Marathon. A self-service cloud environment with monitoring capabilities is mandatory.

The cluster management and application deployment tools will ensure that application dependencies are properly deployed. This will automatically deploy all dependencies that are required in case any are missing. It also ensures that a minimum number of instances are running at any point in time. In case of failures, it automatically rolls back the deployments. It also takes care of rolling back upgrades in a graceful manner.

Tools such as **Ansible**, **Chef**, or **Puppet** will be useful to move configurations and binaries to production. Ansible play book concepts can be used to launch a Mesos cluster with Marathon and Docker support.

Monitoring and feedback

Once an application is deployed in production, the monitoring tools will continuously monitor its services. The monitoring tools and the log management tools will collect and analyze information. Based on the feedback and corrective actions needed, information will be fed to the development teams to take corrective actions, and changes are pushed back to production through the pipeline. Tools such as **APM**, **Open Web Analytics**, **Google Analytics**, **Webalizer**, and more are useful tools to monitor web applications. Real user monitoring should provide the end-to-end monitoring. **QuBit**, **Boxever**, **Channel Site**, **MaxTraffic**, and more are also useful in analyzing customer behaviors.

Configuration management

Configuration management also has to be rethought from a microservices and DevOps perspective. Use new methods for configuration management rather than using a traditional statically configured CMDB. Manual maintenance of a CMDB is no longer an option. The statically managed CMDB requires a lot of mundane tasks to maintain entries. At the same time, due to the dynamic nature of the deployment topology, it will be extremely hard to maintain data in a consistent way.

The new styles of CMDBs automatically create CI configurations based on the operational topology. These should be discovery-based to get up-to-date information. The new CMDB should be capable of managing bare metals, virtual machines, and containers.

Microservices development governance, reference architectures, and libraries

It is important to have an overall enterprise reference architecture and standard set of tool for microservices development to ensure that development is done in a consistent manner. This will help individual microservices teams to adhere to certain best practices. Each team may identify specialized technologies and tools that are suitable for their development. In a polyglot microservices development, there will obviously be multiple technologies used by different teams. However, they will have to adhere to the arching principles and practices.

For quick wins and to take advantage of timelines, microservices development teams may deviate from the practices in some cases. This is acceptable as long as the teams add refactoring tasks in their backlogs. In many organizations, although the teams will make attempts to reuse something from the enterprise, reuse and standardizations generally come as an afterthought.

It is important to make sure that the services are catalogued and visible in the enterprise. This will improve the reuse opportunities of microservices.

Summary

In this chapter, we learned about the relationship between microservices and DevOps. We also examined a number of practice points when developing microservices. Most importantly, we learned about the microservices development life cycle.

Later in this chapter, we also examined how to automate the microservices delivery pipeline from development to production. As part of this, we examined a number of tools and technologies that are helpful when automating the microservices delivery pipeline. Finally, we learned the importance of standard libraries and reference architectures in the microservices governance.

Putting together the concepts of microservices, challenges, best practices, and various capabilities covered in this book makes it a perfect recipe for developing successful microservices at scale.

Index